ANTHEMS OF DEFEAT

Crackdown in Hunan Province, 1989-92

GW00728773

An Asia Watch Report

A Division of Human Rights Watch

485 Fifth Avenue
New York, NY 10017
Tel: (212) 974-8400
Fax: (212) 972-0905

1522 K Street, NW, Suite 910
Washington, DC 20005
Tel: (202) 371-6592
Tel: (202) 371-0124

Cover Design by Patti Lacobee

Photo: AP/Wide World Photos

The cover photograph shows the huge portrait of Mao Zedong which hangs above Tiananmen Gate at the north end of Tiananmen Square, just after it had been defaced on May 23, 1989 by three pro-democracy demonstrators from Hunan Province. The three men, Yu Zhijian, Yu Dongyue and Lu Decheng, threw ink and paint at the portrait as a protest against China's one-party dictatorship and the Maoist system. They later received sentences of between 16 years and life imprisonment.

THE ASIA WATCH COMMITTEE

Introduction

Acknowledgements

This report was compiled and written by Tang Boqiao, former chairman of the Hunan Students Autonomous Federation. Robin Munro, Asia Watch's staff specialist on China, coordinated the research project and edited the report. Jeannine Guthrie, Asia Watch associate, provided production assistance.

Asia Watch would like to express its sincere debt of gratitude toward Tang Boqiao and all of his colleagues still inside China who made this report possible. Their courage and dedication has been a constant source of inspiration.

Introduction

The images of the June 4, 1989 repression in China may have faded from many people's memory, but the human toll continues to be exacted. This report recovers the lost history of the crackdown on the 1989 pro-democracy movement in Hunan Province, where some 1000 activists and demonstrators were detained after June 4 and around 500 are still behind bars today. A comprehensive profile of the repression in one medium-sized Chinese province, the report opens a window on to the previously hidden processes of arbitrary mass detention, wholesale torture and politically-engineered trials that ensued throughout China's vast hinterland following the massacre in Beijing, in areas beyond the purview of foreign journalists and camera crews based in the capital.

The report is the result of a lengthy collaboration between Asia Watch and Tang Boqiao, a leader of the 1989 student pro-democracy movement in Hunan Province who spent 18 months in prison after June 1989 and then escaped from China in July 1991 after being placed on the government's wanted list for a second time. Working in association with a large, underground pro-democracy network with members in many different provinces of China, Tang has provided us with what is probably the most comprehensive account of systematic human rights violations to have emerged from the People's Republic of China in the past 15 years. In order to preserve the immediacy of his account, we have kept it in the first person.

More than 200 cases of political imprisonment in Hunan, almost all of them previously unknown, appear in the report, together with vivid details of the wide range of torture and abuse to which many of those detained have been subjected. Drawing on extensive, first-hand archival sources, the report also includes documents from the 1989 Hunan pro-democracy movement; prosecution bills of indictment and court verdicts; a near-exhaustive list of the prisons, forced-labor camps and jails in the province; and numerous maps. It comprises, in short, the outcome of the most effective large-scale human rights monitoring exercise ever to have been conducted by a group of PRC nationals working from within the country. Asia Watch has independently corroborated and supplemented their account, using a network of other sources, wherever possible.

i

The wealth of information provided by Tang and his underground group -- the All-China People's Autonomous Federation (ACPAF)* -- provides many new insights into the post-June 1989 repression both in Hunan and in China more generally. It shows that the crackdown was far more severe and intense in the provinces, and much wider in scope, than had previously been thought. Whatever the "leniency" of the sentences handed down to activists in Beijing, it is clear that many pro-democracy participants in the provinces suffered the full brunt of the government's wrath. More than 40 prisoners detained in the province in connection with the 1989 movement, for example, arc currently serving sentences of between 10 years and life imprisonment. (Some were charged with violent offenses such as arson and "smashing and looting," but there is every reason to believe, given the well-documented pattern of arbitrary arrests and unfair trials that ensued, that many of them were in fact only involved in peaceful political activities.) The average length of sentence passed on worker participants in the movement was more than eight years.

The report highlights a number of heroes of the democracy movement in Hunan who are virtually unknown outside of China. One of these, a worker named Zhang Jingsheng, became known as the "Wei Jingsheng of the South" - after China's most famous political prisoner and pro-democracy activist. (The two men share the same given name.) Like his Beijing counterpart, Zhang Jingsheng had been imprisoned for his involvement in the Democracy Wall movement in the late 1970s, and after his release he went on to play an active role in the Workers Autonomous Federation in Changsha during May 1989. He was re-arrested and given a 13-year sentence for being a "stubborn anti-Party element."

Other activists became models of courage as much for their behavior in prison as for their role in the 1989 movement. An elderly

---

* A more literal translation of the organization's Chinese name - *Zhongguo Minzhong Tuanti Zizhi Lianhehui* - is "Federation of Autonomous People's Organizations of China." On June 2, 1992, following a decision reached with ACPAF leaders still inside China, Tang held a press conference in Washington D.C. to announce publicly the federation's existence. The identities of the ACPAF leaders and membership remain secret.

retired professor at Hunan University, Peng Yuzhang, was arrested in mid-June 1989 and forced to endure unimaginable torments for his sheer defiance of the prison authorities. He was eventually placed in a psychiatric institution, but not before he had inspired fellow-inmates 40 years younger with his will to resist intimidation.

In a sense, this report on the crackdown in Hunan signals the gradual convergence of China's heavily repressed pro-democracy movement with the current global trend toward the effective monitoring and enforcement of internationally-recognized human rights. Many people in China have taken enormous risks to compile and transmit this material to the outside world, and some of them may well go to prison for their efforts. The task of keeping a close eye on their future fate becomes, with the publication of this report, an item of the greatest urgency in Asia Watch's work and one which is likely to tax our monitoring capabilities to the full.

A much broader task is to build international pressure upon the Chinese authorities to allow full and regular access by acknowledged humanitarian organizations to the vast prison and labor camp systems of Hunan and the other provinces of China. Only when the doors of the Chinese *gulag* have finally been thrown open to such inspection will effective remedies begin to be put in place by the Chinese authorities and the kinds of endemic, systematic violence recorded in this report begin to diminish.

Finally, Asia Watch calls upon the Chinese authorities immediately and unconditionally to release all those currently detained in Hunan Province for the peaceful exercise of their rights to freedom of expression and association. In view of the serious grounds for doubting whether due process of law was observed in the cases of those convicted of violent offenses after June 4, 1989, moreover, the authorities should promptly reexamine all such cases and make public the evidence underlying the convictions.

1. The 1989 Democracy Movement in Hunan Province

The province of Hunan, with a population of over 55 million - ten million more than South Korea with more than twice its area - has been the scene of countless major and often tragic episodes in recent Chinese history. These large-scale social and political upheavals have produced and then destroyed one group after another of outstanding patriots who rose to the challenge of the times. Partial to hot, spicy food and strong liquor, the Hunanese are well-known for their stubbornness, political militancy and general strength of character.

Probably Hunan's best-loved and most famous historical figure was Qu Yuan, a poet and official of the 3rd-4th century B.C. who drowned himself in the Miluo River, near the present-day provincial capital Changsha, in protest at the corruption and impotence of the government. Another much-revered native of the province is Tan Sitong, an intellectual who helped lead the "100 Days Reform" movement in 1898 against Manchu autocracy, and who was later executed by the imperial forces after refusing to flee the ensuing repression. Tan's words, "If I don't shed my blood, who then will?", have inspired generations of Hunanese patriots, including Huang Xing, a colleague of Sun Yatsen and renowned "father of the Chinese revolution."

But the province has also produced numerous great tyrants, ranging from Zeng Guofan, the "Butcher of Hunan" who in the mid-19th century suppressed the massive Taiping Rebellion at the cost of millions of peasant lives, to Mao Zedong, the so-called "People's Emperor" who first united the nation and then inflicted on it such wholesale disasters as the Cultural Revolution. Indeed, an unusual preponderance of Chinese Communist Party leaders have hailed from Hunan. They include such enlightened figures as Liu Shaoqi, Peng Dehuai and Hu Yaobang, and even today's Zhu Rongji (sometimes known as "China's Gorbachev"), but also such hardline ultra-leftist figures as Wang Zhen and Deng Liqun.

From 1949 onward, Hunan Province has stood in the vanguard of the various political campaigns, both benign and repressive, that have swept the country. During the 1989 Democracy Movement, Hunan province experienced the largest and best-organized student and worker-led campaign for democracy of any part of China outside Beijing. The death on April 15, 1989 of Hu Yaobang, the standard bearer of political reform in China, evoked a deep sense of loss among Hunanese - but also a strong patriotic urge to inherit and defend his legacy of reform. During the 1989 movement, there was no sizeable city or district in Hunan which did not have its own autonomous student organization or independent workers' group, and in all parts of the province local residents came out in their tens of thousands to publicly demonstrate, time and time again, their support for the unprecedented movement. This report tells the story, previously unknown, of the 1989 pro-democracy movement in Hunan.

Student activism: a Hunan tradition

During the 1979-89 decade of Deng Xiaoping's "reform and open door" policy, a series of student protest campaigns occurred in Changsha, the capital of Hunan Province, demanding a faster pace of political reform and seeking to promote democracy. The first, a campaign in the summer of 1980 to freely elect student representatives to the local People's Congress, formed part of the nationwide unofficial pro-reform drive which had begun at Beijing's Democracy Wall some two years earlier. It mainly involved students from my own school, Hunan Teacher Training College (now Hunan Normal University), and was led by Tao Sen, a student from the Chinese department's class of 1977, and Liang Heng, who later left China and co-authored the best-seller *Son of the Revolution*.

A vanguard component of the first and only nationwide movement since 1949 for the free election of people's representatives, the 1980 Hunan student campaign lasted for nearly one month and included mass demonstrations, sit-ins and hunger strikes. Tao Sen, who was imprisoned for five years after 1989, led a delegation of student leaders to Beijing to negotiate with the central government and won a number of significant concessions, but these were later revoked and student activists were subsequently purged by the local authorities. The influence and effects of the campaign, however, resonated across the country for several years afterwards.

The second major student movement in Hunan took place in

2

November 1986, when activists at Hunan Normal University again launched a student strike calling for the authorities to observe human rights and the rule of law and to show greater respect for teachers. This campaign, later dubbed the "November 5 Incident" by the central government, spread quickly to include most of the Changsha campuses and was far-reaching in its effects. Preceding the student protests of later that month at the Hefei University of Science and Technology (where Professor Fang Lizhi was then vice-chancellor), it provided the initial inspiration and impetus for the massive wave of student demonstrations in support of democracy which swept China's major cities during the winter of 1986-87. In a counter-offensive launched in January 1987 by hardline Party leaders to root out so-called "bourgeois liberalism," Hu Yaobang was driven from power and replaced as Party general secretary by Zhao Ziyang. Li Peng was appointed as premier, and a severe political chill descended on the country.

The pro-democracy movement in Hunan, however, did not let up. The flashpoint for a third surge of activism occurred in September 1987, when a Hunan University student was beaten to death by a group of People's Liberation Army (PLA) soldiers. This incident sparked off a province-wide protest movement in which students sent telegrams all over the country, and there were rallies on the campuses of Hunan University and other colleges. Local outrage at the student's killing became so great that Deng Xiaoping himself had personally to intervene to restore social order and quell the unrest. He instructed the Central Military Commission to disband the PLA independent division concerned and to dismiss all its officers from their posts, from division commander to platoon leaders. The soldiers directly involved in the murder of the student were all sentenced to death and executed.

The 1989 Democracy Movement

Each campaign for democracy during the decade of reforms had been larger and more influential than the last, and students activists in Hunan all knew that 1989 was likely to produce a major new upsurge of pro-democracy activity throughout the country. Several key anniversaries by chance all happened to fall in that year: the 200th anniversary of the

3

French revolution, the 70th anniversary of China's May 4th Movement[1] and the 40th anniversary of the founding of the People's Republic of China. The high-tide of Deng Xiaoping's political and economic reforms, reached in late 1986, had by early 1989 subsided drastically in the face of an economic austerity program that had generated widespread discontent among the populace, and graft and corruption among Party officials was rampant.

Democracy Salon

At the beginning of 1989, an underground student organization was formed by activists of the Hunan Normal University. It was originally called, variously, the "Arts and Literature Salon" and the "Current Affairs Forum", but eventually the name of "Democracy Salon" *(Minzhu Shalong)* was decided upon. There was no contact with similar salons in Beijing, such as that run by student leader Wang Dan. Besides acting as a general focus for student debate on the topics of reform and democratization, the organization's main role lay in planning and preparing commemorative activities to mark the coming series of anniversaries.

The Democracy Salon's plans for 1989 included, notably, a series of large-scale street demonstrations in Changsha and other cities to promote democracy, oppose corruption and call for accelerated political reforms and a more open system. We proposed a four-point maxim for China's future governance, namely: "Democracy - Rule of Law - Science - Civilization." Although the organization was originally based at Hunan Normal University and carried out most of its planning activities there, it spread quickly during early 1989 to include students from all the institutes of higher education in Changsha. Many of the Salon's members went on to become core leaders of the 1989 Hunan Democracy Movement. The Salon, which met once a week was very tightly organized with officers, members and membership dues.

---

[1] The May Fourth Movement commemorates the day in 1919 when Beijing students staged protest actions against Chinese leaders' acceptance of a decision made by the victorious allied powers at the Treaty of Versailles to give Shandong Province over to Japan as its "sphere of influence." The protest turned into a movement for democracy and national freedom and led eventually to the founding of the Chinese Communist Party.

4

The "April 22 Incident"

The real starting date of the 1989 Hunan student movement fell on April 22, one week after the death of Hu Yaobang, and several days after the first unauthorized mourning activities for Hu had been launched by students in Beijing. (There were several small-scale demonstrations in Hunan before April 22, but these had very little impact.) On that day, the graduate students' associations of both Hunan University and Central-South Industrial University organized a group of around 5,000 students to take to the streets of Changsha and demonstrate publicly in support of their call for "dialogue" between the student representatives and the provincial government. The demonstration went off smoothly, and by around 4:00 pm all the demonstrators had gradually dispersed.

The same evening, however, another group of students took to the streets, carrying floral wreaths and mourning banners and setting off firecrackers as they went. These students were reportedly all from Liuyang, the hometown of Hu Yaobang. It was the weekend, so many ordinary residents of Changsha were out on the streets and joined in the marching column. Soon the whole of May 1st Avenue had become a sea of people. All kinds of slogans, such as "We demand freedom and democracy" and "Smash official profiteering and corruption!", filled the air and gradually a state of considerable chaos began to emerge. I was present throughout the evening and witnessed the whole incident.

Eventually, the mood turned nasty, and some over-excited youths proceeded to completely smash up around 40 of the shops along either side of the street. Very little looting occurred, however, since the incident was essentially an outpouring of pent-up anger and frustration by the crowd against escalating government corruption in recent years. Most of the rioters confined themselves to breaking up and stamping on the objects from the shops (mainly food and items of clothing) that lay scattered around, and few if any really valuable items such as gold or silver ornaments were looted. During the entire incident, no officials from any of the government departments emerged to try to take control or deal with the situation. It was as if the government had simply evaporated.

Finally, after most of the rioting had ended and the crowd had already begun to disperse, more than 1,000 policemen (many of them from newly established anti-riot units) and dozens of plainclothes security agents were sent into the city center to "restore order." By the end of the evening, the authorities had seized and arrested around 100 of the demonstrators - all of whom were later characterized as being mere "beating, smashing and looting elements." It was the same term used to describe student and worker Red Guards after the Cultural Revolution.

The arrests were largely indiscriminate, however, and many of those detained, including some of those later convicted as "ringleaders," had actually played no part in the rioting. Indeed, the person who received the heaviest punishment in connection with the incident, a young factory worker named Li Weihong, had done nothing more than shout slogans urging the crowd to take action. He himself had not engaged in any violence at all. He was eventually handed down a sentence of death with a two-year reprieve. In all, more than 40 of those detained that night were later tried and sentenced by the courts, although the figure officially given was only 27.

The local government immediately relayed this incident to the senior authorities in Beijing. Together with a similar incident which occurred the same day in Xi'an, the capital of Shaanxi Province, it was cited in the April 26 *People's Daily* editorial - "Resolutely Oppose the Turmoil" - as a major grounds for the central government's condemnation of the student movement as a whole. Moreover, the movement was denounced not simply as posing a threat to public order, but as being "a planned conspiracy and turmoil...by an extremely small number of people" with ulterior motives. "Their aim," said the editorial, "was to sow dissension among the people, plunge the whole country into chaos and sabotage the political situation of stability and unity." Concluded the article: "Bans should be placed on unlawful parades and demonstrations and on such acts as going to factories, rural areas and schools to establish ties." From this moment on, plans for the coming repression accelerated across the country.

Commemoration of the May 4th anniversary

After the "April 22 Incident," the Changsha student body felt deeply unsettled and for a time had no idea what to do next. Once the government announced that there had been no students among those arrested, however, everyone felt greatly relieved. After assessing the prevailing situation, a group of core student activists then decided to set up the "May 4 Joint Steering Committee," which was to serve as a guiding body for the Hunan student movement as a whole. The key members of the Steering Committee were myself, Zheng Yan, Xia Siqing, Liu Qiaohui, Long Jianhua and Zhu Jianwen, all from Hunan Normal University; Hao Mingzhao, Lu Siqing, and He Zhiqiang from Central-South Industrial University; and, from Hunan University, Li Zhiping, Shui Li and Shen Yong.[2] A large number of the Steering Committee's members had been very influential in their own institutions and other universities and colleges in Changsha even before the 1989 student movement began. Lu Siqing, Hao Mingzhao, Xia Siqing, Li Zhiping and others had all been cadres of the official student association, and they were all straight-A students.

The first action by the Steering Committee took place on April 27, when students from Hunan Normal University, Hunan University and Central-South Industrial University took to the streets and demonstrated once again. Between 6,000 and 8,000 students tried to march into the provincial administration building. Officials closed the main gate but the crowd pushed it open. Lu Siqing and other students entered the building and met with Wang Fei, the deputy director of the provincial office. The dialogue lasted about two hours and was cordial. The two sides discussed the students' complaints of government corruption, and the officials promised to investigate. When the students left the building, most of the demonstrators were still sitting outside waiting for them.

The following day, several student delegates headed by Lu Siqing were put forward to open a dialogue with Wang Xiangtian, deputy-governor of Hunan Province, and Long Yuxian, chairman of the Provincial Education Commission. The main thrust of the talks concerned discussions on the problem of profiteering and corruption among Hunan officials. The talks proceeded in a friendly and constructive atmosphere, and this marked a turning point in the entire Hunan democracy movement. Henceforth, right up until the time of the June 4 repression, no major state of conflict or antagonism arose between the students and the government. This was one important feature of the Hunan pro-

---

[2] Of these, Long Jianhua, Hao Mingzhao and I were arrested after June 4.

democracy movement which differentiated it quite sharply from that in Beijing.

Between April 27 and May 3, the *May 4 Joint Steering Committee* printed and distributed a large quantity of leaflets and publicity materials in preparation for the May 4 anniversary, including a "Letter to Compatriots", a "Letter to the Students" and a "Letter to the Teachers". At eight o'clock in the morning of May 4, firecrackers were let off in Hunan Normal University, Hunan University, Central-South Industrial University and the Finance and Economics College to inaugurate a "May 4 Joint Action" in Changsha consisting of city-wide demonstrations. The various school authorities ordered all the campus gates to be locked, however, and as a result of this concerted obstruction and interference, only the students from Hunan Normal University, Changsha Railway College and a few other institutions managed to break out and join the demonstration. The rest remained stuck on campus.

As the students gradually converged on Changsha's Martyrs Park, they were joined by large crowds of city residents. By noon, there were 100,000 people gathered together there. After many people from the crowd had been freely allowed to make speeches (each limited to three minutes in length) I made a speech on behalf of the Steering Committee and announced the setting up of the "Joint Action Provisional Committee of Hunan Province Institutions of Higher Education." Immediately after the rally, representatives from all the colleges convened in the same park to hold the inaugural meeting of the Provisional Committee.

Thereafter, the campuses gradually quietened down for a time and no further protest demonstrations took place. During this period, the Provisional Committee held several meetings at the Aiwan Pavilion (a favored recreational spot on Mt. Yuelu, on the banks of Changsha's Xiang River between the Hunan Normal and Central-South Industrial universities, where Mao Zedong held many student movement meetings in the late 1910s), and at the Changsha Youth Palace and other places. These meetings dealt mainly with the problem of how best to develop our activities on a long-term basis, for example by publishing newspapers, setting up study-groups and extending our organizational scale and membership.

During this period, however, the authorities were also busy

preparing their next move. From the time of the April 26 *People's Daily* editorial onward, an intensive official investigation known as the "fight-back and counter-reckoning exercise" *(fangong daosuan)* had been underway in Hunan Province. Dossiers were opened on student activists, and it was made known to us that our "performance" in the coming weeks could be crucial to our future job prospects. In addition, certain key figures who had been active in earlier pro-democracy or student movements were placed under close police surveillance. These included, notably, Zhang Jingsheng, a worker who had spent four years in prison as a "counterrevolutionary" after editing an unofficial journal in Changsha during the 1978-81 Democracy Wall movement, and the former students Tao Sen and Zhou Zhirong, both of whom had been leaders of the 1980 Hunan Normal College free election campaign and subsequently spent time in prison as a result.

On the afternoon of May 4, Zhang Jingsheng was arrested and taken to the Changsha No.1 Jail after making a speech at a students' rally voicing his strong opposition toward the government's attempts to suppress the patriotic students. But in the days that followed, policy lines among the upper echelons of the central government remained unclear, and certain high-ranking supporters of the student movement had not yet fallen from power. The Changsha municipal government, seeing that no large-scale repressive actions had ensued in other parts of the country, had Zhang Jingsheng released within a matter of days.

The Hunan Students Autonomous Federation

On May 13, news reached Changsha that the Beijing students had begun a mass hunger strike in Tiananmen Square. The following day, the Hunan students' Provisional Committee called a meeting in which it was decided that I should travel immediately to Beijing to make contact with the students and assess the situation there. On May 15, some students spontaneously took to the streets of Changsha once again. Several thousand students from different universities converged on the Provincial Administration Building carrying banners supporting the hunger strikers in Beijing, supporting reform, and calling for an end to corruption. The demonstration lasted from about noon to about 5 p.m.

On May 16, the Provisional Committee organized a large-scale joint protest demonstration involving all the Changsha institutions of

9

higher education. On this occasion, Changsha residents from all walks of life joined in, prominent among them being journalists from the news and media units and cadres from the Hunan People's Political Consultative Conference.[3] That evening, the Provisional Committee renamed itself the "Hunan Students Autonomous Federation" (SAF) and started a mass hunger strike of around 2000 students and 100 or so workers outside the provincial government offices. Fan Zhong, chairman of the student association of Central-South Industrial University, acted as general commander of the hunger strike.

During the period of the hunger strike, the SAF held numerous dialogue sessions with the provincial government, demanding that official corruption and profiteering be severely punished and the democratization process steadily continued. But the provincial government adopted a careful wait-and-see attitude; it was clear that the lives of the hunger-striking students were of only secondary importance to them. Essentially, the provincial government was confused and uncertain about how best to proceed. In the absence of a clear policy direction from Beijing, it preferred simply to do nothing. This at least gave us some room for maneuver in the week preceding martial law.

On May 17 and 18, the SAF organized and led further large-scale demonstrations in Changsha, the main purpose of which was to show support for the Beijing hunger strikers and also those on hunger strike outside the Hunan provincial government offices. On each day, several tens of thousands of local people joined the demonstrations.

The situation became increasingly tense. On May 19, one of the SAF leaders, Lu Siqing, tried to commit suicide by slashing his wrists, in a desperate attempt to spur the government to action and win over society. Fortunately, he was discovered just in time and was saved from bleeding to death. At around the same time, another SAF leader, Hao Mingzhao, poured petrol all over himself in the public toilets and was

---

[3] The HPPCC is a provincial body which is supposed to represent all non-communist groups and be the "alternate" representative of the people. In reality, it has acted as a rubber stamp for decisions made by the Communist Party. There is one such body in every province and a national Chinese People's Political Consultative Conference.

about to go the provincial government offices to immolate himself. Luckily, he too was discovered by his class-mates and a tragedy was thereby averted.

Hunan's response to martial law

On the evening of May 19, martial law was imposed in Beijing. That same evening, I returned to Changsha. In view of the rapidly deteriorating political situation, the SAF decided to call off the students' hunger strike and alter it to a peaceful sit-down protest (also in front of the provincial government offices), and in this way to continue the struggle. It was an extremely moving scene that night, with everyone singing "The Internationale" and many of the students crying bitterly. When the Changsha residents heard rumors that the army was approaching Changsha, large bands of them headed off immediately toward each of the main intersections into the city and gathered together to block the troops. In the ensuing confusion, a number of people were arrested by the police, but the SAF sent delegates to negotiate with the provincial public security department and the detainees were soon freed.

In response to the news of martial law, large numbers of students and local residents also took to the streets and demonstrated in many other cities of Hunan Province. In Xiangtan, Hengyang, Yueyang and Zhuzhou, for example, further sit-down protests and hunger strikes were quickly staged in front of the government offices.

In Shaoyang City, tens of thousands of students and local residents marched toward People's Square in the downtown area on the night of May 19 to protest martial law. A number of arrests were made on the spot, and the crowd became angry. Some young people rushed forward, dragging policemen out from their vehicles and setting the vehicles on fire. Several sedan cars belonging to government officials were also stopped and set on fire by the crowd. More policemen quickly arrived on the scene and began indiscriminately seizing the demonstrators. The clashes continued until the early hours of the morning, at which time a section of the crowd broke through the police cordon and forced its way into the offices of the municipal Party committee. As a result, scores of people were arrested that night.

Secret arrests were also made in Hengyang City on May 20, after a large demonstration there against martial law in Beijing in which students and citizens clashed with the police. Official reports claimed that about 100 policemen were injured; from this it was reasonable to assume that the number of civilian casualties was far higher. Many people were arrested in Hengyang over the next few days, though this was denied by the government. After my release from prison on February 13, 1991, I made an investigation into the May 20 incident in Hengyang. Even then, the local people all still expressed strong outrage at the incident. In their words, "The dogs raised up by the people suddenly saw yellow." (In Hunan slang, "seeing yellow" means being treacherous and ungrateful.)

On the night of May 20, the Changsha public security authorities secretly arrested four workers named Dong Qi, He Jianming, Dai Dingxiang and Liang Chao, who had been active in organizing citizens in support of the students. Upon hearing a rumor that the army was entering Changsha, the four hurried to a meeting with student leaders to discuss countermeasures, but were intercepted by the police and arrested on the pretext that they were all carrying small pen-knives (there was in fact nothing unusual about this.) After June 4, they were sentenced to prison terms of between three and five years.[4] The incident was a classic example of the authorities' attempts to find non-student scapegoats to blame for the student movement - so-called "outside agitators" who were supposedly trying to pervert the movement's orientation. In reality, what the government feared most was the growing trend toward collaboration between workers and students.

May 22 brought further serious clashes between demonstrators and the police, this time in Xiangtan City, the hometown of Mao Zedong. The incident was triggered off when officers of the city's Pingzheng Road Police Station indiscriminately arrested some demonstrators. When the local people learned of this, they marched to the police post and gathered outside the main gate, shouting out slogans and demanding the release of all those arrested. The chief of the police post and several other cadres then proceeded to abuse and insult the crowd, and in a fit of anger, some people in the crowd broke into the police station and smashed it to pieces, setting fire to it as they left. Police reinforcements were rushed to the scene and up to ten people were arrested on the spot. (A report in the

---

[4] Hunan Daily, 12 June 1989.

Hunan Daily on June 16 revealed that 23 other demonstrators were arrested in connection with the incident after the June 4 crackdown.)

The Workers Autonomous Federation

On May 20, also in response to martial law, a number of worker activists who had been participating in the pro-democracy movement over the previous few weeks took the major step of formally establishing their own organization: the Changsha Workers Autonomous Federation (WAF). The main WAF standing committee members were Zhang Xudong, Zhou Yong, He Zhaohui, Zhou Min, Wang Changhuai, Zhang Jingsheng and Liu Yi.

Nearly all of the group's members had been actively involved in the hunger strike outside the provincial government offices in Changsha, and had played an important role in helping the students to forge links with the general public. They were tireless in organizing the workers to show support and solidarity for the student movement, and they gave us vital assistance in arranging food and equipment supplies and other logistical backup. The WAF and other worker groups in Hunan never managed to develop organizationally to a scale comparable to that of the student movement, and their prestige and influence among the general public remained considerably less than that of the SAF. But all of the WAF leaders were extremely resolute and dedicated pro-democracy activists, and they subsequently paid dearly for their attempts to form independent labor unions. None of them escaped from China after June 4, and their own story must therefore remain largely untold for the meantime.

Late May: the movement deepens

On May 22, the Hunan SAF decided to reorganize itself. First, we reformed and restructured the student governing bodies of all the participating colleges. Then we had each college reselect their delegates to the SAF, and formed a new standing committee from among those delegates. Those elected to the new standing committee included myself, Fan Zhong, Lu Siqing, Zhu Jianwen, Xia Siqing, Hao Mingzhao, Liu Wei,

Yue Weipeng, Shui Li, Li Zheng, and Hu Hao.[6] Later on, Xia Siqing quit and was replaced by Zheng Yan, a Ph.D student at Hunan Normal University.

By now, the SAF had effectively established itself as the unified voice of the province-wide student movement. Student representatives came to Changsha to participate in the SAF from colleges and universities throughout the province, including Xiangtan University, Zhongnan Institute of Forestry, Hengyang Medical Institute and Jishou University. The SAF dispatched "democracy propaganda teams" to all areas of Hunan to carry out public educational work among local residents, and these were highly influential and effective. In addition, Hunan Normal University's democracy propaganda team (headed by a famous student from the Chinese department nicknamed "Egghead") published a regular newsletter which was widely distributed throughout the province. Contacts with the student movement in other provinces of China were also well developed. One delegation led by Zhang Lixin from Beijing Teachers' College came to Hunan at the end of May.

Fan Zhong and I held full and overall responsibility for the SAF's affairs at this time. Moreover, we organized the sending out of students from all the higher colleges to the various prefectures and cities of Hunan to carry on propaganda and liaison work. On May 24, the SAF organized a massive city-wide demonstration in conjunction with the Changsha Workers Autonomous Federation (WAF). The demonstration went off in a well-disciplined and orderly way, with many different work units taking part - the procession extended for over five kilometers - and it had a considerable social impact. All the drivers from Changsha city's private taxi companies took part in the demonstration, with more than forty taxis altogether taking part in the demonstration column.

---

[6] Fan Zhong and Hao Mingzhao were undergraduates at Central-South Industrial University; Zhu Jianwen was a Hunan Normal University undergraduate; Xia Siqing and Lu Siqing were postgraduates from Hunan Normal University and Central-South Industrial University respectively; Liu Wei was a Changsha Railway College undergraduate; Yue Weipeng was from Hunan Hydroelectric Industry Teachers' College; Shui Li was a Hunan University undergraduate; Li Zheng was a Hunan Finance and Economics College undergraduate; and Hu Hao was a Hunan Medical University student.

After the May 24 demonstration wound up, the SAF convened a plenary session and decided both to continue with the peaceful sit-down demonstration outside the provincial government offices, and, at the same time, to send a group of students to all parts of the province to canvass delegates to the national and provincial People's Congresses. The SAF representatives called upon the delegates to support the students' righteous protest actions and to propose and support a legislative motion to dismiss Li Peng from office. In addition, we installed a sit-down protest group in front of the offices of the standing committee of the Hunan Provincial People's Congress.

Another highly significant event which occurred around this time was the joint drafting and signing, by no less than 60 committee members of the Hunan People's Political Consultative Conference, of a "Manifesto of the HPPCC" in which the delegates to this prestigious official body expressed their clear support for the aims of the student protest movement. The chief signatory of this manifesto was Zou Naishan, a former mayor of Changsha. (In 1990, Zou was dismissed for this by the Provincial Peoples' Congress from his post on the standing committee of the HPPCC.) Many journalists and editors in Hunan also publicly voiced their opposition to Li Peng's declaration of martial law, raising the slogan: "The media must tell the truth!"

Moreover, the workers of Changsha and other cities continued to maintain firm solidarity with the student movement throughout this period. A city-wide strike, which had been planned by the Changsha workers in response to martial law, only failed to materialize because of extreme pressure and intimidation brought to bear by the authorities in the factories.

On May 27, two SAF representatives (myself and Liu Wei) negotiated with Su Qingyun, head of the Provincial Petitions Bureau, with a view to re-establishing a dialogue with the provincial government. Su agreed to engage in dialogue with the students on the government's behalf, on condition that we first of all returned to our colleges and universities and resumed classes. In the end, we reached an agreement whereby the students would return to campus so long as the government began to conduct the dialogue before May 30; otherwise, the SAF would continue to organize its peaceful sit-down protest.

15

On May 28, after a great deal of hard work, the SAF finally managed to persuade the students to temporarily call off the protest and return to their institutions. Before dispersing late that evening, the students held a bonfire-light ceremony in front of the provincial government offices in which we all swore an oath of allegiance. We knelt down, facing toward the five-star national emblem which hung high over the entrance to the government offices, and everyone solemnly took the pledge: "We vow to uphold the ideals of democracy to the end!" A member of the SAF standing committee, Lu Siqing, suddenly raised his head high and with tears streaming down his face cried out, "Emblem of our nation! We won't let you down!"

Many of the students began to cry bitterly at that point. One fine arts student from Hunan University even stood up and threw himself into the bonfire that was blazing away in the square. He was rescued by some fellow-students, his face badly burnt. People in the crowd all around started angrily shouting slogans such as "Down with Li Peng!", "Long Live the Students!" The medical staff from the Red Cross who were present that night wept at the scene. Even the People's Armed Police officers, who were there to uphold public order, couldn't hold back their tears.

When the students finally departed from the provincial government offices, the sound of firecrackers could be heard all along the length and breadth of Changsha's May 1st Avenue. A group of city residents spontaneously organized themselves into a picket squad and escorted members of the SAF back to Hunan Normal University, setting off more firecrackers along the way. That night, even the heavens were moved to tears. The rain fell in torrents until dawn.

Prelude to repression

Again, however, the government vented its anger on the workers. Late on the night of May 28, four leaders of the Changsha WAF who had been participating with the students in the peaceful sit-in protest - Zhou Yong, Li Jian, Zhang Jingsheng and one other - were secretly arrested. Upon hearing of this the following day, the SAF leadership organized a student march on May 30 to the Hunan government offices to protest the arrests and negotiate with the provincial public security department. The effort bore some fruit, for Li Jian and Zhou Yong were set free (only, however, to be rearrested after June 4); the other two were not freed,

16

and Zhang Jingsheng eventually received a 13-year sentence.

By May 29, there was still no news from the provincial government about when the dialogue process would begin. On the morning of May 30, the SAF called Su Qingyun, head of the Provincial Petitions Bureau, to request a final response on the deadline for commencing dialogue, which had expired the previous day. We were informed that Su, together with the provincial Party secretary, had already left Changsha for the Yueyang Lake district to supervise flood relief work. When SAF leaders later relayed this information to the students, they responded with extreme dissatisfaction and anger.

On May 31, several dozen students from Hunan Normal University and Central-South Industrial University went spontaneously to the provincial government offices, wrote out a collective "last will and testament" and started a new hunger strike. On June 1, the SAF organized and led a further city-wide demonstration march and recommenced the sit-down protest outside the provincial government offices. Moreover, we mobilized the entire student population to put into action the so-called "empty campus" strategy *(kong xiao ji)*, whereby the students all simply evacuated their dormitories and went home. (After the June 4 massacre, similar actions were undertaken by the students in Beijing and Shanghai.)

Also in protest at the government's failure to begin dialogue, a group of students from Hunan University, Hunan Normal University and Changsha Railway Institute hoisted their college banners and marched through the streets to Changsha Railway Station, where they laid down on the tracks in an attempt to block the trains. Shortly afterwards, there occurred an ugly incident in which an angry crowd of Changsha residents smashed up all the windows on a No.48 Guangzhou-Beijing express train. The SAF tried its utmost at this time, intervening by all available means, to try to prevent the overall situation from deteriorating any further. We were especially concerned to prevent any possible fatalities.

The final days

Late on the evening of June 3, while the SAF was busy holding a meeting, the news came over the *Voice of America* and other international radio stations that the troops had opened fire in Beijing and were killing students and workers. Realizing how desperate the situation had become, we immediately conducted an emergency review of our options. After an extremely heated debate, the SAF standing committee finally decided (with a small dissenting minority) that on the following day the students would be mobilized to take to the streets to block all traffic, and that we would call upon the entire citizenry of Changsha to boycott markets and stage a general strike.

The people of Changsha and other cities of Hunan were stunned by the news of the massacre in Beijing, and, in a spontaneous public outpouring of grief and anger at the bloody repression, huge protest demonstrations quickly ensued throughout the province. Crowds of students and residents surged through the streets of Changsha, Hengyang, Xiangtan, Shaoyang, Yueyang, Changde and Yiyang for almost a week after June 4, and road traffic in all major cities in the province was brought to a standstill. In Changsha, a mass rally was held outside the provincial government offices on June 6, while no fewer than 100,000 demonstrators congregated on the city's Xiangjiang Bridge alone, blocking all traffic for several days. In Yueyang, a large crowd of angry protesters stormed the offices of the municipal Party committee, government and people's congress, then pulled down all the door signs and smashed them to bits, Only on June 9 did the authorities regain control of the city. Meanwhile, students and workers in Xiangtan not only demonstrated but also held strikes and suspended normal business activities in the city for several days, effectively paralyzing the local government. In an extraordinary departure from normal practice, the Hunan provincial government at first did virtually nothing to prevent all this.

It was clear from the government news bulletins, however, that a nationwide search and arrest operation was about to be launched against leaders of the pro-democracy movement. When a number of violent clashes with the security forces inevitably arose, the government, using these incidents as a pretext, moved in and began the crackdown immediately. Within days, several hundred alleged "thugs and hooligans" (baotu) were behind bars.

From June 6 to 7, the standing committee of the SAF met in continuous session to discuss future strategy and decide upon its next course of action. Eventually, it was unanimously agreed that we would all

18

run the risk of arrest by holding a mass memorial meeting in Changsha Railway Station to mourn the victims of the Beijing massacre. The meeting would also serve as an oath-taking ceremony at which SAF members would pledge their loyalty to the pro-democracy cause and bid a temporary farewell to the people of Changsha.

At 2:00 pm on June 8, with a vast crowd of around 140,000 people in attendance, the mass memorial meeting formally opened. The stage was piled high with floral wreaths, and thin white banners inscribed with funeral couplets were strewn all around. Zhang Lixin (representing the Beijing SAF) and I presided over the memorial meeting. One after another, delegates of the Hunan SAF and WAF, representatives of the Changsha residents, teachers' delegates and spokespersons for pro-democracy groups from other provinces all rose to give speeches. The mood of the meeting was extremely sad and emotional, and when the time finally came for the main memorial oration to be read out, the sound of weeping and wailing drifted upward from the crowd below, filling the air on all sides.[6] Finally, on behalf of the SAF standing committee, I made a closing speech vowing that we would never, regardless of whatever repression might lie ahead, abandon our goal of democracy. "Compatriots, please trust us!", I said. "We of the Students Autonomous Federation love our nation deeply, and we will never waver in the struggle for democracy."

The following day, all the students who had previously remained on campus began to flee. A couple of days later, on June 11, after completing as best we could our contingency plans for dealing with the coming repression, the members of the SAF standing committee also went to ground. On June 12, the provincial government issued an urgent order for the "Two Autonomous federations" (the SAF and the WAF) to disband and for the leaders to turn themselves in to the authorities. On June 17, the public security forces formally began to arrest activists from both groups on a large scale. I myself headed for Guangdong Province, where I was arrested, just over one month later, at dawn on July 13.

---

[6] See Appendix V. below for full translated text of the oration.

19

2. Enemies of the People: the Crackdown in Hunan

Hunan Province, together with Beijing, Shanghai and Chengdu, stood in the front ranks of the 1989 Democracy Movement, and after June 4, the campaign of political repression and judicial retaliation it suffered was among the most severe of any part of China. The following account of the situation in Hunan may give us some idea of the still-untold stories of the repression in many other Chinese provinces, some of which were even less accessible to outside scrutiny in the aftermath of the June 4 crackdown.

On June 9, 1989 at a meeting of senior officers of the PLA martial law units, Deng Xiaoping gave the green light for wholesale repression and round-up operations against the pro-democracy movement to commence across the country. According to Deng:

> *What we face is not simply ordinary people who are unable to distinguish between right and wrong. We also face a rebellious clique and a large number of the dregs of society, who want to topple our country and overthrow our party. This is the essence of the problem....They want to establish a totally Western-dependent bourgeois republic.*[7]

One week later, at a June 16 session of the newly appointed CCP Politburo Standing Committee, Deng added:

> *We must carry the work of suppressing the rebellion through to the end. This is a good chance for us to ban illegal organizations at one go....We must not be soft on those who are*

---

[7] "June 9 Speech to Martial Law Units," by Deng Xiaoping, in *Beijing Spring, 1989: Confrontation and Conflict*, Oksenberg, Sullivan and Lambert (eds.), M.E. Sharpe 1990, pp.377-8.

guilty of the most heinous crimes.[8]

By then, the repression in Hunan was already in full swing. On June 7, at a meeting of senior provincial Party and government officials, Hong Dechuan, provincial Party secretary, called on all regions in the province to take swift measures to round up activists, subdue the disturbances and restore stability. He demanded that a crushing campaign be waged and a rapid, overwhelming victory won. The head of the provincial Politics and Law Committee went further, insisting, "The riotous elements must be uprooted like weeds, so as to eradicate the pestilence once and for all." At a subsequent meeting, a senior public security official instructed, "There must be no mercy whatsoever shown to the riotous elements. Arrests and sentences should be carried out wherever appropriate."

The initial arrests

Within days, Hunan Daily announced that 31 workers and unemployed persons had been arrested, all of whom were described as "criminal elements who participated in the turmoil," although none had yet had the benefit of a trial.[9] They were all later tried and sentenced, with prison terms ranging from three years for Bu Yunhui, a peasant who had lain on the tracks at Changsha Railway Station on June 6 to protest the crackdown, to ten years for Liao Zhijun, a worker at the Changsha Pump Factory who had served in the SAF picket squad.

---

[8] "Full Text of Gists of Deng Xiaoping's Speech to Members of New Politburo Standing Committee [June 16, 1989]," in *ibid*, p.387. In a clear case of giving with one hand and taking away with the other, Deng then went on to say: "Of course, [the rebels] must be treated in light of the seriousness of their crimes. Everything must be based on facts and law. There must be a limit for killing those criminals. We must stress the policy of lenience to those who confess and severity to those who resist." In practice, the latter policy means that anyone detained by the authorities must confess, regardless of whether or not they have committed any offense. To "resist" - i.e. assert one's innocence - is taken merely as proof of a "bad attitude" and results in an even heavier punishment being imposed.

[9] Many of the citations from Hunan Daily given here are taken from undated clippings of the newspaper, so precise reference dates cannot be given. Most of the reports appeared during the last three weeks of June 1989.

Similar mass arrests occurred throughout the province. In Yiyang City, for example, Hunan Daily reported on June 9 that 120 people, "all dregs of society who took advantage of the student demonstrations and sit-ins to incite disturbances, block traffic and create turmoil," had been seized by the public security forces.

In Yueyang City, also on June 9, "Nine bad elements were arrested for involvement in beating, smashing and looting activities." In fact, the nine, all of whom were workers or unemployed persons between the ages of 20 and 35 years, had marched through Yueyang just after June 4 and lain down on the railway tracks to protest the suppression in Beijing. They had then headed to the city government offices, torn down an official door sign and trampled it underfoot. The "ringleader," Guo Yunqiao, was later given a suspended death sentence for this, while the other eight received prison terms ranging from seven to 15 years.

Workers' leaders were among the first to be targeted by the authorities. At dawn on June 9, a young worker named Li Wangyang, the leader of the Shaoyang Workers Autonomous Federation, was arrested in Shaoyang City. Among the charges listed against Li and his colleagues in the *Hunan Daily* were that they had "posted up banners, issued leaflets, carried out liaison trips, spread rumors, uttered reactionary slogans, incited workers to go on strike and proclaimed the founding of a completely independent and autonomous [workers] organization." Li was later sentenced to 13 years' imprisonment.

Similarly, Zhu Fangming, a worker at the Hengyang Flour Mill and vice-chairman of the Hengyang Workers Autonomous Federation, was arrested around June 11 together with Ding Longhua, a standing committee member of the federation. Zhu was later sentenced to life imprisonment; Ding received a six-year sentence. In reporting their arrests, *Hunan Daily* noted that the city's public security bureau had set up a "denunciation telephone hotline" so that "the entire citizenry can be actively mobilized to report and expose criminal elements responsible for the turmoil."

In mid-June, 27 of those detained after the "April 22 Incident" were brought to trial and sentenced heavily. The most severe sentences went to Li Weihong, a young worker in the Hunan Fire-fighting Appliances Factory, who was handed down a death sentence with two years' stay of execution, and Xia Changchun, a worker at the Changsha Port Authority, who received a 15-year prison term.

Banning of "illegal organizations"

On June 12, the Hunan provincial government issued a formal proclamation outlawing the Hunan Students Autonomous Federation and the Changsha Workers Autonomous Federation, and ordering the groups' leaders and core members to report to the public security authorities within five days. Failure to comply with the order would be severely punished by law, said the order, but all those who reported would be dealt with leniently. (In reality, all those blacklisted by the government after June 4 were rounded up and sentenced anyway, regardless of whether or not they complied with the order to turn themselves in.)

By June 16, six leaders of the Changsha WAF had been arrested and four had turned themselves in. Those arrested included the group's founding chairman Li Jian, a later chairman named Zhou Yong, vice-chairmen He Chaohui and Zhang Xudong, and standing committee members Lu Zhaixing, Liu Xingqi and Yang Xiong. The four who reported to the police were vice-chairman and head of propaganda Wang Changhuai, deputy picket leader Cai Jinxuan, picket leader Li Jie and standing committee member Zhou Min. In addition, dozens of members of the Changsha Workers Picket Team were also arrested, although this was not reported by the authorities. The detainees were later sentenced to terms of three to six years' imprisonment. (Zhou Min, who received a six-year term for having made an impassioned speech at the June 8 mass mourning ceremony in Changsha, is now reported to have become mentally disturbed following repeated physical abuse by prison guards.)

By June 17, more than ten leaders of the Hunan SAF had been seized, including the co-chairman of the federation, Fan Zhong, standing committee member Yue Weipeng, and core members Liu Zhongtao (alias Chen Le), Yu Chaohui, Liu Jianhua, Yi Gai and others. They were subsequently held in prison for periods of up to 18 months and then released. Around June 28, the Hunan Daily reported that a total of 23 leaders of the SAF had turned themselves in to the authorities. Most of these were dealt with relatively leniently. (See *Appendix III.A* for details.)

The same article stated that an elderly retired professor of Hunan University, named Peng Yuzhang, had been taken into detention for having acted as a behind-the-scenes adviser to both the SAF and the WAF, and for having participated in the hunger strike outside the provincial government offices in Changsha. Absurdly, the article accused Peng of having "pretended to be a university professor," and said that he had publicly called for a general strike after the May 20 declaration of martial law in Beijing. (Peng suffered severe abuse while in prison and was released in 1990 only to be committed immediately and forcibly to a mental hospital, where he still remains.)

In other cities in Hunan around this time, including Changde, Yiyang, Huaihua, Meizhou, Lianyuan, Loudi and Yongzhou, many other students and citizens were also arrested. *Hunan Daily* reported, for example, that Xiong Gang, a student from Shanxi Province who had been provisional commander of the Autonomous Federation of Students from Outside Beijing, had been arrested after fleeing to his hometown in Hunan's Hanshou County, and that two core members of the Beijing SAF, named Wu Yun and Xu Yue, had also been seized in the province. The subsequent fate of the three students is not known.

The hunt intensifies

After the official banning of the SAF and WAF, the authorities soon began to spread the net more widely. On June 17, the Changsha Party committee established a "Changsha Municipal Leading Group for Investigating and Purging Illegal Organizations," and an extensive clean-up operation was carried out by the city's public security bureau. Scores of printing firms, cafes, restaurants and hair salons were searched and closed down, on suspicion of involvement in the pro-democracy movement, as were certain publishing units of the Hunan People's Press. All of these concerns had their assets seized by the authorities, and their owners and managers were either detained for investigation and interrogation in isolation, or placed under house arrest. In addition, a large number of government cadres were placed under close investigation, on suspicion of having pro-democracy sympathies.

Arrests continued apace elsewhere in the province. According to a June 18 report in the *Hunan Daily*, 31 people were arrested in Xiangtan City for having "pushed their way into public security offices and

24

frantically assaulted the police." Twenty-three of the detainees were workers who had allegedly "burst into the Pingzheng Road Police Station" (a local public security office in Xiangtan) on May 22; the known sentences eventually passed on members of this group ranged four to six years' imprisonment. The other eight detainees, headed by a worker in an electrical machinery factory named Chen Gang, were accused of having burst into the home of the factory's public security chief, who had tried to prevent them from carrying out a protest blockade of part of the factory on June 9, and of having allegedly carted out and set fire to the officer's television set, washing machine and other personal goods. For this act of *lèse majesté*, the courts eventually handed Chen a suspended death sentence.

Similarly draconian punishment was dealt out to nine workers who had earlier been arrested in connection with a riot in Shaoyang City on May 19. According to the *Hunan Daily*, "On June 17, the Shaoyang municipal authorities held a mass public-arrest meeting in Shaoyang, at which Wu Hepeng, Zhu Zhengying, Liu Jiye and six other criminals were formally placed under arrest for such crimes as arson, hooliganism and counterrevolutionary incitement." Wu was later condemned to death with a two-year reprieve, Zhu received life imprisonment and Liu was given a five-year term. The other six received upwards of five year sentences. The report did not indicate, however, which - or how many - of the nine were accused of violent offenses, and which merely of "counter-revolutionary incitement."

For three successive evenings, between June 27 and 29, Hunan Television publicly broadcast a government arrest warrant for me. On July 13, I was arrested in Jiangmen City in Guangdong Province, and towards the end of the month I was taken back to Changsha and locked up in the Changsha No.1 Jail. It was just around then that the rounding up of pro-democracy activists in Hunan was reaching a climax. Almost every police cell in Changsha, including those in the main jails, shelter-investigation centers and detention centers in the city, contained several so-called "riotous elements," and every day, more and more people were being thrown into prison. Moreover, most of the new arrivals around that time were students, teachers, cadres and other pro-democracy supporters who had been arrested purely for opposing the crackdown and expressing views critical of the government. Others were ordinary citizens who had tried to hide students or help them escape after the crackdown.

25

Among the most noteworthy of these "riotous elements," however, was a group of people who were arrested merely for having viewed scenes of the Beijing massacre on video tapes smuggled in from outside China, long after the June 4 incident had passed. In Changsha, anyone found to have seen these tapes was thoroughly investigated by the authorities, and about 30 people were taken into detention and interrogated over and over again until they agreed to say that they had not, after all, ever seen the tapes and had given their solemn word that they would never again speak about them. Thereafter, in Changsha, people would often joke about the "riotous elements who had seen the riot videotapes".

In early July, the central government issued a confidential directive ordering the media across the country to refrain as much as possible from carrying any news items concerning the arrests of Democracy Movement activists. From then on, only the occasional "model report" on such matters, designed to give the general public a periodic warning and reminder, would ever appear in the official press. Repressive activities, however, were neither suspended nor reduced. According to the official *Changsha Yearbook, 1990*:

> *In mid-August, in accordance with the spirit of CCP Central Committee Document No.3, Hunan Provincial Party Committee Document No.10 and Changsha Party Committee Document No.27, the Changsha Municipal Committee established a Leadership Group for Carrying Out the Investigations and Purge. The Municipal Politics and Law Committee then took the lead in setting up an Investigations and Purge Office, and deployed 68 cadres to form a special, full-time group to carry out this work.[10]*

Similar special duty units were also set up in other cities across the province, at great cost in manpower and other resources.

In Hunan Province, the government's round-up operation against student and worker pro-democracy activists continued right through to the end of 1989, and in some cases even beyond. In particular, a

---

[10] *Changsha Yearbook, 1990*, Hunan Publishing House, December 1990.

campaign to investigate and exhaustively document the statements, activities and "political performance" of any citizens suspected of even minor involvement in the pro-democracy movement, with a view to rooting out the broader social bases of support for what had been the greatest challenge to CCP power since 1949, was pursued relentlessly throughout the province until mid-1990. Countless people were subjected to various "administrative punishments" (including several-year terms of "re-education through labor"), were fired from their jobs or demoted, or otherwise had their careers or personal lives ruined by the authorities in this way.

The trials: applying a judicial gloss

The first set of cases to be brought before the Hunan courts, on and around June 15, 1989, was that of 27 people charged with violent involvement in the April 22 Incident. According to an official source, however, a total of 41 persons were eventually tried in connection with the incident. Of these, one person (Li Weihong) was convicted of "hooliganism" and received a suspended sentence of death; seven persons (including Xia Changchun, also convicted of "hooliganism") were sentenced to terms of 10-15 years' imprisonment; 16 persons were handed 5-10 year prison terms; 16 others were given terms of five years or less; and only one was exempted from punishment.[11]

From the outset, all the leaders of the Hunan pro-democracy movement deplored the violent rioting of April 22, and we strove hard to prevent the occurrence of any further such incidents. Indeed, given the subsequent scale of the movement in Hunan, there was remarkably little violence seen throughout, even after June 4. Major questions arose over the court handling of those accused of violent activities during the movement. In the trials of the April 22 detainees, for example, the authorities claimed that 21 public security officers and armed policemen had been injured during the riot, but in a striking departure from the norm, official press reports failed to identify any of those responsible for the alleged assaults. No such charges were laid against either Li or Xia, whose savage punishments were imposed by the court purely on charges of alleged incitement and damage to property.

---

[11] *Ibid*, p.24.

More generally, given the extremely low standards of evidence and judicial process that were applied after June 4, there can be no assurance that those arrested and convicted of violent offenses had actually committed such acts. As the authorities freely admitted, the guiding judicial policy at the time was "rapid reporting of arrests, rapid approval of arrests, and rapid sentencing" *(baobu kuai, pibu kuai, panjue kuai).*[12] The accused's guilt was trumpeted in the official press well in advance of the trials, which were duly held under the firm grip of the Party, so that verdicts of guilty were a foregone conclusion regardless of the merits of the evidence.

From early July onward, a wave of trials of leading pro-democracy activists and demonstrators was carried out across the province. The most notable feature of the trials was that almost all the defendants were either workers or ordinary urban residents. This reflected a clear and deliberate policy by the central government to scapegoat non-students for their alleged "manipulation" of events, and had two main objectives. One was to provide supporting evidence for the official conspiracy theory of the 1989 pro-democracy movement, whereby "well-intentioned but misguided" students were said to have been led astray and exploited by "outside elements with ulterior motives." (This theory was necessitated by the overwhelming support shown to the movement by the general public, and determined also that the student leaders themselves had to be given relatively minor punishment.)

The other overriding objective of the government was to crush all signs of emergent unrest and independent labor organization among the urban workforce. The CCP has had long and rich experience in controlling China's students and intellectuals, but perhaps its greatest fear in May-June 1989 was that its crucial ability to keep the workers well in line had finally begun to slip.

Chen Gang

A clear example of the way in which workers were victimized by the courts is provided by the case of Chen Gang. In early July, the Xiangtan Intermediate People's Court tried Chen Gang and seven other

---

[12] Ibid, p.24.

workers from the Xiangtan Electrical Machinery Plant on charges relating to the incident on June 9, mentioned above, in which a police officer's home was broken into and some of his belongings burned. The incident had been sparked off by a group of students from the Changsha Railroad College, headed by Chen's younger brother, Chen Ding, who had come to the Xiangtan Electrical Machinery Factory to urge the workers to strike. Moreover, Chen Gang himself had not even been present at the scene of the subsequent break-in at the policeman's house.

At the time of the Chen brothers' initial detention, the charge brought against both of them was "counterrevolutionary propaganda and incitement." Shortly afterwards, Chen Gang was formally indicted by the procuracy and the charge was changed to one of "robbery." The following day, the court opened to try the case, but by then the charge had been changed again, this time to "hooliganism." Only one day had elapsed between issuance of the indictment and the trial itself, leaving no time at all for preparation of a defense, and Chen Gang was duly sentenced to death. (In April 1990, the judgment was altered to death with a two-year reprieve.) Chen's seven co-defendants received sentences ranging from five years to life imprisonment. Chen's younger brother, Chen Ding, the student who, if anyone, had initiated the confrontation, was tried separately on a charge of "counterrevolutionary propaganda and incitement" and sentenced to one year's imprisonment. In mid-1990, he was released and allowed to resume his studies at college.

Many of the other harsh sentences imposed by the Hunan courts on workers during July - for example, the suspended death sentence for Guo Yunqiao of the Yueyang WAF, and the life sentence passed on Zhu Zhengying of Shaoyang City - have already been mentioned. Between August and September, however, dozens of other democracy movement activists in Changsha City were also tried and given heavy sentences, bringing to well over 200 the total number of those convicted since the onset of the crackdown.

Perhaps the most shocking of these cases involved Yao Guisheng, a member of the Changsha WAF, and two others, one a resident of Guangzhou named Hu Nianyou and one a resident of Lian County in Guangdong surnamed Chen (given name not known.) All three were arrested in Zhuzhou City for attempting to help WAF leaders escape from Changsha after June 4. At their trials in the Changsha Intermediate

Court in September 1989, Yao Guisheng and Hu Nianyou were convicted on spurious charges of "robbery and assault" arising from an argument in which they had been involved with a taxi driver over the fare for the WAF leaders. They were sentenced to terms of 15 years' and life imprisonment respectively. Chen was condemned to death, however, and was duly executed on December 26, 1989.

From the October 1 National Day until early 1990, a further series of trials was carried out in Hunan. In these, many influential figures who had been active during previous phases of the pro-democracy movement were sternly dealt with by the authorities and heavily sentenced. They included people who had been previously convicted for "counterrevolutionary activities" or for various "political mistakes"; so-called "rightists" and others who had regularly borne the brunt of the CCP's periodic political score-settling campaigns; and others who had long suffered persecution simply on account of their "complicated" family or individual backgrounds. Most of these individuals were ones whom the authorities had branded as being especially stubborn and persistent "reactionaries." In addition, many more members and leaders of the various Hunan regional WAFs continued to be brought to trial.

Zhang Jingsheng

Among the best-known of the "stubborn and reactionary" cases tried around this time was that of Zhang Jingsheng, the veteran pro-democracy activist who had founded and edited the unofficial journal *Wanderer (Liulangzhe)* in Changsha during the 1978-81 Democracy Wall movement. After the crackdown on that movement in spring 1981, Zhang was convicted of counterrevolution and spent four years in jail, where he quickly became known as the "Wei Jingsheng of the south" (the characters for both men's given names are identical.) While in prison, he wrote many protest poems which were set to music and are now sung by political prisoners and others in jails and labor camps throughout China (see *Appendix IX*). After his release in 1985, he was kept under close surveillance by the authorities.

During the 1989 Democracy Movement, Zhang Jingsheng was active in the Changsha WAF, although not in any leadership capacity. On May 4, he gave a rousing speech in the Martyr's Park to a large crowd of demonstrators, citing from his own experiences to illustrate China's need

30

for greater political democratization and official tolerance. He was loudly cheered by the crowd, but later that evening he was detained by the public security authorities and held for several days. Zhang took no part in any of the more radical actions undertaken during the 1989 movement, such as the blocking of traffic or laying down on railway tracks. He merely gave a few speeches at public gatherings and wrote some influential, though moderate, articles for the movement.

To the authorities, however, these were details of scant importance. Zhang was rearrested on May 28, following his participation in the student oath-taking ceremony earlier that evening outside the provincial government offices, and in December 1989 he was finally put on trial at the Changsha Intermediate Court on a charge of "counter-revolutionary propaganda and incitement." One of the main accusations made against Zhang at his trial was that, "While serving a previous prison sentence, the accused composed a large quantity of songs about prison life, the content of which was extremely reactionary." Originally, the provincial government had planned to impose a three-year sentence on Zhang. When the Beijing authorities got word of the case, however, they branded Zhang a "stubborn anti-Party element" and ordered that a figure "1" be placed in front of the scheduled "3." The order had come directly from the senior political authorities, and the Hunan court had no option but to meekly carry it out, despite widespread opposition within the local bureaucracy. Zhang is currently serving his 13-year sentence in the Provincial No.1 Prison in Yuanjiang.

Overview of the trials

Common to all the political trials carried out in Hunan Province after June 4 was an almost complete lack of regard for due process. First, in nearly all the cases, guilt was predetermined by the Party's "politics and law committees," which exist at all levels of the judicial, procuratorial and police hierarchy for the sole purpose of exercising so-called "unified leadership" by the Party over law-enforcement matters. In some cases, instructions as to the disposition of cases and level of sentencing were issued directly by the central Party authorities in Beijing. Second, in no cases were defense lawyers allowed to enter pleas of not guilty on behalf of their clients. Third, no prosecution witnesses were summoned to appear in court, thus depriving both the accused and their lawyers of any opportunity to cross-examine the state's evidence. Instead, written statements from these "witnesses" were produced in court and quoted from in piecemeal fashion by the prosecution, and any attempt to challenge their veracity was disallowed. And fourth, most of the cases were held *in camera*, and defense witnesses requested by the accused were not permitted to appear or give evidence.

In general, the harshest and most arbitrary sentences were imposed on pro-democracy activists who were brought to trial during the months immediately following the June 4 crackdown. The level of sentencing remained unconscionably high for the remainder of the year, however, and only began to return to (for China) somewhat more "normal" levels after the lifting of martial law in Beijing in January 1990. Several leading democracy activists were taken to court and tried each month during 1990, mostly on charges of "counterrevolutionary propaganda and incitement." These included university and college teachers, government cadres, students, workers, private businessmen and even some peasants, and the sentences handed down generally ranged from two to five years' imprisonment. An important factor behind this more lenient treatment was undoubtedly the increasing international pressure brought to bear upon the Chinese government in 1990 over human rights issues.

Another clear and consistent pattern in the trials was that detainees of low social status were dealt with much more harshly than those with status. Workers, and particularly unemployed people, faced harsher penalties as a matter of course, with average levels of sentencing starting at around five years and rising, in some cases, all the way to life imprisonment or even death, though usually with a two-year reprieve. Students, intellectuals and government cadres generally fared much better. I myself, for example, was tried by the Changsha Intermediate Court on July 17, 1990 on a charge of "counterrevolutionary propaganda and incitement." Despite having been branded as one of those chiefly responsible for the province-wide "turmoil and chaos," I received a mere three-year sentence. It was the highest passed on any student in Hunan. I was released on parole in February 1991. A small number of other students were sentenced to prison terms, mainly for "common criminal" offenses, but the leading members of the Hunan SAF were for the most part eventually acquitted and set free.

A final hallmark of the trials was that defendants who pleaded not guilty were branded as persons with a "bad attitude," and were invariably punished more severely than those who bowed to the inevitable and expressed contrition. In fact, the more convincing and powerful a defense case that such persons managed to put forward, the sterner and more vengeful, usually, was the response of the court.

The central government was well pleased with the performance of the Hunan judicial authorities in crushing dissent in the province. On November 27, 1989, the Supreme People's Procuracy in Beijing conferred upon the Changsha Municipal Procuracy a "National-Level Advanced Collective Merit Award for Curbing the Turmoil and Suppressing the Counterrevolutionary Rebellion." On January 5, 1990, the Supreme People's Court conferred the same honor upon the Changsha Intermediate Court.[13]

Statistical summary of arrests and convictions

By mid-1990, well over 1000 people had been detained or taken in for so-called "shelter and investigation" in Hunan Province on charges arising out of involvement in the 1989 pro-democracy movement.

Of these, about 25 per cent, or roughly 300 persons, were detained in Changsha alone. These included the nearly 100 persons held after the April 22 Incident (of whom at least 40, and probably many more, were tried and sentenced) and also 140 "major riotous elements" (i.e. pro-democracy leaders) detained in the city between June and late December 1989. According to an official source, 66 of those 140 had been placed under formal arrest, and 46 already tried and sentenced, by year's end; seven persons had been sent for several-year terms of re-education through labor; 53 had been "released after education"; six had been transferred to other jurisdictions for trial; and eight remained in investigative custody.[14] In fact, however, the actual trial and conviction rate in Changsha was considerably higher than that claimed by the authorities, and at least 80 persons remained in untried custody in the

---

[13] *Changsha Yearbook, 1990*, p.108.

[14] *Ibid*, p.105.

city by the end of 1989.[15] In addition, several dozen more pro-democracy activists were arrested in the Changsha region in the course of 1990.

As regards the rest of Hunan, over 100 people were arrested from each of the province's other four main cities, namely Xiangtan, Shaoyang, Yueyang and Hengyang, and only slighter lesser numbers from the cities of Changde, Yiyang, Zhuzhou, Loudi and Huaihua. In addition, several dozen were arrested in the towns of Chenzhou, Lingling and Xiangxi.

At a conservative estimate, well over 65 per cent of all those detained in the province, or around 750 persons, were eventually either tried and sentenced to terms of imprisonment or reform through labor, or else were sentenced by the public security authorities to 2-3 year terms of re-education through labor. (Confidential government figures cited below, however, suggest that this may well be a considerable underestimate.)

The present report contains details of 219 pro-democracy activists detained in Hunan Province after June 4, 1989, of whom 172 (or just under 25 per cent of the total estimated convictions for the province) were sentenced to terms of either labor reform or labor re-education. Of the 219 detainees, 150 reportedly remained in prison or in labor re-education camps as of May 1992, while only 67, or less than one-third, had been released. The overall disposition of these cases by prisoner category is shown in *Table I*.[16] (For individual case details, please refer to *Appendix I*, below.)

Applying this average one-third release rate to the total convicted

---

[15] In late 1989 I was still being held in Changsha No.1 Jail, and those in untried detention in that jail alone at the time included Zhang Xudong, He Zhaohui, Xie Changfa, Tang Changye, Zhong Hua, Zhang Jie, Li Shaojun, Yu Chaohui, Chen Le, Zhou Min, Long Jianhua and Fan Zhong. Many more untried pro-democracy activists were still being held in other jails and detention centers in Changsha at that time.

[16] See note at end of chapter for explanation of the table.

Table I: Treatment of 213 Pro-democracy Prisoners in Hunan Province

Statistics based on Appendix I		Sentenced Prisoners		Detained without trial then freed	Total
		No.	Average Sentence		
Workers	Excl. lifers + death w/rep.	(79)	(6 years)	7	97
	Incl. lifers + death w/rep.	90	8.1 years		
Students		19	2.2 years	16	35
Intellectuals		32	4.5 years	5	37
Journalists		7	4 years	3	10
Businessmen		9	3 years	4	13
Cadres		11	5 years	3	14
Peasants		7	3.3 years	0	7
TOTAL		173	4.3 years	38	213

population for Hunan, it can be inferred that around 500 of those detained since June 1989 in the province probably still remained in prisons, labor-reform camps or labor re-education centers as of May 1992.

Confidential report on political imprisonment in Hunan

Compiling detailed information on the repression in China, especially in the provinces, is a daunting task, and while every effort has been made to confirm the information on political prisoners set forth in this report, a small margin of error may still remain.

The following remarkable figures can, however, be cited with absolute certainty, for they come from a highly-classified report compiled by the Hunan judicial authorities themselves. The document in question is entitled "Outline Report on the Numbers of Turmoil Elements Committed to Prisons in Hunan Province by the End of 1990." The term "turmoil elements" *(dongluan fenzi)* refers solely to political prisoners detained after June 4, 1989 on account of their involvement in the pro-democracy movement. The scope of the report, moreover, is confined to those pro-democracy detainees who had already, as of December 31, 1990, been tried and sentenced in court. (In China, only convicted criminals are sent to prisons; those still awaiting trial are kept in jails and detention centers.)

According to the report, a total of no fewer than 594 "turmoil elements" had been committed to the seven main prisons in Hunan Province by the end of 1990.[17] Sixteen of those were women, since they were sent to Changsha Prison, the province's only jail for female prisoners. The report even noted the successive batches in which those sent to each of the main prisons had been organized to commence "political study." **Table II** shows the core information from the report.[18]

As mentioned, only convicted criminals are ever sent to actual prisons in China. Furthermore, only two classes of convicted prisoners are ever sent to prisons: so-called "common criminals" who have been sentenced, on average, to terms of seven to ten years and above, and also the majority of "counterrevolutionaries" or political prisoners. Non-political prisoners serving lesser sentences are usually sent to labor-reform camps instead to complete their sentences.

---

[17] All 145 of the pro-democracy prisoners noted in the government report as having been committed to two of these seven prisons - namely Chenzhou and Huaihua prisons - are excluded from the purview of *Appendix I*, below, since Asia Watch was unable to obtain information on any of the individuals held in those two places.

[18] The "one late arrival" listed in the report under Longxi Prison was Tang Boqiao.

Table II: Figures from secret government report

Name of Prison	No. of "Turmoil Elements" by end of 1990	Commenced "political study" in batches of
Provincial No.1 Prison (Yuanjiang Prison)	121	24, 49 and 45 (+ three late arrivals)
Provincial No.2 Prison (Hengyang Prison)	98	16, 54 and 27 (+ one late arrival)
Provincial No.3 Prison (Lingling Prison)	106	28, 50 and 25 (+ three late arrivals)
Provincial No.4 Prison (Huaihua Prison)	77	55 and 22
Provincial No.5 Prison (Chenzhou Prison)	68	40 and 28
Provincial No.6 Prison (Longxi Prison)	108	33, 51 and 23 (+ one late arrival)
Changsha Prison	16	6 and 10
TOTAL	594	594

Hence, the figure of 594 "turmoil elements" committed to prisons in Hunan after June 1989 probably only includes those who were convicted of "counterrevolution" and those who received heavy sentences for such alleged crimes as arson and assault. It would include neither those who received lesser terms of imprisonment for other "common" criminal offenses during the 1989 movement, nor the many peaceful protestors who were sentenced without trial to terms of "re-education through labor." Given that the average length of sentence in the case of those committed to prisons is considerably higher than that for all other penal institutions in China, moreover, it is reasonable to assume that the great majority of the 594 "turmoil elements" cited in the confidential Hunan government report are still behind bars in the province today.

Notes to Table I:

  * Categories in the table refer to the following: "Workers" includes both factory and service-sector employees, and also unemployed persons. "Students" includes both undergraduate and graduate students. "Intellectuals" includes university, college and high-school professors, as well as scientists, doctors, technicians and musicians. "Journalists" includes newspaper reporters, editors and television journalists. "Businessmen" includes private entrepreneurs, managers and salespersons. "Cadres" includes state administrative personnel, Party functionaries and ranking officials.

  * *Appendix I* lists details of 219 named prisoners or ex-prisoners; the six persons not covered in *Table I* include one who was executed, one who died in prison and four who remain in untried detention. In addition, *Appendix I* mentions 12 others reported to have been tried and sentenced but whose names are not known.

  * Sentences of both life imprisonment and death with reprieve are taken, for purposes of the table, as being equivalent to 25 years' imprisonment. In China, the longest sentence of fixed-term imprisonment that the courts can impose is 20 years. Life sentences begin at that level, and often mean life. Those sentenced to death with a reprieve are either executed at the end of the two-year probationary period, or else are left to serve out at least the equivalent of an average life sentence; most will never be released.

  * There were 12 sentences of known length passed on students, totalling 26 years; the average known sentence for students was thus 2.2 years. (No college student in Hunan is known to have received a sentence exceeding three years. However, one high-school student, a 15-year-old named Liu Xin, received a 15-year sentence; this was excluded from the averaging here, as it was so much higher than any of the other sentences on students.) In addition, there were six sentences of unknown length passed on students; they have been arbitrarily assigned the average term of 2.2 years here.

  * There were 29 sentences of known length passed upon intellectuals, averaging 4.5 years each. In addition, there were two intellectuals whose sentences were not known. They were each assigned the average of 4.5 years here.

  * One of the seven journalists, Yu Zhijian (an editor), received a sentence of 20 years' imprisonment. Since this was far higher than any of the other sentences on journalists, it was excluded from calculation of the average figure given here. When the sentence on Yu is included, the average sentence for journalists rises to 6.3 years.

  * Six businessmen received known sentences averaging three years. A seventh, Li Zimin, received a 15 year sentence which greatly exceeded any other in the category and so was excluded from calculation of the average. Two other businessmen received unknown sentences, and they were assigned average three-year sentences for purposes of this chart.

38

* Ten cadres were sentenced to known terms averaging five years. One other was sentenced to an unknown term and was assigned the average for purposes of this chart.

* The average terms of detention for the various categories of those listed in the column headed "Detained without trial then freed" are not known. These were mostly students who were held for periods of several months to a year before being released. An unknown number of people remain in untried detention in Hunan Province in connection with the 1989 pro-democracy movement.

3. Some Prominent Cases of Abuse and Injustice

Behind the prison gates in China, one sees the regime's veneer of "socialist humanitarianism" stripped bare, revealing the underlying brutality of the system in its clearest form. After my arrest on July 13, 1989, I changed overnight from a university student into an imprisoned "counterrevolutionary criminal," and over the next 18 months I was detained in seven different jails and detention centers in Guangdong and Hunan provinces.[19] While there, I witnessed numerous flagrant violations of basic human rights being committed by the prison authorities.

The first place I was taken was the Jiangmen City No. 1 Jail, and it was there that I met my first case of unjust imprisonment. The person's name was Zhang Xinbiao, a young fellow of strong character. As soon as I entered the cell, I noticed that Zhang was wearing leg irons. Perplexed by this - he was the only one of over 20 prisoners who was wearing shackles - I asked him what on earth he had done to deserve such treatment. He answered, in a matter of fact way, that it was because he had sworn and spat at a cadre. He had been shackled continuously from the moment, more than four months earlier, when he was first admitted to the jail. I was shaken by this information: how was it possible that in our country a person could be thrown into chains simply for daring to argue with a government official? Frankly, at the time I only half believed what he was telling me. Until then, I had always naively believed that the kinds of people who ended up in jail - shackled or not - must have committed unforgivable crimes and were merely getting their just deserts. Surely, the People's Government would never allow such things to happen?

But this was just the beginning. I soon realized that such sights were an everyday part of the prison scene and my eyes were quickly opened to the ugly realities all around. My way of thinking began to

---

[19] These included detention centers in Jiangmen City and Xinhui County; Guangdong Province Detention Center No.1; Changsha No. 1 and No.2 Jails; Shaoyang Jail; and Longxi Prison. In all, I spent time in 16 different cells.

change, and I felt increasing anger and contempt for the callous hypocrisy shown by the Chinese Communist prison authorities towards those whom they branded, often quite arbitrarily, as criminals. In the name of so-called "thought reform" and "recreating useful members of society," they thought nothing of destroying a man's spirit. Particularly in the case of political prisoners, indeed, this was seen as a necessary part of the "reform through labor" process (although physically, so-called "common criminals" often received worse treatment.)

The following are only a few of the more egregious examples of the kinds of systematic degradation, punishment and indignity that have all too frequently been inflicted upon detained pro-democracy figures in Hunan since June 4, 1989. Some of these individuals have already been released, and their stories are thus readily available. At least one is now dead. The others remain behind bars, and the information on their cases has been obtainable only through secret channels.

The "Mao portrait" case

Perhaps the best-known group of political prisoners currently being held in Hunan Province are three men - Yu Zhijian, Yu Dongyue and Lu Decheng - who defaced the giant portrait of Mao Zedong which hangs in Tiananmen Square by throwing ink and paint-filled eggshells at it on May 23, 1989. This case was reported worldwide at the time, and the public desecration of the Great Helmsman's image in this way so infuriated the Party leadership that the case was labelled as one of the foremost "counterrevolutionary incidents" of the entire 1989 Chinese pro-democracy movement.

Yu Zhijian, aged 27, was formerly a teacher at the Tantou Wan primary school in Dahu Township, Liuyang County, and Yu Dongyue was a fine arts editor for the *Liuyang News*. Lu Decheng, 28, worked for the Liuyang branch of the Hunan Provincial Bus Company. (Other notable figures from Liuyang include Tan Sitong, the late 19th century reformer, and Hu Yaobang.) The three were tried by the Beijing Intermediate Court in September 1989 on charges of "counterrevolutionary sabotage" and "counterrevolutionary propaganda and incitement" and sentenced variously to life, 20 years and 16 years' imprisonment.

According to the authorities, the three men had travelled from

41

Hunan to Beijing on May 19, 1989, having already displayed "counter-revolutionary" banners and given "counterrevolutionary speeches" in Changsha. In addition, Lu was accused of having organized a Liuyang branch of a group called the Hunan Delegation in Support of the Beijing Students. (The three probably went to Beijing as representatives of that body.) Regardless of whether or not one endorses their provocative act of defacing the Mao portrait, the fact remains that under any more civilized judicial system the men would have received at most short-term prison sentences for "disturbing the peace."

After their secret trials, Lu and the two Yus were transferred under armed guard back to Hunan from Beijing to serve out their sentences at the Provincial No. 3 Prison in Lingling. Ever since their initial detention, the three have consistently refused to admit that their protest action had any "counterrevolutionary intent" (a necessary factor for determination of guilt by the courts in such cases.) Because of this evidence of "bad attitude" on their part, they were subjected to manifold forms of severe torture and ill-treatment from the outset. After the men were transferred back to Hunan, the Lingling Prison authorities were instructed by Beijing to incarcerate them in a "strict regime" unit.

Conditions in such units vary from place to place in China, but they are usually extremely grim. (I myself was held under "strict regime" at Longxi Prison for several months, but because I was a university student and did not make any conspicuous trouble, I was assigned to teach Chinese language classes to the other prisoners.) In the case of the three "portrait desecrators," whose crimes were compounded by their "refusal to confess and submit to the law," one of the harshest prison measures - solitary confinement - was imposed. The solitary confinement cells at Lingling Prison are just over two square meters each in area. They have no ventilation or heating, which makes them freezing cold in winter and unbearably hot in summer, and they are almost pitch-dark. In addition, the cells are damp and sanitation is extremely deficient. Prisoners are only allowed to leave these cells for brief, thrice-daily meal periods during which they must eat their food while walking around in a tiny exercise yard.

According to the regulations, prisoners may only be held in solitary confinement for a maximum period of two weeks, and Lu Decheng was returned to a shared-cell regime after six months. Yu

Zhijian and Yu Dongyue, however, have been kept in solitary confinement ever since late 1989. According to reliable inside sources, Teacher Yu Zhijian's health has deteriorated dramatically as a result of his ongoing 30-month ordeal. He has dramatically lost weight and now appears severely emaciated and skeletal. Yu Dongyue, the one-time fine arts editor, has become badly disturbed psychologically, to the extent even of having lost control of his excretory functions. On top of this, both men have been subjected to a range of overt physical tortures, ostensibly because they uttered "reactionary statements" about certain government officials.

According to the prison leadership, the two men have "completely failed to reform their reactionary nature." Other cadres at Lingling Prison, however, are reported to be greatly dissatisfied with the inhumane treatment still being meted out to the two Yus. International attention to the plight of Yu Zhijian and Yu Dongyue is now urgently required.

Peng Yuzhang

A retired professor of Hunan University now in his seventies, Peng Yuzhang showed active support for the students throughout the 1989 pro-democracy movement by participating in our various sit-ins and hunger strikes. He was arrested at his home in mid-June, 1989, and thrown into Changsha No. 1 Jail. Despite his advanced years, Professor Peng showed real spirit. Every day, he would shout out loudly from his cell, "Why are you detaining me!", and "I demand to be released!" This overt show of resistance did not go unpunished for long. Peng was eventually taken from his cell and placed on a device known as the "shackle board" - a horizontal plank roughly the size of a door, equipped with metal shackles at the four corners and a large hole at the lower end. The offending prisoner is laid upwards on the board, and his hands and feet are secured by the four shackles. The hole allows the prisoner to perform basic bodily functions. Although highly illegal, this inhuman instrument of torture can be found in most of the jails and prisons in Hunan Province. Its existence, of course, is a closely guarded secret.

After I was escorted back from Guangdong to the Changsha No. 1 Jail in July, every night I used to hear Professor Peng's distressed cries of protest from his punishment cell. "Let me out!", "I need to take a bath" and "We are not afraid!", he would shout out. He remained very sensible

43

and coherent, however, and took care to never utter extreme slogans. Sometimes he would even sing the old primary school anthem, "Learn from the Good Example of Lei Feng." At the last line ("Stand firm and never waver!"), his voice would rise to a crescendo, as he bravely sought to give heart and encouragement to the rest of us. We, in turn, would cry out in unison: "Professor Peng! A good example!"

At one point, I could bear it no longer and roared out a demand that he be released from the "shackle board" immediately. The only response I got from the jail warden, however, was that Peng was "psychiatrically ill," and that this, precisely, was why he had to be kept in shackles. Appalled and enraged by this, I argued with the cadre that under Chinese criminal law, far from being subject to such additional torments, the mentally ill are in fact meant to be "exempt from prosecution." He then replied that since there was as yet no concrete proof of his illness, Professor Peng did not qualify for this exemption and so could not be released. The truth of the matter, I discovered later, was that prison officials in Hunan deliberately use the "shackle board" punishment as a means of determining whether unruly prisoners who show signs of mental illness are genuinely disturbed or whether they are just feigning it. In Peng Yuzhang's case, the ordeal lasted for more than three months. When finally he was taken off the "shackle board," he was a mere shadow of his former self.

Some time later, while I was being taken down one of the jail corridors to an interrogation session, I happened to pass by Peng, who was just then being brought back from one himself. All shrivelled and dried up, he was barely conscious and was being carried out on a warden's back. I began to say, "Professor Peng, you've suffered so much...", but my voice became choked with sobs and I couldn't go on. Somehow, he managed to smile at me - just like before, in May 1989 when we held the sit-in protest together outside the Changsha government offices. "Don't worry, Little Tang," he said. "I'll be all right." That was the last time I ever saw him. Some days later, a pre-trial investigator told me that the hospital had given a clear diagnosis of psychiatric illness on Peng's part, and so the government had decided to release him and allow him to return home. I felt greatly relieved.

Much later, upon my own release in February 1991, I found out that Professor Pang had in fact been forcibly committed to a psychiatric asylum immediately after his release from the Changsha No. 1 Jail. In effect, the authorities had contrived to pass a life sentence on him by other means. Since then, none of Professor Peng's friends or relatives have been allowed to visit him in the psychiatric asylum, and there are reports that he may have committed suicide soon after being admitted there.[20]

Zhou Zhirong

Zhou Zhirong, a graduate of the Hunan Normal College (which later became Hunan Normal University), was prior to the 1989 pro-democracy movement a geography teacher at the Xiangtan No. 2 Middle School. He entered college at the age of only 15, in the class of '77 - the first group of students to be enrolled since the Cultural Revolution on the basis of competitive examinations. During the 1980 student protest campaign at Hunan Normal College against official interference in that year's free elections to the local legislature, Zhou emerged as a dauntless activist and was one of the last to give up a collective hunger strike staged by the students.

During the 1989 pro-democracy movement, Zhou, 32 years old, gave numerous public speeches in Changsha, Xiangtan and elsewhere to promote democratic ideas. He did not, however, join in any of the student or worker organizations. After the June 4 crackdown - despite the brutal heat of the Hunan summer, he put on a black woollen coat bearing the Chinese character for "sadness" on the front and the character for "mourning" on the back, and staged a lone sit-in protest with his eyes closed outside the Xiangtan municipal government offices.

He then fled Xiangtan for several months, before eventually and

---

[20] Other sources speculate that the authorities may simply have disposed of Peng in the same way that they did Chen Guangdi, a well-known political activist who was imprisoned in Hunan toward the end of the Cultural Revolution for having served as an adviser to a radical Red Guard group called the "Hunan Provincial Proletarian League" *(Sheng-Wu-Lian.)* Chen's body was found in 1975 at a rubbish dump at the Pingtang Labor-Reform Farm, Changsha. According to the government, Chen had "committed suicide to escape punishment." By coincidence, Chen, like Peng Yuzhang, was also a teacher at Hunan University.

after much thought deciding in September to report voluntarily to the public security authorities. He was seized on the spot and carted away to be locked up in the Xiangtan Jail. From that time onward, his life became an unending round of gross torment and abuse. At first, the prison authorities treated him, if anything, somewhat more politely than the so-called "common criminals." But Zhou's character was such that he used to insist on having the few formal rights that were left him as a prisoner respected, and he would often complain when this did not happen. Soon, the prison cadres began to fear and resent him, and eventually to hate him.

At first they just used to scold and humiliate him, but then later they instructed his cellmates to begin tormenting him. From then on, the other prisoners would not allow him on to the sleeping platform at night, so he had to sleep on the concrete floor. During the daytime, they forced him to scrub the floor endlessly, hour after hour, long after it had become spotlessly clean. As he scrubbed, he was made to sing songs like the opening theme to "Clever Yi Xiu" (a popular Japanese animated film) - the lyrics having first been altered to include the line "Hurray! Let's scrub and clean this floor! Hurray! Let's polish it all the way into the cassia blossom room!" (In prison slang, "cassia blossom room" means the toilet cubicle at the end of the cell.) In the evenings, they even made him imitate bird and animal calls - in short, they tried in every way imaginable to demean and humiliate him.

"How do you like it now?", the prison cadres would ask him spitefully. Again, Zhou's character was such that while he would never clash with his fellow prisoners, he used to break into the most vehement curses when taunted by a prison guard or other official. He used to tell them that he was already being more than polite enough to them, simply by considering them as human. They couldn't believe their ears. He would never submit to them - this was his way of retaining his human dignity. Every time a cadre ordered him to kneel, for example, he would refuse. They would interpret this lack of subservience as a major challenge to their authority, even seeing it as a source of personal humiliation, and they would promptly beat the shit out of him. The other prisoners all came to regard him as a sheer madman.

In early 1990, Zhou was brought to trial and sentenced to seven years' imprisonment for "counterrevolutionary incitement," reduced after appeal to five years. His defense argument at the trial consisted of two points. First, he was not guilty, because none of the various speeches he had made during the 1989 movement were counterrevolutionary in nature. And second, he denied that he had, as claimed by the prosecution, "turned himself in" to the authorities, since that would have implied an admission of guilt on his part. A man of forthright and outspoken character, Zhou knew all along that by taking this principled stand he would surely be dooming himself. Ironically, the only part of his defense that the court accepted was that he had not, after all, "turned himself in." As a result, not only was he denied the reduced punishment accorded to those who were held to have done so - he was even sentenced more heavily.

Zhou was sent to Longxi Prison, in a remote mountainous part of Shaoyang, several months before me, and we spent time in the "strict regime" unit there together with other political prisoners. Latterly, he even tried to organize secret political discussions between us, and for this, seven or eight of us were put into solitary confinement for seven days in the prison's "black rooms" - windowless, pitch-dark boxes of less than two meters in area. Prior to that time, Zhou had still not properly recovered physically or psychologically from the ill-treatment he had suffered in Xiangtan Jail. He was prone to sudden outbursts of wild and erratic speech, alternating with periods of deep depression and silence.

On February 12, 1991, Zhou was transferred to a solitary-confinement punishment unit at the Provincial No. 3 Prison in Hunan's Lingling Prefecture. Once there, he was put on a "shackle board" and kept there, without respite, for a full three months. When he showed continued resistance by shouting at his jailers, a filthy rag was stuffed in his mouth, to be removed only at feeding times. According to an inside source, Zhou had become severely psychiatrically disturbed by the time of his eventual removal from the "shackle board" in May 1991.

What makes Zhou Zhirong's story all the more sad is that his father died early and his sick mother now lies paralyzed and bed-ridden at their home in a poor, remote village, with only Zhou's younger brother left to look after her. Zhou wrote to his friends from prison, begging them to help his mother out financially, so they started sending her small sums of money. But after a few months the authorities found out about it and the friends were interrogated by the police and told to stop "giving assistance to a counterrevolutionary family." One day, when Zhou's younger brother was on his way to visit Zhou at the Xiangtan Jail, he became involved in a traffic accident and his leg was crushed by a tractor. As they say, troubles never come singly in life.

Fan Zhong

Another political prisoner whom I saw with my own eyes being cruelly mistreated was Fan Zhong. A student in the class of '85 at Central-South Industrial University, Fan was at the time of the 1989 pro-democracy movement chairman of the official students union, vice-chairman of the provincial students federation and a member of the Chinese Communist Party. Although initially reluctant to involve himself in the movement, he eventually did so and soon rose to become a standing committee member of the SAF. When I travelled to Beijing in late May to assess the situation there, Fan acted as SAF chairman.

Arrested at the end of June 1989, he was first held in the Changsha No. 2 Jail, before being transferred in mid-July to Changsha No. 2 Jail where he was kept in Cell 6, just a few doors away from my cell. Whenever I was taken out for interrogation, I passed right by Fan's cell and had the chance to see him and exchange a few words. He would always flash me a quick V-for-victory sign, and initially he was full of optimism. As time passed by and hopes of an early release began to fade, however, his mood sank and his eyes took on a dark and lost expression. Shortly after the 1990 Spring Festival, he came close to mental collapse and began shouting out loudly and making big scenes. (On another level, this was actually a form of resistance).

The jail officials soon marked Fan down as a troublemaker, and before long they took to pulling him out of his cell and giving him what they used to refer to in jail slang as a "reaming." This is a form of punishment commonly found in Hunan jails, and involves being given repeated shocks by an electric baton to sensitive parts of the body. The somewhat obscure nickname "reaming" (*jiao*) derives from the fact that when the cadres torture prisoners in this way, they not only go for places like the neck, face and ears, but quite often even push the baton inside the victim's mouth and start twisting it around from one side to the other - as if reaming out a hole. Each time this happened to Fan and I would hear his agonized cries of pain, I felt my heart being pierced by a knife.

Finally, they put him on to the "shackle board" and then he really did start to go crazy. The first thing we would hear on returning to our cells after work in the evening would be Fan's shouts of "You bastards are going to die a bad death!", "Let me out of here!" and "I'm so angry I could die!" Sometimes he could be heard barking like a dog, quacking like a duck or crowing like a chicken. At other times he would just lie there talking to himself all night long, right through until daybreak. In the daytime, he would sometimes be carried out for another dose of electric "reaming" or handed over to a bunch of prisoners to be tormented by them, falling asleep when his body could eventually stand no more. On one occasion, unable to bear the loathsome spectacle any longer, I called one of the prison cadres and requested that Fan's punishment be halted. He told me that Fan had brought the whole thing on himself by pretending to be mad, when in fact he was perfectly sane. I asked how they could possibly justify treating prisoners like this. But I might as well have saved my breath. The cadre replied that Fan had violated prison rules and stirred up trouble, and so it was essential that he be punished.

Fan's condition deteriorated day by day. He lost all control over his bowel and urinary movements and even began to stop responding physically to the electrical assaults. In the end, when he could no longer differentiate between different people or objects, the cadres no longer doubted that Fan really did have psychiatric problems, and for a while they more or less stopped beating him with the electric batons. But by then Fan had lost all physical coordination, which often led to him being teased and tormented by the other prisoners. They would vent all their pent-up frustration and resentments against Fan, either by stuffing dirty socks or cloths into his mouth, pouring cold water over his body (this was during a bitterly cold winter) or just kicking him. All the while, Fan was just lying there, fixed to the "shackle board" and unable to move or do anything but endure the torment.

Three months went by before the higher authorities acknowledged the situation as being at all serious - and only then because they realized that if the facts became known outside the prison there would be widespread public discontent and strenuous criticisms would be raised. They then did an enormous amount of so-called "ideological work" on Fan, and he was only released from the "shackle board" after he had given an undertaking that he would stop all his protests and not make any more trouble. No one made any attempt to stop the bullying by his fellow prisoners, however, and it continued right up until his release in late 1990.

The next and last time I met Fan Zhong was in mid-July 1991, shortly before I escaped from China. We talked through the night, and he poured out all his feelings about the terrible experience he had been through. Thinking back on it all, I too felt overwhelmed with emotion. He and I were true friends in adversity. Fan told me that he was no longer in contact with anyone anymore, and that until the social system changed, he would not dare to re-enter society again. As I left his place, the thought occurred to me: if the government wouldn't even spare a youth like him, someone who had been raised in the teachings of the Party from earliest childhood, then the government must surely be blind. It was, to coin a phrase, creating its own grave-diggers.

Chen Gang

Immediately after his conviction in June 1989, Chen Gang (the Xiangtan worker who was sentenced to death in June 1989 on trumped-up charges) was put into handcuffs and leg-irons - the usual practice for condemned prisoners in China. He secretly wrote out a last will and testament and entrusted it to be passed on to his younger brother, Chen Ding. In the letter, Chen expressed the hope that his younger brother would never abandon his ideals or the pursuit of justice.

Chen's fellow workers at the Xiangtan Electrical Machinery Factory, however, refused to accept the court's verdict against him, and several tens of thousands of them prepared to stage a protest strike. The mood was extremely tense and explosive, and the case was referred upward through ever higher levels of the bureaucracy for resolution, and as a means of holding the strike at bay. On several occasions, Chen was taken from his cell by armed guards in preparation for execution, only to be sent back inside again later.

In early April 1990, workers at the Xiangtan Electrical Machinery Factory heard that Chen was to be executed on April 22 and spread the news all around. The following day, the entire factory workforce came out on strike. This incident alerted those at the most senior levels of government to the depth of popular local feeling over the issue, and showed the strength of the people. A series of official "studies" then followed, at the end of which, in May 1990, the judicial authorities altered the sentence on Chen Gang to one of death penalty with a two-year stay of execution.

Throughout this 10-month period, from initial imposition of the death penalty to the final review and reduction of sentence, Chen Gang had been kept shackled hand and foot. One can scarcely imagine the mental and physical suffering he must have gone through as a result of this brutal, and entirely unnecessary, punitive measure.

After my release from prison, I made a special trip to the Xiangtan Electrical Machine Factory, hoping to meet with Chen's parents. While having lunch at a local restaurant, I asked the proprietor if he knew their address. Upon hearing that I was Chen's friend, the restaurant owner became very excited and began telling me all the latest news. Apparently, the security section chief whose belongings had been burned in the original incident had since been transferred to a post elsewhere, because the local people used to stare at him angrily all the time and stones were often thrown at his home at night. Chen's mother, it turned out, was an old teacher at the factory kindergarten, and people all said that she was a good and kind woman. Chen Gang's younger brothers and sisters were all said to be coping well. But now, a once happy family had been plunged into tragedy. "The Chen brothers were indeed unfortunate!" said the restaurant owner, with mixed sadness and anger.

My friend then quietly told him that I was a student leader who had been jailed together with Chen Gang, and pointed to my head. (In prison, my head had been shaved, so I normally wore a hat to avoid attracting attention). The owner was surprised and delighted, and his family all came over and began asking me many questions, including all about Chen Gang's current condition and about our experiences in jail. They said that everyone in the area wanted to know if Chen Gang had any chance of being released in the near future. I comforted them as best I could, saying I believed that the day would not be too far off. Before I left, the restaurant owner and his family toasted me with a glass of wine and declined all attempts to pay my bill. My friend and I then went to the Chen family home, but the door was locked and nobody was there. We next went to the kindergarten where Chen's mother worked, but still there was nobody. So I had to return to Changsha without having seen Chen's mother. I had met many people who loved and cared about the family, however, and I was moved and comforted by this fact.

Li Maoqiu, Zhang Zhonghui and Liu Fuyuan

Three of my fellow prisoners in Cell 12 of the Changsha No. 1 Jail were pure cases of unjust imprisonment. The oldest was a man named Li Maoqiu, 53 years old, a senior engineer at the Changsha Non-Ferrous Metals Design Institute and latterly a millionaire. The youngest was a 16 year-old lad named Zhang Zhonghui, who had been falsely accused of theft. The other, a severely ill man named Liu Fuyuan, had been accused of economic crimes. (Although ostensibly unrelated to the 1989 pro-democracy movement, his arrest was a direct consequence of the indiscriminate "law and order" campaign which accompanied the movement's suppression.)

In 1986, Li Maoqiu went off the payroll[21] of the Nonferrous Metals Design Institute in order to set up a private business. By 1989, less than three years later, the business had expanded to include a chicken farm, a dog farm, a salted goods shop and a roasted snack shop.[22]

After the outbreak of the 1989 Democracy Movement, Li, who felt strongly about the escalating problem of official profiteering and government corruption in China, demonstrated his firm and unconditional support for the protesting students by donating over 10,000 *yuan* to our fighting fund.[23] This gesture of financial support was much appreciated by the student movement in Hunan.

---

[21] *Tingxin liuzhi*, a fairly common procedure whereby employees of state enterprises can sometimes seek other employment while retaining their original job-benefit package.

[22] Around this time, a friend of Li's named Zhou Zhenhua, a lecturer at the Central-South Industrial University, set up a technology development enterprise called the Central-South Materials Company. Li Maoqiu invested more than RMB 270,000 *yuan* in the company, but in early 1989 it went bankrupt and Li lost most of his money.

[23] One US dollar equals approximately 5.20 *yuan*.

At the end of June 1989, however, the public security authorities secretly arrested Li and threw him into the Changsha No. 1 Jail for interrogation and investigation. (Li was an obvious target for political scapegoating: both his maternal grandfather and his father-in-law had been students at the Whampoa Military Academy in the 1920s and went on to become high-ranking Guomindang generals.) For some time, the authorities' attempts failed to bear fruit, and they were at a loss as to what to charge him with. Finally, in mid-1990, the Changsha Procuracy brought formal charges of economic fraud and sealed up all his property, including even his home electrical appliances. His wife, a woman named Yu Ziyu, was distraught and made several unsuccessful suicide attempts.

In jail, Li Maoqiu always maintained a high level of self-composure and integrity, and he would often say to us: "A true gentleman can be killed, but he cannot be shamed" *(shi ke sha, bu ke ru.)* Deep down, however, he was overwhelmed with feelings of sadness and anger at his situation. One evening in late 1990, he suddenly just died. The authorities later announced to the assembled prisoners that the cause of death had been "an explosion of the coronary arteries" *(xin xueguan baozha)* - an explanation which we all regarded as being nothing more than a cynical lie. Thereafter, whenever anyone else died in the prison we would be sure to refer to the event as an "explosion of the coronary arteries."

At least Li had done something wrong in the government's eyes by donating money to the students. The case of Zhang Zhonghui, however, was an utter miscarriage of justice. Zhang, who had just turned sixteen and was still legally a minor, had been arrested with several others in June, 1989 and accused of theft. In early 1990, the procuracy brought formal charges against him and in May of that year he had his first public trial. But because the evidence against him was insufficient, the trial was suspended and Zhang was returned to jail. (Elsewhere, of course, insufficient evidence would have been grounds for immediate release, but not in China.)

What with one delay after another, the case dragged on to the end of 1990, until finally Zhang's family petitioned the government and, at the same time, made public the results of fingerprint tests taken at the scene of the crime which demonstrated Zhang's innocence. On seeing the evidence, the workers at the factory where Zhang had worked rose up in arms, the accusation against Zhang was swiftly withdrawn and he was released as not guilty. Through a sheer injustice, he had spent a year and a half in prison. It later emerged that the real reason for Zhang and the others having been arrested in the first place was simply that they had offended the son of the factory security chief.[25]

As for Liu Fuyuan, his case was similar to that of Li Maoqiu - he had been slapped with a charge of economic crime for purely political reasons. In his youth, Liu had come under the influence of the Cultural Revolution pro-democracy activist, Chen Guangdi, and become involved in dissident activities. The government, however, had never been able to pin anything specific on him. With the crackdown on the 1989 pro-democracy movement, the authorities decided to sweep up all alleged "dangerous elements" without further distinction, and Liu Fuyuan was one of the many who were unjustly imprisoned as a result.

By the time of my departure from Changsha No. 1 Jail in October 1990, Liu had not eaten for more than a month. He suffered severely from kidney stones, and every night would roll around and scream in pain. His body weight had dropped from over 80 kilograms when he first arrived at the prison, to under 40 kilograms by the time I left. The doctors who were brought to examine him all recommended that he be released on bail pending trial, so that he could begin to receive proper treatment. But a leading official of the Changsha Municipal Public Security Bureau was resolutely opposed to the idea. "Let him die in jail," said the official in October 1990. I never managed to find out what later became of Liu.

---

[25] Security cadres at state enterprises are often appointed directly by and responsible to the local police. Thus, they are much more like policemen than like private security guards.

4. Widening the Purge

In the 1989 crackdown, the authorities did not confine themselves to carrying out only the more obvious repressive measures, such as large-scale arrests, expedited trials and heavy sentences. They also resorted to more subtle methods of persecuting and punishing pro-democracy activists, including job dismissal or demotion, exile to the remote countryside, various administrative punishments and marathon doses of "ideological re-education." Since tens of thousands of students and many times more workers and ordinary citizens had participated in the 1989 democracy movement in Hunan, it was clearly not feasible for the government to arrest all of them. Toward the rank-and-file supporters of the movement, therefore, the authorities adopted a policy of "attacking the few and educating the many."

In China, the law is only one instrument for maintaining the political and social order. It is also the least commonly used. Countless "directives," "documents" and "policies," all formulated by the Party, exist for this purpose, and they carry considerably more weight than the law. Of the estimated 100 million or so people in China who have fallen victim to the endless "political movements" waged by the authorities over the past 40 years and more, only a small minority were ever actually tried in court and sent to prison. The vast majority were simply branded with the Party's hate-term of the day: "landlords," rich peasants," bad elements" and "rightists" in the 1950s, "capitalist-roaders" and "revisionists" in the 1960s, "hangers-on of the Lin Biao/Gang of Four clique" in the 1970s, and "bourgeois liberals" and "turmoil elements" in the 1980s. Then they were subjected to a barrage of mental and physical persecution, professional ruin, public humiliation and social ostracism. Following the defeat of the 1989 pro-democracy movement, a similar tragic scenario was played out yet again throughout the country.

Province-wide investigations

Following the June 4 massacre, the Hunan authorities conducted a comprehensive investigation to identify all those in the province who had ever participated in any of the pro-democracy groups or demonstrations. Tens of thousands of students, workers, ordinary citizens and even government officials were "ferreted out" in this way, and many were branded as "major targets for re-education." Internal Party documents repeatedly stressed the need to pursue the investigations with the utmost thoroughness and severity, and each "battlefront" in society - that is, each different sector, department or profession - was instructed to draw up its own detailed plan of action for implementing the purge. The official score-settling was especially intense in Changsha, the provincial capital.

The lucky ones among those investigated were simply ordered to "perform introspection and repent their ways." A large number, however, were eventually subjected to so-called "administrative discipline" by their work-units. Such discipline included expulsion from college or university; dismissal from public employment; being placed on probation within the work-unit for a period of six months to two years; having "demerits" entered in personal dossiers; and being issued formal "disciplinary warnings." Most were forced to attend so-called "political study classes" so that they could be brainwashed into giving up their dissident ideas. Others were dragged before mass public rallies around the province and subjected to humiliating denunciation and criticism. (The Communist Party's methods of "re-educating" people are many and various.)

The combing-out operation continued right through until May 1990, by which time several tens of thousands of activists across the province had been identified and punished. The authorities stipulated that all those found to have committed "political errors" during the 1989 pro-democracy movement would be denied promotion until further notice and would under no circumstances be eligible for employment in key posts or positions of trust. In a more positive, self-congratulatory vein, it was required also that every locality had to muster a group of so-called "outstanding youth": students and other young people who had "taken a firm and clear-cut stand against the turmoil." These worthies were paraded in the media and rewarded with important government posts, and they even received cash bonuses.

The purge was pursued somewhat differently among the various sectors of society. The workers, as discussed above, bore the brunt of the arrests and sentencing side of the crackdown, but in the wider investigation and purge they fared much the same as other sectors. A certain proportion of the workforce in a given factory would be singled out for public criticism, demotion or dismissal, but simply too many workers had joined in the demonstrations, and to amplify the purge would have been unnecessarily risky for the authorities. In the main, therefore, they relied upon exemplary criminal proceedings against selected workers in order to instil a deterrent effect among the workforce as a whole.

In the universities, colleges and scientific establishments, teaching staff who had "committed errors" during the democracy movement were treated more harshly than those of their students who did so. Minor punishments included being organized to take part in "study classes," having salary docked, or receiving a Party warning or some administrative-disciplinary sanction. More serious cases brought outright dismissal (a dire prospect for most academics in China, who often have nowhere else to go.)

After my release from prison, I visited a number of university teachers who had been pro-democracy activists during the 1989 movement. The great majority of them had, by way of punishment, been put through "study classes," a vague and nebulous concept which covers a multitude of sins. For some people, this involved actually being sent to a political study group to receive "ideological education." For less fortunate individuals, it meant being sent down to some work-unit at the grassroots to undergo "re-education by the masses." While for the really unlucky ones, it entailed being forcibly rusticated to some backward and impoverished part of the countryside to take part in the so-called "socialist education movement."

Forced rustication

The Hunan "socialist education movement", which began in the summer of 1989, was a highly significant event, for it turned out to be the prototype for a massive campaign of the same name which was launched throughout the country in 1990. The campaign's ostensible purpose was to mobilize urban resources to help "raise the political and cultural level" of the peasants. In reality, it served to a large extent as a means of punishing pro-democracy intellectuals and officials. In March 1990 in Changsha alone, a city with a population of just over 1 million people, at least 50,000 young government cadres and university teachers were sent down to villages throughout the province to perform agricultural labor.

According to the government, those sent down to the countryside were only supposed to remain there for three months. But a large number of them, those branded as being seriously "bourgeois liberal" or just plain "incorrigible" have still, almost three years later, not received their "certificates of reform" from the local authorities. They look set to remain in the countryside making "contributions to socialism" indefinitely. The majority of the young cadres sent down after June 1989 had only recently graduated from university and so tended to be the most enthusiastic about reform and democracy. In the countryside, however, little attempt was made to utilize their skills and training. As for the university and research institute staffers who were sent down at the same time, professors of mathematics are now having to teach elementary arithmetic to the peasants, and holders of doctoral degrees in philosophy are being forced to teach basic literacy classes.[25] Since March 1990, when the "socialist education movement" was launched nationally, several more armies of urban individuals, each over 10,000-strong, have been dumped into villages all over Hunan to "undergo reform." In each batch, there has been a certain group of people who will never be allowed to return. They themselves refer to their plight as "forced banishment."[26]

Bureaucratizing the purge: the students

University and college students suffered relatively less harassment in the wider purge. As everyone knows, the 1989 pro-democracy

---

[25] Among several dozen people I know personally who were sent down in the "socialist education movement" and have not yet been allowed back to the cities are: Jiang Caoxin, from the general office of the Hunan provincial government; Li Chuan, from Hunan provincial television; Li Manyu, from Central-South Industrial University; and Deng Chaohua, Jiang Jianwu and Wan Zhongxue from Hunan Normal University. Some of them have been married for many years, but now have to live separated from their spouses.

[26] In Chinese, *chong jun*, the term used in imperial times to describe the forced sending into exile by the emperor of out-of-favor officials. Such people were usually sent to the remote desert areas of the far northwest or to the malaria-infested swamplands of Yunnan.

movement began on the campuses, and students formed the highest proportion of activists throughout the entire movement. Faced with this fact, the authorities "ingeniously" decided to adopt a strategy of divide and rule to deal with the students afterwards. Soon after June 4, all the universities and colleges organized a one-month long "study course in political ideology." At Hunan Normal University, Hunan Agricultural College, Changsha Railway College and other places, they even set up "intensive training courses" in the subject. The purpose of these classes was not, however, to punish student activists immediately, but rather to establish an overall hierarchy of guilt and to assign each student to one of three categories.

The first category, known as "dangerous turmoil elements" *(dongluan weixian fenzi)*, were punished by means of administrative sanctions and restricted job assignments after graduation. Those placed in this category were the ones whom the authorities believed could not, in the short term, be "educated and persuaded" out of their beliefs. They therefore had to be actively punished, and the best way to do this was to assign them a job in some remote, rural area where the local people's low level of political awareness and the practical difficulty in maintaining contact with other student activists would effectively neutralize them and prevent them "stirring up trouble" again.

The second category, those known as "wavering radical elements" *(dongyao buding de jijin fenzi)*, were dealt with by a combination of threats and promises. Most students placed in this category proved unable to withstand the sheer force of government propaganda after June 4, and in the end were persuaded to renounce their ideas about democracy. Superficially, the authorities did not punish or discriminate against such students in any way, but their activities were all carefully noted down in their personal dossiers. Provided they stayed out of trouble, no further action was taken, although they had little chance of ever gaining a position of trust. But if they were caught engaging in pro-democracy activities again, then the old score would be settled along with the new one. (Many student activists of the 1989 movement who had also participated in the winter 1986-87 student movement were punished on the basis of this rule.) Those who didn't toe the line were penalized either by bad job placements or even, in some cases, by getting no job assignment at all. (This had been almost unheard of prior to 1989.)

The third category comprised "students who acted on impulse and made mistakes through a momentary lack of understanding" *(yi shi bu ming zhenxiang, ganqing chongdong fanyou cuowu de xuesheng)*. Such students were not punished by the authorities, apart for being made to undergo "ideological education. They too, however, were barred from subsequent employment in Party or government organs, key enterprises or any of the other departments offering good working conditions.

The intense stress and anxiety caused among students by the post-June 4 settling of accounts resulted in a number of tragedies. A male student from Hunan University's forestry department (class of '87) and a female student from Hunan Normal University's history department were both so devastated by their protracted interrogation that they committed suicide. The male student, who lived in Room 411 of Dormitory 11, lay down on the railroad track and was run over by a train. The woman, who lived in Dormitory 7 of Hunan Normal University, wrote out her will and then jumped to her death from the twelfth floor of the Moshan Hotel, after loudly shouting some slogans. The government viewed this incident as being extremely sensitive and all information on it was strictly suppressed.

The net outcome of the campus investigations in Hunan was roughly as follows. By the end of 1990, more than 40 students from my own school, Hunan Normal University, had either been expelled, placed on probation, had a major or minor "demerit" marked in their personal dossier or been given a serious warning or a caution.[27] At the Changsha Railway College, 23 students were expelled and 37 received lesser punishments.[28] In addition, groups of between 10 and 50 students were similarly penalized at each of the following: Hunan University, Hunan Agricultural Institute, Central-South Industrial University, Hunan Water Conservancy and Electrical Power Normal College, Hunan College of

---

[27] These included Xia Siqing, Zheng Yan, Liu Chaohui, Zhu Jianwen, Qin Jianxin, Nie Qinglong, Nie Weihong, Li Wenjun, Bai Hua, Qu Zhaowu, Luo Weiguo, Chen Jianwei and He Zhongxia.

[28] The expelled students included Liu Wei, Li Lanlan, Li Chunyuan, Jia Jinfeng and He Guanghui. In early 1991, some of the 23 were readmitted to the college.

Finance and Economics, Changsha University, Hunan Communications College and Changsha Basic University.

Most of those punished had been members of either the Hunan SAF or the various autonomous campus federations. Indeed, out of all my friends who were active in these organizations, there was not one who managed to avoid some form of official discrimination or retaliation. Those expelled from college found life very difficult thereafter, since no one would employ them and they had to spend all their time and energy searching for ways to support themselves - which is just what the government intended. Many of my friends from the former SAF leadership remained destitute for a long time after June 1989, before eventually finding work outside the province in places like Shenzhen, Guangzhou, Hainan and Xiamen. Some of them are still unemployed and have to rely entirely on help from their families to support themselves.

Plight of released dissidents

The plight of pro-democracy activists who were sentenced to prison terms after June 1989 and have since been released, however, is still worse. For the most part, they have become a new class of highly-educated, unemployed vagrants, discriminated against by the authorities at every turn. Most firms and companies are afraid to hire them because of their "counterrevolutionary" records, and they are barred from employment in colleges and State-run enterprises. If they try to set up small private businesses, they are harassed by the public security authorities and usually denied the necessary operating permits. Those not originally from the cities have been stripped of their urban residency permits, and their only options are thus either to remain unlawfully as "black city-dwellers" or to return to their homes in the countryside and become "repairers of the planet" *(xiu diqiu)* - that is, farm laborers.

Zhou Liwu

The experiences of Zhou Liwu, formerly a teacher at the No.2 Light Industrial College in Changsha, typify those of many recently-released dissidents in Hunan. Zhou was sentenced to two years in prison on a charge of "counterrevolutionary propaganda and incitement" for his involvement in the 1989 movement. After being released in early 1991, he went back to his old college, only to be informed that he had been

61

fired from his post there long ago. He then returned to his parents' home in the countryside to recuperate for a while, hoping that he would soon receive good news and believing that the government would be sure to find some use for a talented university graduate such as himself. (Zhou's graduation thesis in philosophy won widespread local academic acclaim.) But he remained in limbo for months. Eventually, not wishing to be a burden on his parents any longer, he headed for Changsha in search of work.

Several collective enterprises in Changsha were keen to hire him, but they finally all refused on the grounds that he had a "problematic personal history." Thinking that some of the coastal cities might be less concerned about enforcing the government's repressive policies, he then borrowed 300 yuan and went south to Guangzhou City, where he finally found employment with a Taiwanese joint venture company. His boss was so pleased with him that he quickly put him in charge of personnel matters. All went well until the end of the first month, when he was suddenly fired. According to the boss, he had come under such pressure from the government for hiring Zhou that in the end he had no choice but to fire him. Subsequently, Zhou found other positions in joint venture companies, but he was always fired within the first month following renewed government threats and pressure on the management. Finally, Zhou gave up and went back to his home village, where he now scrapes out a living as a peasant.

Other students I know who have encountered the same problem since being released from prison include Tan Liliang, formerly a teacher at Loudi Vocational Normal College; Zhang Xiaojun, formerly a teacher at Changde's Taoyuan Normal College; Zeng Ming, formerly a teacher at Central-South Industrial University; and Jiang Fengshan, formerly a teacher at Xiangtan University. Each time any of them found jobs, the government invariably found out about it and had them fired. During 1991, for example, Tan Liliang had to change jobs no fewer than 20 different times.

Mo Lihua

One of the most outstanding activists of the 1989 pro-democracy movement in Hunan was a woman named Mo Lihua (the name means simply "Jasmine"), formerly a teacher at the Shaoyang Vocational Normal college. She went to Beijing during the movement, returning to Hunan shortly before the June 4 massacre. She later made passionate public speeches denouncing the crackdown, including one at a mourning ceremony on June 5 in which she called it "a bloody repression of the people by a fascist government." Her husband resigned from the Party after June 4, and when Mo was eventually arrested he went to the Shaoyang public security bureau and demanded (unsuccessfully) that they arrest him too. Tried by the Shaoyang Intermediate Court on December 21, 1989 on charges of "counterrevolutionary propaganda and incitement," Mo was sentenced to three years' imprisonment and sent to the women-only Changsha Prison. (See *Appendix VIII.C* for full text of the court verdict.) In mid-1991, she was released early on parole - but only to find that a couple of months previously she had been fired from her college teaching post.

A gentle and sensitive intellectual, she nonetheless showed her strength of character by deciding to head south in search of work, leaving behind her husband and a seven-year old daughter. As she was about to leave, however, a government official arrived and laid down a set of "rules" for her parole. She was not allowed to leave the school where they were living, and she was especially forbidden to travel to other parts of the country; she even had to get the authorities' prior permission to visit friends and relatives in Shaoyang. She was, to all intents and purposes, under a form of house arrest. Since then, she has been stuck in a state of futile and enforced inactivity, with no job, no money and no future.

Pan Mingdong

One of the more inspirational stories of the post-June 1989 suppression in Hunan is that of Pan Mingdong, a former boxing coach in the provincial Commission for Physical Education. Pan is a big, kind-hearted man with a strong sense of justice. His father, although a veteran of the "Autumn Harvest Uprising,"[30] was executed in the 1950s as a

---

[30] The Autumn Harvest Uprising was a series of attacks carried out, on Stalin's orders, by the Communist Party forces against Guomindang-held cities in Hunan and other southern provinces in the summer of 1927. The failure of the uprising prompted Mao's retreat to the Jinggangshan mountains along the Hunan-Jiangxi border and led to the formation of the Red Army.

"counterrevolutionary" for allegedly opposing Mao's line (he was posthumously "rehabilitated"), leaving Pan's mother to bring up him and his younger sister all on her own. He knows life at the grassroots, having spent several years as a peasant and several as a worker.

In October 1989, Pan was arrested on suspicion of having drafted the "Declaration of Hunan Autonomy," a radical manifesto which was issued on June 8 by a group called the "Preparatory Committee for Patriotic Self-Governance by the People of Hunan," calling for a military rebellion against the Li Peng government. (Many PLA officers, among others, were investigated in connection with this startling document; see *Appendix VII* for full translation.) But the prosecution could produce no evidence, and Pan was administratively sentenced instead to two years' "re-education through labor." His mother was devastated and took to her bed for most of the next two years, surviving only thanks to the constant care and attention of her daughter and the generosity of neighbors.

When Pan was released in late 1991 from the Changsha Xinkaipu Labor Re-education Center (known outwardly as the Hunan Switchgear Factory), he went to the public security bureau to reclaim his possessions which had been confiscated at the time of his arrest. The police refused, however, and to this day he has still not been given them back. He cannot find a job, and he and his mother now rely on regular small donations from his many friends.

An incident I remember from one day soon after June 4, 1989 vividly illustrates the irony and injustice of Pan's treatment by the government. We were on the run together, sitting on a train headed south, when suddenly a gang of about 20 young thugs burst into the carriage and began systematically robbing the terrified passengers of all their valuables. (Such crimes are becoming increasingly common all over China nowadays.) No one dared confront or resist the robbers, and they made a clean sweep of the carriage. But then one of them began to fondle a pretty young woman sitting next to us. Having taken her last two *yuan*, he stroked her on the cheek and said, "Why, that's not even enough for my pack of cigarettes."

At this, Pan Mingdong leapt to his feet and took up a martial-arts combat stance in front of the man. "Okay, tough guy, let's see what you're made of now!", he hissed. The thug pulled out a huge knife, but began to back off nervously. Stopping what they were doing, the rest of the gang slowly started to close in on Pan, their weapons also drawn. But Pan just coolly stood his ground. "Fine," he said, "I can easily handle all you creeps at once!" Just then, one of the armed police guards on the train came into the carriage, his pistol at the ready. After sizing up the situation, he looked over at Pan and said, "What're you making trouble for? This has nothing to do with you." The members of the gang just laughed and put their weapons away, then drifted back toward the far door and moved on into the next carriage. But the police officer made no move to arrest or even challenge them - and it was then we realized that he must actually be in cahoots with them. (No doubt, he would be getting his share of the loot later on.) As he slipped quietly away, the passengers all stood up and applauded Pan. They never got their valuables back, but at least the young woman's honor had been defended.

Incidents like this revealed clearly the true character of pro-democracy activists like Pan, and gave the lie to the cynical government propaganda depicting us as being mere "thugs" and "hooligans." In this case, as in many others, it was a so-called "counterrevolutionary" who stood up for the common people - and a corrupt government functionary who let the real thugs and hooligans go scot free.

Purging dissent within the Party: the Yin Zhenggao Affair

With the onset of the June 4 crackdown, the Hunan authorities availed themselves of the opportunity to wreak vengeance upon a number of senior and mid-ranking provincial Party officials who had been rocking the boat by criticizing government corruption and promoting political reform. Foremost among these was Yin Zhenggao, until November 1988 the pioneering vice-mayor of Yueyang City and a man often referred to in Chinese pro-reform circles as "Hunan's Gorbachev." Soon after taking office in 1985, Yin initiated three major projects, all of which benefitted the city's quality of life and economy and greatly endeared him to the local people: improving environmental protection, building up the urban infrastructure and renovating major historical sites such as the Yueyang Tower.

He was also a model of moral rectitude, and demanded clean government on the part of his subordinates. For this, the residents of Yueyang gave him the affectionate nickname of "Clear Skies Yin" (*Yin*

Qing Tian).[30] Among his many pathbreaking political innovations was the setting up of a new government body called the "Office of Discussion and Criticism" (*Jiang-Ping-Ban*) which held regular open meetings at which members of the public were invited and encouraged to expose corrupt activities within the local Party and government administrations. People flocked to these meetings, and each session was extensively broadcast on Hunan Television the same evening. The effect was astonishing. For the first time in China since 1949, a measure of real, direct accountability had been introduced into the political process, and officials all over Yueyang City soon began to feel the pinch of public scrutiny. Corrupt local officials were weeded out and punished, and, under the threat of possible public exposure, others began to tone down or even dismantle their operations. Vice-mayor Yin, of course, who was only 45 years old at the time, made many enemies in high places as a result.

His downfall came in late 1988, after he had broken all known rules by denouncing at a municipal Party committee meeting his own superior, Mayor Tan Zhaohua, for flagrant graft and bribe-taking. The case was sent up to the provincial disciplinary commission for decision, but the latter bounced it right back down to the Yueyang authorities - all of whom were firmly under the patronage of Mayor Tan. In November 1988, Yin was suspended from all duties, accused of "conspiring to usurp power" and a major Party investigation was launched into him and his entire circle of associates. The Yueyang students and general public rose up in outrage, staging a series of large-scale protest demonstrations across the city over a several-week period. (These protests were, in effect, the first salvoes of the nationwide pro-democracy movement of the following year.) Other solidarity actions included a conference entitled "Symposium on the Yin Zhenggao Phenomenon," organized by Huang Yaru, professor of politics at the Yueyang Vocational Normal College, specially to provide a forum for critics of the attack on Yin. The central authorities in Beijing followed these events, which soon became known nationwide as the "Yin Zhenggao Affair," with the greatest concern.

The official investigation, during which time Yin and his circle

---

[30] "*Qing Tian*" was the term traditionally used in China to denote an upright and incorruptible local magistrate.

remained on ice, continued right up until the outbreak of the pro-democracy movement in May 1989. Some weeks prior to then, however, a journalist by the name of Mai Tianshu had arrived in Yueyang to prepare a long investigative article on the incident for publication in *Reportage Literature (Baogao Wenxue)*, the country's foremost political *exposé* news magazine. The editor in charge of this article, which was titled "Living Sacrifice" *(Huo Ji)* was Liu Xiaoyan, daughter of China's most famous investigative journalist, Liu Binyan. Moreover, the introduction to the article was written by Su Xiaokang, principle author of *River Elegy*, a controversial television series which had scathingly dismissed several millennia of Chinese culture and was screened in late 1988 and early 1989 to the consternation of the country's hardline elderly leaders.

Days before the article's scheduled publication in May 1989, the propaganda department of the Party central committee in Beijing issued an order banning all distribution of that entire issue of *Reportage Literature*. At great personal risk, however, some officials took a large number of copies of the magazine from Beijing to Hunan by car and secretly distributed it among the various government departments and the recently-formed autonomous student bodies - including the Hunan SAF. I myself sent a student from Hunan University to Yueyang to investigate the matter, and upon his return the SAF passed a resolution to begin lobbying the Hunan Provincial People's Congress with a view to winning their support for Yin Zhenggao and his cause. The majority of the congress delegates were right behind us, and they angrily denounced the local Party authorities' campaign of persecution against Yin.

After June 4, the retaliation began in earnest. Yin Zhenggao and several of his closest colleagues were placed under house arrest, and up to 50 other leading and middle-ranking Yueyang officials in his circle were formally arrested. Many of them were eventually tried and given heavy prison sentences. The most severe sentence went to Qin Hubao, a senior cadre in Yin's "Office of Discussion and Criticism" (ODC) and one of those who had secretly smuggled the banned copies of *Reportage Literature* down to Hunan from Beijing. Qin was convicted in the Yueyang Intermediate Court in December 1989 on a charge of "counter-revolutionary propaganda and incitement" and sentenced to ten years' imprisonment.

At least eight other officials from Yin's administration were also tried on the same charge and received sentences ranging from three to five years. They included Mei Shi, editor-in-chief of the *Yueyang Evening News*, who received a four-year sentence; Yang Shaoyue, former head of the ODC, sentenced to five years; Wu Weiguo, also a cadre in the ODC, five years; Xie Yang, first secretary of the Yueyang Communist Youth League, three years; He Aoqiu, assistant professor in Chinese at the Yueyang Normal College, three years; Zhang Jizhong, a reporter for the *Hunan Daily*, three years; Cheng Cun, reporter for the Yueyang bureau of *News Pictorial* magazine *(Xinwen Tupian Bao)*, five years; and Huang Yaru, the professor who had organized the solidarity conference for Yin Zhenggao at Yueyang Normal College, five years. All eight are currently being held in Hunan Provincial No.2 Prison in Hengyang City. Dozens of other journalists and state cadres were given a range of administrative punishments in connection with the Yin Zhenggao Affair. For the journalists, among the lightest of these was a ban on publication of their works for up to two years.

In keeping with Party tradition, the authorities neither arrested nor imprisoned Yin Zhenggao himself, preferring to victimize his colleagues instead. (They provided a softer target, and it is considered bad for "inner-Party unity" to destroy a senior comrade.) But Yin is now unemployed and near destitute, living in a tiny apartment with his wife at her work-unit, the Chongshan Metallurgy Plant. Perhaps the only source of comfort to him, however, is that the local people still refer to him as "Clear Skies Yin."

Suppression of renewed pro-democracy activism, 1989-92

The political changes that began to sweep through Eastern Europe less than six months after the onset of the crackdown in China only confirmed the Beijing leadership's fears about the emergence of "Gorbachev-style" figures at home. They also hardened the leadership's resolve to crush any future dissident trends in society at an early stage, and punishment for those who continued to organize underground for democracy after June 1989 has been correspondingly severe. In March, 1991, for example, 15 and 11-year prison terms were imposed on two graduate students at Beijing's Qinghua University, Chen Yanbin and Zhang Yafei, for producing a pro-democracy journal called *Iron Current (Tie Liu)*.

The authorities have dealt secretly with all such cases and made strenuous efforts to prevent them from becoming public knowledge. In Hunan, where the pro-democracy movement began to regroup relatively quickly after the body-blow of June 4, 1989, numerous isolated acts of repression have been carried out by the authorities over the past two years. The following are only a few such incidents on which firm information has become available.

In December 1989, news of the popular uprising in Romania and the fall and execution of Ceaucescu was greeted with exultation in Changsha, causing the local authorities to place the security forces on high alert. Students at the Central-South Industrial University planned to stage a celebratory demonstration, but large numbers of police were dispatched to block the main gate and seal off the campus. All the official banners and posters on campus proclaiming the glories of socialism were plastered with graffiti over the next few days, and a number of students, including Cai Feng of the physics department, were arrested and held for several months.

In the wake of the Romanian events, the central authorities issued an internal directive ordering the provinces to further boost the crackdown on dissent. In Hunan, several student and worker activists who had escaped arrest after June 4 were promptly hauled in. Zhong Hua, a 24-year old environmental planning student at Hunan University who had been head of the school's picket squad in May 1989 and had organized a lie-in on the railroad tracks at Changsha Station late that month, was arrested in March 1990. He went on trial in July, charged with "disrupting traffic order," and was sentenced to three years' imprisonment.

Around the same time, two scientific researchers named Ah Fang[31] and Zhang Jie, who in September 1989 had left their jobs at the Changsha Nonferrous Metals Design Academy in order to establish a private company, were arrested together with their entire company staff. The authorities branded the company as being a front organization for pro-democracy activities, and in mid-1990 both Zhang Jie and Ah Fang were convicted of "forming a counterrevolutionary organization" and

---

[31] This was the man's nickname; his actual name is not known.

sentenced to five years' imprisonment. It is not known what became of the other staff members.

In March 1990, a student in the foreign languages department of Hunan Normal University, named Long Jianhua, was detained and imprisoned for two months after the authorities discovered that he had decked out his bed to resemble a coffin and hung from it a poster of Hu Yaobang edged with black silk.

In April 1990, a group of workers were arrested in Changsha for having printed and distributed on the city's streets a large quantity of protest leaflets in advance of the first anniversary of the June 4 crackdown. The workers, all of whom had been detained and then released by the authorities the previous year for being members of the Changsha WAF, included three employees of the Hunan Electrical Battery Factory named Yang Rong, Wang Hong and Tang Yixin. The group's underground printing plant was uncovered by the authorities and destroyed, and the three men were charged with "forming a counter-revolutionary group." They have not yet been brought to trial, but the authorities have reportedly instructed that they be given long prison sentences.

In the early hours of May 1, 1990, dozens of big-character posters were pasted up on walls all around the Changsha Railroad Station, denouncing the June 1989 crackdown and raising criticisms on a range of issues including the sincerity of Deng Xiaoping's ten-year reform program and the wisdom of China's 1979 military incursion against Vietnam. The posters were swiftly torn down by the police, and from then on until after the first anniversary of the June 4 crackdown, the security forces throughout Hunan Province were placed on maximum alert. In August that year, several activists who had been detained the previous year and then released, including Liu Yi, the former treasurer of the Changsha WAF, were arrested once more and charged with the crime of "posting up counterrevolutionary slogans." They have not yet (so far as is known) been brought to trial.

In the summer of 1990, in the course of a nationwide "campaign to crack down on crime," more than 50 "common criminals" were executed in Changsha alone, ostensibly to "create a peaceful social atmosphere" in advance of China's hosting of the Asian Games. A number

70

of private businessmen who had given financial support to the 1989 pro-democracy movement in Hunan are said to have been arrested on charges of economic corruption and severely punished during this campaign.

In February 1991, two brothers from Hengyang City named Li Lin and Li Zhi, both activists of the pro-democracy movement who had escaped to Hong Kong in July 1989, returned to Hunan after their families had been explicitly assured by local officials that they would not be punished if they did so. The brothers were arrested almost immediately. After being beaten and tortured in custody, the two were finally released and allowed to leave China following a major campaign of international pressure on their behalf. In May 1991, however, a young railway worker named Tang Zhijian was arrested for a second time on charges of having helped the Li brothers escape from China in July 1989. The authorities have secretly pressured Tang to confess to a false charge that he received money for helping in the escape, while at the same time publicly claiming that he is being held on charges of stealing a tape-recorder.

On June 4, 1991, students at Hunan Normal University, like those at Beijing University, let off firecrackers and smashed small bottles to commemorate the 1989 crackdown.[32] As a result of this incident, I myself was placed on a wanted list for a second time, having been released on parole only four months earlier, and so had to flee the country. In Guangzhou, also on June 4, a technician from a foreign joint venture company, a graduate of Qinghua University, wrote out a memorial banner bearing the words "The martyrs to democracy are not forgotten - the democratic movement will live forever." The man (name unknown) then took the banner to the Sun Yatsen Memorial Hall and placed it in front of Sun's statue, and was immediately arrested. There has been no further news on his fate since then.

With the collapse of the Soviet Communist Party in August 1991, the Chinese authorities again clamped down on dissident activities. In Hunan, one of the casualties of this was a 32-year old man from

---

[32] The Chinese for "small bottle," *xiao ping*, is evocative of Deng Xiaoping's given name, and smashing bottles thus represents a form of political protest.

Yongzhou City named Duan Ping, formerly a teacher in Qiyang No.1 Middle School. Duan had spent two years in Changsha's Xinkaipu Labor Re-education Center after June 1989 on account of his involvement in the pro-democracy movement. After his release in mid-1991, he opened an electronic games parlor. Following the failure of the coup in the Soviet Union, Duan was rearrested merely for expressing his support for those who had resisted the coup-plotters. In September 1991, he was sentenced without trial to a further three years' re-education through labor and sent back to Xinkaipu.

Li Shaojun, a physics student in the class of '88 at Hunan University, has been arrested no fewer than three times since June 1989. A founding member of the Democracy Salon and treasurer of the Hunan SAF, Li fled to Guangzhou after June 4 but returned to his hometown of Hengyang that August because he was penniless. He was arrested, held in Changsha No.1 Jail without trial until December 1989 and then released. In August 1990, he was again taken into detention after he telephoned a friend of his overseas who was a member of the Chinese exiled dissidents group, Federation for a Democratic China (FDC). He was freed again shortly after the end of the Asian Games. In early November 1991, Li was arrested for the third time, again in Guangzhou, and accused of "colluding with reactionary foreign powers" and "engaging in counterrevolutionary activities." He was sent back to Changsha No.1 Jail, and there has be no further word on his situation. (So capricious have the authorities been in his case that they may even release him yet again.) Li's father is a senior engineer in a car plant and his mother is a middle school teacher. He writes under the pen-name Li Aiju.

Finally, a 26-year-old man who was my personal bodyguard during the 1989 pro-democracy movement, Luo Ziren, was arrested for the second time in November 1991. Formerly a worker in the Changsha Cigarette Factory, Luo served during the 1989 movement as a SAF "special picket" and was responsible for guarding the organization's headquarters and protecting the SAF's main leaders. He was constantly by my side during the latter part of the movement. After June 4, 1989 he returned on our advice to his home province of Guizhou, but was arrested shortly thereafter and sent back to Changsha for interrogation. In November 1990, he was unexpectedly freed. Abandoning his job, however, he soon became involved once again in pro-democracy activities, and in November 1991 he was arrested again in Guiyang City, the capital of Guizhou. The authorities have accused Luo of "organizing a group of social degenerates" to produce and distribute "large quantities of reactionary posters." No word has been heard of him since his arrest, but he is likely soon to be formally charged with "counterrevolutionary propaganda and incitement" and given a heavy sentence. Luo is a brave and dedicated pro-democracy activist, and his friends are now deeply concerned about him.

5. Torture and Ill-Treatment in Prison

During the year or so that I spent as a prisoner in Changsha No.1 and Changsha No.2 Jails, I witnessed and experienced many of the different kinds of torture and punishment that are commonly used nowadays within the Chinese Communist prison system. Reflecting on that experience now, after my escape from China, it feels to me almost like a year spent in an ancient Roman gladiator arena.

Torture and ill-treatment are rampant in Chinese jails, and the Changsha No.1 and No.2 Jails are certainly no exception. The cadres there know that so long as they don't actually beat a prisoner to death, they need have nothing to worry about, for there will be no repercussions. Prisoners transferred to those two jails from other prison facilities in Hunan, moreover, used to tell us that the problem was even worse elsewhere. Indeed, prison officials themselves boasted to us that Changsha No.1 and No.2 were "the most civilized and well-disciplined" jails in the whole province.

Prisoners in Changsha, like those held elsewhere in China, are routinely subjected to two broad categories of torment. The first is torture and ill-treatment inflicted directly by prison guards and other officials themselves. The second is that inflicted, usually at the instigation and direction of prison officials, by specially appointed prisoners known as "cell bosses" (*laotou yuba*). While both categories of abuse have the effect of turning a prisoner's life into a kind of living hell, the latter can often, if anything, be the more fearsome.

I. Abuses by prison officials

Few people in China would willingly work in prisons, and especially since the start of the economic reforms, the rewards and prestige of the job are low. Increasingly, only the most brutish and uneducated types of people end up working in the prison system. They torture and abuse for two main reasons: one is to vent their anger and frustration, while the other - slightly more subtle - purpose is to create an atmosphere of terror and intimidation among the prisoners. Simply put, this makes it easier for the prison staff to "maintain order."

The following are the main types of torture and abuse commonly inflicted upon inmates by prison staff directly.

1) **Electrical assault** (*dian ji*). This is probably the most widespread form of torture used by officials - and also, according to some, the most "civilized." Electric batons, which first appeared on the Chinese law-enforcement scene in the mid-1980s, are now standard issue for police and prison officials, and the latter are liberally empowered to use them. Although the central authorities have drawn up detailed regulations governing the use of such implements, these are almost completely ignored.[33] In practice, prison staff regard their electric batons as being merely convenient tools for punishing and terrorizing the prisoners.

In Changsha No.1 and No.2, the scenario for such an assault is usually as follows. The prisoner is ordered to kneel down and face the wall, with his back straight and both hands raised high and pressed against the wall. The guard or other official then switches on the electric baton and touches it a few times against the metal cell-door or the lock, causing electric sparks to fly forth and giving out a sinister, crackling sound. Once the prisoner has been put into the required state of terror and anxiety, the guard then begins poking the back of his neck with the live electric baton. This makes him scream out in pain and turn his head around involuntarily, begging the guard for mercy. As a result, however,

---

[33] The gist of the regulations was summed up as follows in an article which appeared in *China Legal News (Zhongguo Fazhi Bao)* on February 15, 1985:

"The use of police batons is restricted to situations where an escaped criminal resists when being pursued in accordance with the law; where warnings have proven ineffectual when dealing with incidents of riotous assembly or gang fights among criminals; and where the need for self-defense arises following sudden attack by criminal elements. The use of police batons should be restricted to overpowering one's opponent and should cease as soon as the criminal acts of the felon have been curbed. In using a police baton for such purposes, the infliction of unwarranted mortal wounding should be avoided. We must strictly guard against and firmly rectify the continued use of police batons against criminals who have already been overpowered; the use of police batons against criminals guilty of everyday infringements of prison rules or discipline; indiscriminate poking or hitting; and random punishment."

75

he then suffers severe shocks to the face and mouth, making him whip his head back around again, at which time the guard will administer further electrical shocks to his ears. The cycle is usually repeated until the victim collapses from the pain or passes out.

Occasionally, prisoners become so inured to electrical assault that they never actually pass out. In such cases, the guard adopts the alternative method of holding the live electric baton steadily against a fixed point on the victim's body, until the flesh starts burning and smoke begins to rise. At that point, another part of the body will be selected and the punishment repeated. In prison jargon, this treatment is often sardonically referred to as "electro-curing therapy" *(dianliao)* - as if the flesh were actually being "cooked".

2) **Down-on-knees whipping** *(gui bian)*. This frequently encountered form of punishment in Changsha jails is, in some ways, sufficiently bizarre as to probably constitute a local invention. Far from reflecting the dignity of the "state," it reminds one superficially of the domestic chastisement of a young child by its irate parents. The procedure is as follows: the guard orders the prisoner to pull down his trousers and kneel down facing the wall, with back held straight and hands pressed against the wall well above head height. He then begins whipping the victim's exposed buttocks with a thin bamboo switch measuring around two feet long and half an inch wide.

In the course of the whipping, the following dialogue will typically occur. Guard: "Have you been well behaved lately?" Prisoner: "Yes, I have, sir!" Guard: "Oh yes? If you'd been well behaved, then why would I be whipping you right now?" (This forces the prisoner to backtrack.) Prisoner: "Perhaps it's true, sir, maybe I have been badly behaved!" Guard: "Badly behaved, eh! Well, in that case, I'll just have to whip you some more!" The performance continues until the prisoner breaks down (usually after about 30 to 50 strokes of the cane), starts to beg for mercy and promises henceforth to obey the guard's every word. The guard then admonishes the prisoner with a few final words, and one of the older inmates will often rise on cue and tell the prisoner to say: "Thank you kindly, Mr. Cadre."

This type of punishment serves the obvious purpose of inflicting intense physical pain on the prisoner, and the continuing discomfort he experiences when sitting or lying down afterwards makes him "reflect on his errors" for some time to come. But it also serves the additional purpose of leaving scars on the buttocks. Such scars make the prisoner fearful of ever having to undergo the same treatment again, since any guard seeing them the next time will promptly identify him as being a "recidivist" and will whip him all the more severely.

3) **Chains and fetters**. In China, prison cadres are authorized by law to chain and fetter prisoners. According to the prison regulations, which all cadres and inmates are supposed to learn by heart, "Those who violate the regulations shall in minor cases be given education and criticism; in more serious cases, they shall be admonished and may be made to wear implements of restraint." The phrase "implements of restraint" (jieju) clearly refers to chains and fetters, while the word "admonished" means, in practice, corporal punishment. Only two types of restraint are officially permitted, namely handcuffs and ankle-fetters. In reality, however, a wide range of different implements are found in current use, some of which, such as chains, are explicitly banned by the government. Time limits are also supposed to apply, except in the case of condemned prisoners awaiting execution. (They are fettered hand and foot from the time of sentencing, and often from the time of initial arrest, right up until the moment of execution.)[34] In practice, such time limits are completely ignored.

---

[34] The article cited above gave the following summary of the rules:

"Handcuffs may be used on arrested escapees and on criminals in custodial transit. In the case of criminals sentenced to death and awaiting execution, both handcuffs and ankle-fetters may be applied simultaneously. Upon approval by the top leadership of the labor-reform unit in question, handcuffs or ankle fetters may also be applied to criminals who (in the course of undergoing prison control and reform) escape, commit arson or other violent acts, create disturbances in prison or seize weapons, or who sabotage the equipment, property or discipline of the labor-reform unit or camp. During the time in which such implements are applied, the criminal should be given intensive education, and once the dangerous behavior has ceased and been eliminated, the implements should be removed. Apart from the case of condemned criminals awaiting execution, a maximum period of 15 days for the use of handcuffs or ankle fetters applies. It is fundamentally incompatible with the civilized governance of China's labor-reform organs to regard handcuffs and ankle fetters as being instruments for the torture or punishment of criminals."

77

The following are the various kinds of handcuffs, chains and ankle-fetters that I personally saw being used in Changsha No.1 and No.2 Jails.

(i) *"Country cuffs" (tushoukao).* Although this type of handcuff has long been banned by the authorities, it remains in widespread use. The handcuffs consist of one centrally-placed iron strip hinged at the top to two semi-circular strips. Each part has a small hole at its lower end, and the device is clamped shut by threading these together with a padlock. A range of different handcuff sizes is kept available, so that regardless of how narrow a prisoner's wrists may be, the guards will always be able to find a pair that clamps shut tightly. In fact, the main purpose of this type of handcuff is to cause the prisoner maximum discomfort, by obstructing circulation through the wrists and causing blood to well up painfully in the hands. ("Country cuffs" are also sometimes known as "tiger cuffs," since wearing them can give the sensation of being gnawed at by a wild animal.)

The handcuffs can be applied in three different ways: a) with the hands pointing to the front; b) with the hands pointing to either side, in opposite directions; and c) with the hands behind the back and pointing in opposite directions. Of the two frontward styles, the second is the worst, since it makes eating and other necessary tasks extremely difficult. Rearward handcuffing is the worst of all, since not only do all manual operations become virtually impossible, but also the blood flow is severely restricted and the pain is such that one cannot sleep at all.

(ii) *"Finger cuffs" (shouzhikao).* As the name suggests, this type of handcuff is applied only to the fingers. Such cuffs are only ever used "internally" within the prison system and are never seen by members of the public. They consist of two pieces of rough metal wire crudely welded together, resembling a pair of finger rings set side by side, and are used exclusively for the purpose of punishing prisoners. To fix them in place, the prisoner's thumbs are inserted into the two holes and the open ends are then pinched shut using a pair of pliers. One word alone sums up these cuffs: tight. After a day or less of wearing them, the prisoner begins to experience intense pain, as the thumbs become ever more bloated and swollen.

(iii) *"Ankle fetters" (jiaolianliao).* These are standard leg irons, used to chain the prisoner's feet together in various different ways, and are available in a range of different weights and sizes. The lightest type weighs around eight kilograms, while the heaviest can extend to over 30 kilograms. All prisons and detention centers in China are obliged by law to be equipped with such fetters. In the standard variety, the chain connecting the two ankle-rings can be easily varied in length, depending upon how close the prisoner's feet are to be shackled together. Although this basic type of leg fetter can often be quite heavy, the prisoner can usually still move around without too much difficulty. It is most commonly applied to those prisoners condemned to death and awaiting execution. However, it may also be used as a form of punishment in the case of common criminals who have infringed some regulation or other.

(iv) "*Rod fetters*" (*zhiliao*). This type of fetter differs from the standard variety in that, in place of a connecting chain allowing a certain degree of mobility, the ankle-rings are joined by a fixed iron bar of approximately one and a half feet in length. Again, it is most often used as a direct form of punishment. Prisoners shackled in this way experience extreme difficulty and discomfort in moving around, since the feet are always kept at a fixed distance apart. Sleeping is also difficult, for the slightest leg movements while lying down at night result in pain to the ankles and wake the prisoner up.

(v) "*Multiple fetters*" (*lianhuanliao*). This device, consisting of several sets of ankle fetters chained together in a row, is used as a means of shackling several prisoners together by the legs simultaneously, usually as a form of collective punishment. The largest number of prisoners I ever saw being shackled together in this way in Changsha No.1 Jail was eight. An extremely inhumane form of punishment, it allows almost no individual movement by those being shackled. When one prisoner wants to go to the toilet, for example, all the others have to accompany him and stand next to him while he performs.

(vi) "*Shackle board*" (*menbanliao*). This is the cruellest and most barbaric form of shackling that I saw used during my own term of imprisonment, and also among the worst that I have heard about from elsewhere. The device consists of a large wooden door laid flat and supported by four low legs, and equipped with a set of handcuffs secured to each corner. A hole situated toward the lower end allows the attached victim to perform (after a fashion) normal bodily functions.

Among those personally known to me who were subjected to such shackling are several pro-democracy prisoners arrested after June 1989 and also a number of common criminals with whom I subsequently shared cells. In addition, 26 condemned criminals who were executed in Changsha on June 9, 1990 were all fixed to "shackle boards" throughout the two days prior to their execution. The sufferings of those made to undergo this particular form of punishment are almost indescribable.

(vii) *"Full shackle set"* (*lianliaokao*). This consists of standard handcuffs and standard ankle fetters, but with the two being joined together by either a steel chain or a fixed steel bar. The device comes in various shapes and sizes. The most common, the type with the connecting chain, is that applied to prisoners awaiting execution. Depending on the weight of the chains used, movement can be more or less difficult. Those prisoners able to move usually attach a strip of cloth to the chains that lie looped on the floor. This allows them to lift the chains up by their hands when moving around, which makes walking slightly easier.

Two other types of the "full shackle set," those having a steel bar placed between the handcuffs and ankle-fetters, are used solely and blatantly by prison officials as instruments of punishment and inflict severe physical and mental damage upon those subjected to them. They are known as the "standing up" and "sitting down" varieties. In the former, a steel bar of more than one meter in height is set vertically into the ground, with fetters at the base and cuffs attached to the top end. Prisoners attached to this device are physically unable to sit down and must remain standing at all times. Sleep is impossible because of the pain caused in the wrists and ankles if one slumps downwards. Most prisoners are unable to last more than two days on this device.

In the "sitting down" variant, the fixed vertical pole is only a few inches high, forcing the prisoner to remain in a crouched or seated position all the time. Some prisoners are shackled in this way for as long as a month. Typically, the legs and buttocks become all swollen with blood after a few days, and sores quickly appear. Sometimes, the flesh begins to fester and decay.

4) **"Martial arts practice"** (*liao quan jiao*). During my time in Changsha No.1 and No.2 Detention Centers, there were several young prison guards whose greatest enjoyment in life seemed to come from

beating up the prisoners. They are Cadre Luo, Cadre Lu, Cadre Chen, Cadre Yao and Cadre Yang, and also another man named Yang who is one of the so-called "No.2 Cadres." (This is prisoners' jargon for those hired from outside to work as temporary prison guards. Many of these guards are local villagers who in fact have no legal authority to engage in such work.) All these cadres have been awarded the epithet "Killer" (*Sha*) by the prison inmates.

In the case of "Killer Luo" (*Luo Sha* - real name: Luo Jian), for example, physically tormenting prisoners had become second nature, and he used to beat people up on the slightest of pretexts. Quite often, he would summon a prisoner out of his cell and then suddenly and without warning attack him savagely. It usually went like this: Luo would call out the name of a certain prisoner and order him to step out of his cell into the corridor, kneel down and face the wall. Once the victim was in place, he would casually spin around and land a flying drop-kick to the man's back. After that, he would walk around for a while, and then repeat the same thing again, over and over. The performance would come to an end only when the prisoner had finally been battered senseless to the ground.

All the while, Killer Luo would be sure to maintain an air of complete coolness and nonchalance. His specialty, however, was that he never looked at his victim directly. Also, unlike the other guards, he never used his fists, only his feet. This was apparently because he feared dirtying his hands.

The "No.2 Cadre Yang," by contrast, appeared somewhat fairer and more conscientious, for at least he always used to "pick a fight" with the prisoners before beating them up. (Despite this courtesy, the prisoners would never, of course, dare to fight back.) Yang's belligerence was attributed by the prisoners to the fact of his lowly status as a mere "No.2" cadre.

5) **"Saochai descending from the mountain top."** The term *saochai*, meaning "those who sweep up the firewood," is prison slang for officers of the People's Armed Police (PAP), who are employed by the prison authorities to patrol the prison's safety perimeter and prevent any escapes. The phrase "descending from the mountain-top" refers to the periodic occasions on which PAP officers are ordered down from their watch-towers to conduct so-called "lightning raids" on the prisoners' cells.

These raids are ostensibly carried out for the purpose of inspecting the prisoners' cells and checking that no forbidden goods or objects are being concealed there. (According to regulations, however, checking the cells is the regular guards' responsibility. The PAP's sole duties are to prevent escapes and quell any prison riots or disturbances.) In Changsha No.1 Jail, these "saochai raids" took place on an average of once a month.

The real purpose of the raids was simply to allow the PAP into the cells for a so-called "contact session" with the prisoners - that is, an opportunity to beat up and terrorize them, in a display of crude military force. At each of these sessions, the PAP would suddenly arrive in the cell blocks brandishing special, military-issue leather belts in their hands. As soon as they threw open a cell door, they would immediately start lashing out at random at the terrified prisoners within, whipping and beating them with the belts. The ostensible reason for this violence was that they had to "drive back" anyone who might be hurriedly trying to conceal forbidden items. Some PAP officers would specifically pick out certain prisoners and start laying into them exclusively, shouting out things like, "Let's see if you dare challenge us now!" Since the PAP are mostly just powerfully-built and uneducated thugs, these "*saochai* raids" invariably used to leave the prisoners in a state of complete physical and psychological terror.

6) **Solitary confinement** *(jin bi)*. Previously, Changsha No.1 and No.2 Jails had no system of solitary confinement, although many other detention facilities in Hunan Province certainly did, and still do. In 1990, however, Changsha No.1 began building a solitary-confinement punishment block, and it was fully constructed by the time I left the prison. As a "cell delegate," I was once taken by cadres on a conducted tour of this special unit. The solitary cells resembled square metal boxes, measuring about 1.5 meters in height, width and depth, and without any window whatever. The door leading into the cell was less than one meter high. As the cadres explained to us, once inside, a prisoner could neither lie down properly nor stand up straight. I privately thanked heaven that I had never been consigned to one of these "black boxes," I'm not sure I could have withstood the experience. (The solitary confinement cells at Longxi Prison, in which I was placed for seven days in January 1991, were almost comfortable by comparison with those at Changsha No.1.)

II. Abuses by "Cell Bosses"

In addition to all these different types of punishment and abuse inflicted by the prison staff directly, Changsha No.1 and No.2 Jails, like all other prisons and labor camps in China, operate a complex and deeply-entrenched system of internal terror and control known as the "cell boss" system. This system is the scourge of prisoners' daily life, for it undermines all guarantees for even their most basic physical safety and security. Although strictly banned by the government, the cell boss system flourishes throughout the Hunan prison system. Moreover, the prisoner-thugs who act as the cell bosses are specifically appointed to play that role by prison officials themselves. These prisoners act as the latter's direct agents within the cells, and as a reward for this service they receive specially favorable treatment and conditions.

Prisoners are usually even more afraid of these cell bosses - the system's unofficial hit-men - than they are of the actual prison staff. Cell bosses have numerous specific ways and means of tormenting other prisoners and of making their lives intolerable. The twenty main varieties of such unofficial persecution and torture are described below, together with an outline of their officially-intended functions within the Chinese prison sub-culture.

(i) *"Paying respects to the cell god" (bai lao men)*. This is a technique commonly used to punish and intimidate new arrivals to the prison cells. Its purpose is to make the newly arrived prisoners submit symbolically to the cell boss's authority. The procedure is as follows. First, the new prisoner is ordered to kneel down in front the "cassia blossom vase" (*guihua tong*: prison jargon for the toilet bucket,) holding several rice-straws.

Second, just as if he were offering incense at a Buddhist altar, he has to offer forth the rice-straws in both hands and perform the so-called "three prostrations" before the "cassia blossom vase". These are: 1) a prostration to his mother *(yi bai qinniang)*; 2) a prostration to the prison cadres *(er bai ganbu)*; and 3) a prostration to the cell boss *(san bai laotou)*.

Third, the new prisoner has to insert one of the straws, the kind used to make the bedding quilts used in the cells, into the "cassia blossom vase" and blow forcefully through it, making bubbles froth up from the

83

contents of the bucket and sending forth a foul smell. The cell boss will then ask the prisoner: "Is the cassia blossom fragrant?" The prisoner must immediately reply, "Yes, it smells lovely."

Finally, the prisoner has to suck some of the contents of the toilet bucket up through the straw. The cell boss again asks, "Does the cassia blossom taste sweet?", and the prisoner must reply "Yes, delicious." With this, the ceremony of "paying respects to the cell god" is formally concluded. If, however, the new arrival has failed in any way to perform as required, then new and still worse humiliations await him.

(ii) *"Electric shock treatment" (chu dian)*. Here, the cell inmate is ordered by the cell boss to go into the "cassia blossom chamber," that is, the toilet cubicle, located between the cell proper and the outside exercise yard, and to stretch his hand around the dividing wall into the cell and grope around for the "electric light switch." (Actually, there are no light switches or electric sockets in any of the cells.) The cell boss then gets one of the other prisoners, or sometimes he will do it himself, to crack some hard object like a wooden stool or the sole of a shoe down against the prisoner's fingers without warning. The prisoner will scream out in pain, just as if he'd received a sudden electric shock.

(iii) *"The sandwich filling" (jiaxin mianbao)*. This entails the prisoner being simultaneously struck on the back and chest. First, the victim is ordered to stand in front of the cell boss (or someone designated by him), facing toward the side. The cell boss then repeatedly strikes hard against the same spot on the prisoner's back and chest, until he develops an unbearable sensation of being unable to draw breath. This punishment can generate an intense feeling of fear and claustrophobia in the victim.

(iv) *"Jetplane ride" (zuo feiji)*.[35] The cell boss orders the prisoner to stand on the edge of the raised sleeping platform, of which there is one to each cell, facing across the side corridor toward the opposite wall. He

---

[35] This term, *zuo feiji*, is more commonly used in China to refer to another kind of punishment (often used by Red Guards during the Cultural Revolution) in which the victim's arms are pushed straight up behind the back, forcing him to bend down low at the waist. The backward-stretched arms make a "V" shape, rather like the outline of a jet plane.

then has to lean forward and support himself in a rigid, slanted posture against the wall, with a cup wedged firmly between his head and the wall. The cell boss then knocks the cup away with a stick or some other object, causing the victim to fall forward and strike his head against the wall, with the full force of his body-weight behind the impact. Repeated several times, this creates a sense of nausea and vertigo (thought to be reminiscent of being in an airplane at take-off), not to mention causing bruises to the head.

(v) *"Eating the golden carp" (chi jiyu)*. This is the easiest and most convenient method of inflicting punishment within the cells, and simply involves the cell boss repeatedly hitting the lower part of a prisoner's face with the sole of his shoe. In the process, small pieces of filth from the shoe usually drop into the victim's mouth. Also, the sole of the shoe somewhat resembles the shape of a golden carp - hence the name.

(vi) *"Heroic martyrdom" (yingyong jiuyi)*. This type of punishment, while not necessarily causing any serious physical damage to the victim, nonetheless often generates in him a considerable degree of psychological stress and anxiety. The name evokes the scenario of a condemned prisoner being dragged to the execution ground and shot. The process is this. First, the cell boss orders two of the other inmates to "apply the leg fetters" (actually, just a piece of cloth tied around the victim's feet.) The cell boss, pretending to be a judge, then declares that the death sentence has been imposed and orders that the prisoner be "dragged out and executed." The two stooges promptly drag him across the floor by his hands and make him stand near the cell wall.

At the sound of "gunfire" (in fact, just a "ping" sound emitted by the cell boss), the prisoner has immediately to fall directly backwards, landing flat on the cell floor. Prisoners who have experienced this punishment several times learn quite quickly how to fall backward without hurting themselves too much. But first-timers, especially if they are overly anxious, often crack the back of their heads hard against the stone floor, sometimes knocking themselves out.

(vii) *"Hammer clanging" (qiao xiang zhui)*. This is one of the more painful punishments commonly used within the cells, although it seldom leaves any permanent damage. It consists of the cell boss striking repeatedly at the victim's ankles with a wooden stick or some other hard

85

object. The name of the practice is derived from the percussive noise it creates, which is thought reminiscent of a particular style of folk-music performance known as the "Hebei Hammer" *(Hebei Zhuizi)*.

(viii) *"Bouncy bouncy" (tan bengbeng)*. This kind of punishment is meted out as a warning. The cell boss tucks his forefinger and middle-finger in firmly under the thumb, and then begins flicking the victim hard on a spot right in the center of his forehead, using each finger in turn. This is repeated over and over again, until eventually a large dark bruise appears over the spot.

(ix) *"Lotus-wrapped egg roll" (gun hebaodan)*. A type of punishment clearly intended purely for the amusement of the cell boss, this one can nonetheless induce a protracted sense of nausea in the victim. It works like this. The cell boss selects a prisoner and tells him to kneel down, grasp his feet in both hands, and lean forward as far as possible, tucking his head in tightly so that his body assumes a ball-like shape. Another inmate is then ordered to push the victim forward and begin rolling him around all over the cell floor, until finally he becomes so dizzy that his body uncoils involuntarily and he comes to a halt. Someone else then forces the victim to his feet and orders him to stand still - something which he finds impossible to do, since he is swaying around uncontrollably. Eventually he collapses on the ground, and the whole process is then repeated all over again. If continued for long enough, the victim will be left feeling nauseous, giddy and extremely uncomfortable for the next several days.

(x) *"Staying upright thrice" (san bu dao)*. This is a relatively straightforward type of abuse. The cell boss simply punches a prisoner on the chest as hard as he can three times in a row, and if the prisoner remains standing up, without having shifted his feet, then he passes the test. If he does not, on the other hand, the punishment will continue for as often as the cell boss feels inclined. (Many prison guards, especially younger ones, also like to perform this trick.)

(xi) *"Riding a donkey back to front" (dao qi maolü)*. This is another of the many ways used by cell bosses to humiliate and demean their fellow inmates. The chosen prisoner is made to kneel down on all fours, on either the cell floor or the sleeping platform, and the cell boss then sits astride him facing to the rear and orders him to crawl around. As the prisoner does so, the cell boss beats him continuously on the buttocks with either his hand, a pair of chopsticks or some other hard implement.

(xii) *"Clubbing the dreamer" (pu meng gun)*. Cell bosses use this method to deal with any prisoners who will not readily submit to their authority or who fail to be subdued by a simple beating. The usual procedure is that late at night, when the defiant prisoner is soundly asleep, several other inmates will be directed by the cell to assault him. Some of them first wrap a cotton quilt tightly around his head and upper body, and the others then begin kicking him viciously, stamping on his body and battering him about the head. The victim, of course, is completely unable to fight back, and because of the quilt, his shouts and screams are completely inaudible outside the cell. All but the toughest of prisoners usually cannot withstand this treatment, and most will quickly begin begging the cell boss for mercy. The latter will only give the word for the beatings to stop once he is fully satisfied of the prisoner's submission.

(xiii) *"Cassia blossom perch" (guihua deng)*. This form of punishment is rife in virtually all the detention cells in China equipped with toilet buckets ("cassia blossom vases.") It entails the following. Usually around ten o'clock at night, after the guards have finished inspecting the cells and counting all the prisoners, the cell boss orders the prisoner slated for punishment to go to the toilet cubicle and squat on top of the "cassia blossom vase" for the entire night. (The cell boss has only to utter the words "Go perch!" and the victim will know what is in store for him.) The toilet buckets used in the cells are around two feet high and more than one foot in diameter around the top; the rim is a mere quarter of an inch wide. If the person perched on it loses concentration or falls asleep for even a moment, the "cassia blossom vase" will topple over and the muck will spill all over both the floor and himself. A terrible smell spreads throughout the cell, and the victim invariably gets punished for this with a severe beating.

(xiv) *"Playing the electric piano" (tan dianzi qin)*. This is a kind of game played by cell bosses as a way of passing the time. Although innocuous as compared to the other measures described here, it nonetheless serves to remind the prisoners of their depersonalized and subservient status within the cell. At the given order, at least eight inmates line up in a row and call out their numbers - "One, two, three..."

- in sequence. These numbers correspond to the standard notes of the musical scale: Do, Re, Me, etc., and the prisoners are ordered to remember their allotted notes. Another inmate, usually someone with a bit of musical knowledge - then stands in front of them brandishing a pair of chopsticks and proceeds to strike them smartly on the head in accordance with the notes of a particular tune. Whenever a member of the lineup feels the chopsticks landing, he must immediately sing out his own note. In this way, the tune takes shape and the cell boss gets his entertainment. The prisoners, of course, are reduced to mere piano keys - and any who miss their cue get punished for it later.

(xv) *"Learning to count" (xue shushu)*. This is a special type of punishment often favored by cell bosses as a means of sowing discord and antagonism among the other prisoners, thereby boosting their own dominant position. If used often enough, it leaves the prisoners incapable of uniting together in any form of resistance. It goes like this. Two inmates who are known to be close to each other are ordered to take turns counting backwards - "100, 99, 98..." etc., all the way to "3, 2, 1." If the person doing the counting happens to make a mistake, then the other one has to slap him across the ear, and then start counting backwards himself. If he in turn slips up, then he gets a slap on the ear from the same person he hit earlier. And so on, counting and hitting, back and forth. At the start of the process, neither person is usually willing to slap the other one very hard. But by the time the game has gone a few rounds, ill-feeling and anger inevitably begin to build up, and the slaps get harder and heavier. By the end of it, the original friendship can be in tatters.

(xvi) *"Embracing the cassia blossom vase" (bao guihua tong)*. This is yet another means by which the toilet bucket - as in the case of the "cassia blossom perch" - gets pressed into service as an instrument of punishment. At night, after the guards have inspected the cells and counted the inmates, the person to be punished is told to go and wrap his arms around the "cassia blossom vase" and remain there motionless the whole night. If any of the other prisoners need to use the toilet during the night, the victim must stay in position and endure it all without complaint. (In the Changsha jails, hardly a night went by without someone receiving this punishment.)

(xvii) *"Blind man groping an elephant" (xiazi mo xiang)*. The aim of this type of punishment is, as in the case of "learning to count," to try to break down any sense of friendship and solidarity among the prisoners. Unlike "learning to count," however, numerous prisoners are involved, rather than just two. The cell boss selects at least four prisoners, one of whom has to cover his eyes with a piece of cloth and play the "blind man." This involves groping at the other prisoners in turn and trying to guess their identities. If he guesses wrongly, the "blind man" will be given a slap around the ears by the person being groped, and he must then continue the routine with all the other prisoners until he manages to guess someone's name correctly. The latter person will then become the "blind man," and the game begins anew.

(xviii) *"Eating red-cooked meat" (chi hongshao rou)*. This is a form of beating in which the cell boss punches the prisoner repeatedly on the lower jaw. The name arises because the puncher, his fist resembling a slab of "red-cooked meat," slams the victim's upper and lower teeth together with each blow, as if he were "eating."

(xix) *"Playing dead" (ban siren)*. A game used for punishment purposes. Two prisoners are placed back-to-back and ordered to bend forward low at the waist, their backs forming a kind of horizontal platform. A third prisoner is then lowered on to this platform and made to stiffen his whole body - just like a corpse lying in a mortuary. A large sheet is then placed over his entire body, covering the head and leaving only the feet exposed. If this "game" is continued for long enough, all three prisoners will eventually begin to feel extremely uncomfortable.

(xx) *"Learning the regulations" (xue jiangui)*. Originally, this was a regular type of activity whereby cadres made the cell bosses responsible for teaching the other inmates the prison regulations. Gradually, however, it evolved into a type of punishment. It goes as follows. Several prisoners are ordered to read aloud in turn from a copy of the prison regulations, substituting the word "box" *(kuangkuang)* for any characters they do not understand. (Each character of the regulations is printed in a separate box on the page.) While each prisoner is reading, another one counts up the number of times he says "box." At the end, the prisoner is forced to give himself one hard slap on the face for every character he has failed to recognize. (Many common criminals are either illiterate or semi-literate, so the number is usually quite high.) After a brief lesson in how to read the characters in question, the prisoner is then made to recite the regulations all over again - followed by a further round of self-inflicted punishment for any mistakes. The process will be repeated over and over again until either the cell boss gets bored or the prisoner gets the text right.

The above catalogue of tortures and punishments includes only those most commonly encountered by prisoners in Hunan's Changsha No.1 and No.2 Jails. Numerous other kinds of torture and ill-treatment are widely employed by cadres and cell bosses both there and in the countless other prisons, labor camps and re-education centers throughout China.

To conclude, one other cruel kind of torture that is sometimes used by cadres in the Changsha No.1 Jail, namely "electric shackle treatment" *(dianliaokao)*, should also be mentioned. The existence of this type of torture, in which electric shocks are transmitted to the prisoner's body through shackles applied to the wrists and ankles, is a well-kept secret within the prison system. It is resorted to by prison officials, after all other punishments have failed to produce results, as a means of dealing with those prisoners who either create disturbances or who pretend to be crazy. It is sometimes also used against people who are in fact mentally ill. Ostensibly, this to done to "establish their true condition" (this would be culpable enough, were it true), but actually it is just a form of punishment treatment designed to stop such people from being "troublesome."

The torture proceeds as follows. The prisoner is shackled, hand and foot, to a specially designed board (one similar in shape to the "shackle board" described above), and a high-voltage alternating current is then administered via the shackles. Like the electric baton, the shock is of a low enough current that death cannot ensue, but the pain is unbearable, and it makes the prisoner want to die. The electric shocks are continued until the prisoner begs for mercy and guarantees that he will henceforth be entirely submissive.

In short, the range of abusive practices found in Chinese prisons and jails is diverse, complex and frightening. These practices should be condemned by all forces for justice and humanity throughout the world.

6. The Hunan Gulag

The territory of Hunan Province is home to one of the largest systems of prisons, labor-reform camps, labor re-education centers, jails, shelter-for-investigation centers and detention centers in the whole of China. *Appendix X*, below, lists details of 142 of the various custodial facilities that make up this vast, gray archipelago of state retribution. Forty-eight of them are prison, labor-reform camps or labor re-education centers where prisoners who have been sentenced either judicially by the courts or administratively by the police are sent to serve out their terms of imprisonment. These include, at a known minimum, seven large prisons, one of which is for women, and one smaller prison; 22 labor-reform camps including two for women; 16 labor re-education centers; and two juvenile detention centers. The remaining 94 units on the list are all either local jails, where prisoners charged and awaiting trial are kept, or else administrative holding and investigation centers of various sorts.

Prisons *(jianyu)* are high security units, and are used to incarcerate two types of sentenced criminals: those convicted of serious "common criminal" offenses who are serving sentences of around 10 years or more, and all those convicted of political offenses or so-called "counter-revolutionaries." Labor-reform camps *(laogai zhidui* or *laogai nongchang)* are often but not always located in the countryside, and generally hold criminals who have been sentenced to terms of less than 10 years. Juvenile offender centers *(shaonian guanjiaosuo)* are designed to hold all young criminals under the age of 18, except for those convicted on political charges. Labor re-education centers are for those sentenced directly by the police, without benefit of any trial.

Jails *(kanshousuo)*, shelter-for-investigation centers *(shourong shenchasuo)* and detention centers *(juliusuo)* are used to hold all those who have yet to be sentenced. In principle, jails are meant only for prisoners who have already been formally charged and are awaiting trial, while detention centers are for all those who have not yet been charged or who are destined for various forms of administrative detention. Shelter-for-investigation centers, which have no proper legal status, are meant to hold only those "who roam around from place to place committing crimes and whose identity is unclear." (In fact, they are used as a convenient

91

dumping ground for all those whom the authorities choose to arrest without first having obtained sufficient evidence of guilt.) In many parts of Hunan, however, these demarcatory guidelines do not apply, since many localities have only jails but no detention centers or shelter-for-investigation centers.

Prisons

The seven main prisons in Hunan are Yuanjiang Prison (Provincial No.1), Hengyang Prison (Provincial No.2), Lingling Prison (Provincial No.3), Huaihua Prison (Provincial No.4), Chenzhou Prison (Provincial No.5), Longxi Prison (Provincial No.6) and Changsha Prison. The two largest are Yuanjiang and Hengyang prisons, which hold more than 6,000 and 7,000 prisoners respectively. They are also the oldest, having already been in use at the time of the Guomindang regime. The populations of the other five prisons range from around 2,000 to 5,000.

Each prison is assigned a role in economic production, and publicly all are called factories. Provincial Nos. 1, 2 and 3 prisons are responsible for turning out automobile parts and accessories, for example, and the second is presented to the outside world only as the "Hunan Heavy Motor Vehicle Plant." Provincial Nos. 4, 5 and 6 prisons are mainly engaged in mining and quarrying activities. Longxi Prison, the place where I was sent after my trial and which thanks to its remote and barren location is known locally as "Siberia," is a marble quarry, producing partly for export. Changsha Prison is used mainly to hold female prisoners from all parts of the province, but it also accommodates a small number of adult male prisoners. It comprises several different factories, involved variously in garment making, handicraft production, engineering, machine-building and printing.

Conditions of detention in the prisons are better than those in the other types of facility, and the forced manual labor is usually less strenuous. Because of the high security regime in prisons, however, freedom of movement is even more restricted there than in the other units. Cells range from between 10 and 40 square meters in size, and the average number of inmates in a cell is usually around 20. A uniform daily schedule is operated in the prisons, stipulating the precise times at which inmates have to rise, wash, eat, work, join in political study sessions and go to bed. Any breach of the rules results in punishment.

As regards diet, prisoners generally have meat in their meals two to three times a week, although this varies between different prisons and brigades. The basic fare is just rice and plain vegetables, with scarcely a drop of edible oil to be found. The rice allowance is more or less sufficient, however, to stave off hunger pangs, and while new prisoners often feel hungry, they generally adjust to the diet after a few weeks inside.

Prisoners are each paid a government allowance of 2.30 *yuan* (less than US$0.50) per month, which has to be spent on toothpaste, toothbrush, face towel and soap. Throughout the year, only cold water is available for showers. Several hundred inmates have just one toilet room to share, so the facilities are always stinking and unsanitary.

Upon first arriving at the prison, newly convicted prisoners are put into "prison induction teams" *(rujiandui)* for a period of three months, so that they can be taught the prison regulations and subjected to preliminary disciplining. There is extensive "political study," the main purpose of which is impress upon new arrivals the need to obey the regulations without question. At the end of this time, prisoners are assigned to one of the various production teams to commence forced manual labor.

According to prison regulation, the daily working hours for a prisoner are restricted to a maximum of eight. But in practice, prisoners usually have to work at least ten hours, and some even have to work as much as 16 hours a day. This depends mainly on the type of labor to which one has been assigned and the daily quotas that have been fixed for the job. In general, those working in prison factories, performing such tasks as machinery assembly, find the labor considerably less strenuous than do those of their counterparts assigned to work in mining or quarrying.

In recent years, along with the improvements in living standards in society at large, some prisons have begun to provide basic amenities and even a few recreational facilities, for example a television room and a basketball court. Prisoners are usually only permitted to watch television once a week, but Sunday in the prisons is a rest day, and inmates are allowed to play poker or chess then. (To play these games at any other time is strictly forbidden.) Nowadays, there is generally a basketball court for each brigade, but it is mainly used for purposes of letting inmates take their daily exercise stroll at specified times. At all other times during the Sunday rest day, inmates have to remain in their cells. They are not permitted to make contact with, still less to visit, inmates in the other brigades, teams or cells.

Each prison has its own set of rules, some of which apply nationally, while others are drawn up by the local prison authorities themselves. Any violation of the rules results in immediate punishment, ranging from reprimands, use of shackles, short-term solitary confinement and placement in a "strict regime" unit within the prison, all the way through to long-term solitary confinement within the strict regime unit. The latter is used to punish prisoners who seriously violate prison rules, and specific measures include raising the prisoner's daily forced-labor production quota; making him remained seated and motionless, staring at the wall for many hours each day, so that he may "repent his sins"; placing him in prolonged solitary confinement; and a vague category referred to only as "punishment regime." This latter can range from such things as reduction of daily food rations and greatly raising the daily work quota, all the way up to gross physical punishment and torture. Prison cadres claim privately that they would find it impossible to operate and keep order within the prisons unless they had such severe punitive measures as this at their disposal.

Labor-Reform Camps

By comparison with the general regimen of the labor-reform camps, however, that found in the prisons appears relatively humane. Apart from such atypical labor-reform camps as the Changsha Match Factory (Provincial No.9 Labor-Reform Detachment), where administration is relatively orderly and civilized, life in the Hunan labor-reform camps and farms is often little more than a battle for survival.

As mentioned above, the 22 known labor-reform camps in Hunan (each of which is identified numerically) are used to hold prisoners sentenced to terms of less than 10 years. They do not generally take in either political prisoners or juvenile offenders. Most of the camps operate as agricultural farms, while a small number engage in manufacturing or mining. Some of the camps are enormous. Two of the largest, namely Jianxin Farm, located near Yueyang City, and Cendan Farm in Xiangyin

County, each have more than 20,000 inmates. In the Provincial New Life Coal Mine near Leiyang City, and in the Changsha Cement Factory near Pingtang, the camp populations range from 5,000 to 10,000. Most of the other labor-reform camps hold somewhere between 1,000 and 5,000 inmates.

The camps fall into two broad categories: agricultural farms, and factories or mines. The living conditions in the farms are the most harsh, whereas labor-reform camps organized as factories or mines are rather similar to the prisons. Just as in the prisons, for example, the latter operate production-related incentive schemes which allow prisoners to have their term of sentence progressively reduced. The adjustments are made on the basis of how many credit points a prisoner can obtain. Those who observe strict discipline and manage to finish their assigned production quotas on time are periodically awarded one credit point, equivalent to one four-and-a-half days' reduction of sentence. The system also works in reverse, however, and failure to meet the quota results in loss of the credit point and a corresponding increase in sentence.

Most of the labor-reform camps in Hunan, apart from a few which were already in existence in the 1950s, were set up during the early 1970s. These include Jianxin Farm, Bainihu Farm and the Pingtang Cement Factory. These camps were in a deplorable state in their early stages, but things have improved somewhat in recent years. At present, the government's subsistence allowance for a labor-reform camp prisoner stands at 29.50 *yuan*, just a little lower than that for a prison inmate. (They receive food and items of daily necessity to the value of just over 30 *yuan* per month.) Prisoners have to provide for any of their own daily sundry needs over and above this bare minimum, however, and most depend on their families for even the barest of luxuries.

Labor-reform camps are located in the countryside, where life is hard and the work is strenuous and unremitting. Take Jianxin Farm, for example, which has over 20,000 prisoners. The farm is divided into brigades *(dadui)*, which are in turn subdivided into squadrons *(zhongdui)* and then teams *(fendui)*. There are over 1,000 prisoners in a brigade, several hundred in a squadron, and several dozen in a team. At first sight, the farm looks just like a small town, complete with living quarters for over 100 cadres and officials, and there are also shops, a cinema, a market and a hospital. The farm has all the attributes and facilities of a normal settlement - except that they are for the exclusive use of the labor camp staff alone.

The squadron forms the basic nucleus of camp life for the inmates. (The squadron in the farm is similar to the brigade in the prison.) All the members of a given squadron live together in an area surrounded by walls on all sides, and members of one squadron are not allowed to communicate with those of any other squadron. On the surface, life is much the same as in the prisons. The difference, however, lies in the far lower living standard and in the much more strenuous nature of the forced manual labor required on the farms. Prisoners in the farms have to work all the year round, moreover, and are only entitled to two or three days' rest altogether, during the Chinese New Year Festival. They have no Sundays off, and so the only other time they get a rest is when it rains heavily.

At busy times such as seed planting or harvesting, the work is unrelenting. The prisoners have to get up before dawn and begin work in the fields when it is still dark. They have their lunch in the fields as they work. (Special duty prisoners prepare lunch for the whole team in advance and bring it to the fields when they leave for work in the morning.) All prisoners have to work until nightfall before being allowed to return to their cells. Currently, prisoners engaged in farm work are each assigned a production quota, and failure to meet it normally results in punishment, such as a beating or being locked up in shackles. The guards, their truncheons in hands, stand behind the prisoners the whole time as they work in the fields, and beat any of them whom they consider to be slacking. The sight of one person treating another like an outright slave in this way is deeply offensive. When they return to the camp from the fields in the evenings, the prisoners all just fling themselves on to the sleeping platform immediately, fully clothed, and are asleep within minutes. None of them would even think of taking a shower before sleeping, and the stench of unwashed bodies all around them is the least of their worries.

The forced labor sites are usually located in areas near to the city suburbs. The cadres in charge mark out on the spot the boundary of the day's security zone, and any prisoner stepping outside the zone runs the risk of being shot. Few people, therefore, ever try to escape while working in the fields. However, there are times when prisoners do defy orders. One such moment is when a prisoner's hunger for food, stimulated by the sight of fresh vegetables on display right there in the fields, overcomes his fear of being discovered in the act of pulling them up, still covered in mud, and eating them. The prisoner will get a beating, but the taste of the fresh vegetable will often be considered worth it nonetheless.

Violence is rife in the camps, with both frequent fights breaking out among the prisoners themselves and extensive resort to force on the part of the cadres and guards. In Jianxin Farm, for example, prisoners who fail to complete their production quotas find themselves either being summoned after work to the so-called "education room" and used as human targets for martial arts practice by the guards, or else simply being visited in their cells and beaten up right there. As in the prisons, certain of the guards are known only by nicknames acknowledging their prowess in this field, for example "Killer Lei", "Desperado Tan" and "Three-Blows Wang" (a particularly violent individual who was known to have knocked a prisoner unconscious with only three blows.)

Self-maiming

Some prisoners in the Hunan labor camps try deliberately to maim and injure themselves, hoping that their self-inflicted disabilities will gain them a temporary respite from the miseries of camp life, the rigors of forced labor and the constant threat of physical violence. They even sometimes hope, although vainly, that becoming disabled will increase their chances of securing an early release from prison.

Cases of self-maiming occur quite frequently in the camps. The main aims of prisoners who injure themselves are, first, to secure a respite from the daily grind of forced labor, and second, to be released on bail to seek medical treatment (*qubao houshen*: a measure specified in China's criminal procedure law.) In addition, some prisoners use the opportunity of being sent to a hospital outside in order to escape and go on the run. There are several types of such self-imposed injury. One type involves injecting kerosene (often mixed in with rotten food) into the blood stream, via such parts of the body as the abdomen, legs or even the head. After a while, the affected part will begin to swell and fester, and the authorities usually have little choice but to allow the prisoner out on temporary bail for treatment.

Another method used by prisoners is to deliberately break their own limbs. This is done by placing the arm or leg between two heavy pieces of slate and then striking down hard on the slate with either a pick or a sledgehammer. When the slates splits into two, the prisoner's limb will often fracture as well, so rendering him incapable of performing manual labor. Other commonly used methods include swallowing harmful herbs or medicines which induce the symptoms of such serious contagious diseases as nephritis and hepatitis; swallowing small pieces of razor blade; slashing open the abdomen; and severing the leg tendon. Again, the prison authorities often have little choice in such cases but to grant the prisoner temporary bail. (Labor-reform units, especially those operating as farms, have only rudimentary on-site medical facilities and so cannot treat such conditions by themselves.)

Some prisoners did actually succeed in getting out of prison this way, although rarely for very long. The most gruesome instance of self-maiming that I came across in prison was that of a prisoner who used a twin-hook device, which he had specially designed for the purpose, to gouge out his own eyes. The injury was irreparable - but the attempt to secure release on bail backfired. For the prisoner in question was serving a life sentence, and the camp commander strictly adhered to a regulation which lays down that lifers are not eligible for release on bail.

Rather than respond humanely to what in some camps was fast becoming a near-epidemic of self-mutilation - by, for example, reducing the forced-labor quotas and starting to treat prisoners more fairly - the authorities instead decided to step up deterrence. In 1988, a directive was issued ordering that all requests by prisoners for release on bail to seek treatment for injuries which had been self-inflicted were to be turned down. In spite of this hardline attitude, however, the incidence of self-maiming in the camps has showed no signs of decrease. According to former labor-camp prisoners, hardly a day goes by without some such incident arising.

Strict regime units

Prisoners who regularly break camp rules are dealt with by committal to the "strict regime unit" (*yanguandui*), a highly punitive regime where a host of imaginative abuses and indignities lie waiting in store. The strict regime unit at Jianxin, for example, is a veritable house of fun, being characterized by a series of punishment ordeals known collectively as "Playing the Three Games." The first one, called "Clinging Gecko," involves the prisoner having to kneel down on the ground, with his hands raised above head height and pressed against the wall, for several-hour-long periods. The strain on the muscles soon becomes excruciating, and eventually the prisoner will collapse on the ground in a state of shock.

The second "game," which is known as "Golden Chicken Standing on One Leg," entails the prisoner having one arm handcuffed to the foot on the opposite side and then having the other arm chained high up above head height. In this way, the prisoner is left to stand on only on leg, and when exhaustion sets in the leg buckles under him, thereby wrenching his arm socket.

The third delight is called the "Pillar Standing Feat," and involves the prisoner being made to stand atop a pillar of around one meter in height with his hands chained behind his back and fixed to the wall. After 24 hours of this ordeal, at most, even the strongest of prisoners become exhausted and unable to prevent themselves from nodding off or falling asleep. When this happens, the prisoner falls off the pillar, with his full body weight behind him, and again wrenches his arms.

Juvenile Offender Centers

In addition to the prisons and labor reform camps, there are two large Juvenile Offenders Institutes in Hunan. These institutes are part of the labor reform system. One is situated in Wangchengbo in the suburbs of Changsha, and the other is in Chenzhou City. They are called the Changsha Juvenile Offenders Institute and the Chenzhou Juvenile Offenders Institute. The former was set up quite recently, and the latter no more than 10 years ago.

Such centers hold in custody nearly all offenders under the age of 18 who have been given court sentences. (Two categories of juvenile offenders - namely political prisoners and women - are committed to prisons to serve out their terms.) There are about 5,000 prisoners in the Chenzhou Juvenile Offenders Institute and somewhat fewer in the Changsha unit. Both are engaged in matchbox production. ("Chenzhou matches" are manufactured by the former; "Changsha matches," sold throughout the country, however, are manufactured by the Hunan No.9 Labor Reform Camp, which is known outwardly as the Changsha Match Factory.) The Changsha Juvenile Offenders Institute also produces packing bags.

Supervision is even more rigid in these institutions than in the adult prisons and labor-reform camps, and young offenders are allowed less freedom of movement. Throughout the year, they are required to work indoors in prison factories located inside the institute compound; they are not allowed to work outdoors. Upon reaching the age of 18, juvenile offenders are transferred either to adult prisons or to labor-reform camps, depending upon their terms of sentence.

Labor Re-education centers

China's system of "re-education through labor" was originally learned and borrowed from the Soviet Union. It is a form of so-called "administrative detention" and is designed for those who "commit misdemeanors" which are "not serious enough to qualify for criminal sanction." In practice, it means that anyone who falls foul of the public security system can be locked up by it for up to three years without ever having had a trial. Until less than three years ago, there was not even any provision for appeal to the courts. (The current right of appeal, moreover, is largely a futile formality.)

There is little real difference between the living conditions for "labor-reform" criminals and those for "labor re-education personnel." Indeed, the two types of prisoners are often held in the same labor camp, although organized into different teams. One crucial difference is that if a person sentenced to a labor reform camp is subsequently found to have been sentenced by mistake, his case will be said to be a miscarriage of justice. It is a different story, however, for someone wrongly sentenced to labor re-education. The authorities will not acknowledge such a case as being a miscarriage of justice, on the specious grounds that "it wasn't even a criminal sanction anyway." In the eyes of the people in the street, they both amount to incarceration just the same.

In Hunan, there are 16 known labor re-education centers of diverse sizes. On average, there is one center in every district or in every city. The larger ones are the Changsha Xinkaipu Labor Re-education

Center (known publicly as the Hunan Switchgear Factory, a well known production enterprise), the Zhuzhou Lukou Labor Re-education Center, the Hengshan labor Re-education Center, and the Lengshuijiang Labor Re-education Center. Among them, the Changsha Xinkaipu Labor Re-education Center is the most well-known, being regarded nationally as a model labor re-education unit. Usually somewhat smaller than labor reform camps, their populations range from between 1,000 and 10,000. The largest, those at Changsha, Hengshan and Lengshuijiang, all have populations of over 5,000. Most have under 5,000.

Life in labor re-education centers is roughly the same as that in the labor reform camps. The one marked difference is that if those undergoing re-education have a "good performance" they can ask after certain intervals for parole for the purpose of home visits. Inmates in labor re-education centers are not described as prisoners. They are identified as "re-education personnel," since they belong to the category of so-called "contradictions among the people," namely "non antagonistic" ones. (Overtly political criteria such as these, of course, have no rightful place in a country's system of legal justice.) As for labor, production activities in labor re-education centers are mostly in machinery and other light industries, with a small number involved in mining. The Changsha Xinkaipu Labor Re-education Center, for example, is a factory producing various types of electrical switchgear. Several smaller-scale centers such as the Changqiao Labor Re-education Team and the Changsha Silk Factory are also local manufacturing enterprises. Persons in the labor re-education centers are divided into teams (publicly known as workshops.) There are engineers and technicians among these persons. The atmosphere in the centers is less tense and less dull as compared with labor reform camps, since prisoners are serving sentences of usually less than three years.

There are also at least two Women's Labor Re-education Centers in Hunan. They mostly hold women accused of engaging in prostitution or other petty crimes. In the Changsha Center, the population is more than 1,000. The Zhuzhou Center is by far the largest.

Jails and detention centers

The numerous pre-hearing custodial centers *(kanshou jiguan)* in Hunan Province are also worthy of mention here, since many pro-democracy activists were held in custody in them after the June 4 crackdown for periods ranging from a few months to well over one year, before finally being released. The various types include jails *(kanshousuo)*, shelter-for-investigation centers *(shourong shenchasuo)* and detention centers *(juliusuo)*. The larger cities, such as Changsha, Hengyang, Xiangtan, Zhuzhou, Yueyang and Shaoyang, are equipped with all three types of centers, whereas in the counties or smaller towns there is often only one jail, and no shelter-for-investigation center or detention center. But each county has at least one jail, the larger of which can hold several hundred or even a thousand or more prisoners, while the smaller ones only hold around a hundred.

Of the three types, jails are usually the most properly run - although all the pre-hearing holding centers in Hunan might best be described as "wrestling rings." The shelter-for-investigation centers and detention centers, however, can only be described as being like the proverbial "Palaces of the King of Hell" *(Yan Wang Dian.)* Almost all pro-democracy activists detained in 1989 were consigned to jails from the outset, with only a very few being detained in the other two types of holding centers. This mainly reflected the government's prejudgment of them all as being guilty, but it was also because jails are all guarded by the People's Armed Police, which is only true in a minority of the other two types of detention facility. The reason given by the authorities themselves for preferring the former in our case was that otherwise - so great being "the people's anger" toward us for having upset the tranquillity of the socialist idyll - they would be unable to protect us from being beaten up by the other prisoners.

Most of the various types of holding centers are grossly overcrowded. In the jails, detainees generally have less than one square meter of floor space each. The better-run ones have small exercise yards adjoining each cell, and prisoners are allowed out for short periods each day to walk around in them. The detention centers and shelter-for-investigation centers usually have no exercise yards, and prisoners remain in the cells 24 hours a day. In the two detention centers I know most about, namely the Changsha East District and the Changsha Suburban PSB detention centers, the cells are less than six square meters in area. At the height of the "crackdown on crime" campaign in mid-1990, 20 or more prisoners were commonly packed into a single cell, leaving an average of only 0.3 square meters of floor space for each prisoner. At night, the lucky ones were jammed like sardines on to the sleeping platform, while others had to sleep under it (they were referred to in the local prison slang as "coal miners" *(wa mei)*. The rest simply had to stand around all night and await their turn to sleep during the daytime.

Throughout the pre-hearing detention network, the so-called "cell boss" system is rife. Sometimes there will only be one or two cell bosses per cell, but some cells may have up to five or six. When the cell door slams shut, their word is law, and they abuse and torment the other prisoners on a mere whim. For instance, when they feel like having a bit of fun, they just spit on the floor and order some hapless inmate to get down on his knees and suck it up, licking the spot clean afterwards. Almost no one would dare to refuse, so total is the cell bosses' power. They especially enjoy seeing the prisoners fight among themselves at their instigation.

The jail diet is grossly insufficient and of extremely poor quality. This is hardly surprising, given that the subsistence allocation for each prisoner is a mere 24.50 *yuan* per month. In addition, some jails and detention centers force the inmates to perform long hours of entirely unpaid manual labor in the cells. In Changsha No.1 Jail, where I was held, for example, we had to sit right there on the cell floor making matchboxes day after day, and we never received a single cent. (Prison labor, if properly administered, can be a quite acceptable practice in the case of sentenced criminals. But it is not so in the case of those held in jails and detention centers, since they have not yet even been tried and found guilty.)

On average, detainees are held in these various holding centers for periods of between three and six months before being put on trial. After conviction (only a tiny minority of defendants are ever acquitted by the courts), they are dispatched to either prisons or labor-reform camps to serve out their sentences. (In the case of labor re-education, the opinion of the local public security chief suffices to clinch the judgment; the authorities do not even bother with the formality of a trial.) Some detainees, notably major economic criminals and certain types of political prisoners, however, remain in the jails, shelter-for-investigation and detention centers for far longer, sometimes for as long as two to three years, if the authorities for any reason consider their cases to be "particularly complex."

103

The forced-labor production regime: Longxi Prison

I was incarcerated in Longxi Prison, western Hunan, from November 1990 until February 1991. Although the workforce there is made up entirely of prisoners, Longxi Prison is actually a large-scale marble quarrying plant, known to the outside world as the "Shaoyang Marble Factory." The following is a brief account, based on my own direct experience and observation, of the economic production, marketing and exporting activities of Longxi Prison.

Situated near Longxipu Township in Xinshao County, Shaoyang Municipality, the prison lies about 250 kilometers to the southwest of Changsha, the provincial capital, and about 50 kilometers from Shaoyang City. Far off in the mountains of Xinshao County, the location of Longxi Prison is without doubt the most remote and secluded of all the prisons in Hunan Province. The prison has approximately 2,000 inmates, around 70 of whom are political prisoners serving sentences ranging from two years' imprisonment to death with a two-year reprieve. The remainder are common criminals whose terms of imprisonment are generally in excess of 15 years.

The basic nucleus of prisoners' work and daily life in Longxi Prison is the brigade *(dadui)*. (A prison brigade has equivalent status to that of a section *[ke]* in the wider government administrative structure.) The prisoners are organized into six brigades, a prison induction team, a headquarters squadron *(zhishu zhongdui)*, a headquarters brigade *(zhishu dadui)* and a medical corps. Apart from Brigade No.6, which is responsible for mechanical and electrical work, all the brigades are directly involved in production activities.

The division of labor among the five production brigades, each of which comprises an average workforce of between 200 and 300 inmates, is as follows: Brigades No.4 and 5 engage in quarry operations and are called "field brigades" *(waigong dui)*. Brigades No. 1, 2 and 3 are responsible for processing the raw marble material into finished products. Prisoners assigned to the two field brigades work at marble quarries in the mountains, where core operations include rock blasting, marble cutting and transportation of the marble blocks back to the processing plant. The three brigades involved in raw-materials processing are mainly responsible for grinding and polishing the blocks of quarried marble and

104

then turning them into finished products. The production line is primitive, the only equipment being the basic stone-grinders and polishers.

Prisoners work under a strict system of production norms and must complete their daily quotas. Failure to do so means punishment. Poor performers generally have their sentences increased in accordance with a pre-set sliding scale. In more serious cases, however, offenders are either sent to the strict regime unit or placed in solitary confinement. Time spent undergoing either of these punishments is discounted, moreover, for purposes of calculating a prisoner's remaining length of sentence. Indeed, an extra day is added to the original prison term for each day of the punishment.

The most dangerous production task carried out by prisoners at the quarrying and mining sites is the laying of dynamite for blasting operations. Many prisoners suffer injuries or even permanent disability in the course of this. For prisoners with only minor injuries, the prison provides basic medical attention. But if a prisoner suffers serious injury or encripplement, he must simply resign himself to his fate. For in nine out of ten cases, the authorities will insist that the injuries were "self-inflicted," constituting an act of defiance and a deliberate attempt to evade productive labor, thereby disqualifying the victim from being allowed out on bail for medical treatment.

The finished marble products shipped from the prison comprise mainly goods for use by the building and construction industry, such as marble floor-slabs, wall tiles and decorative plaques. The prison also produces marble handicraft items such as office paper weights, table-lamp stands, vases, ashtrays, signature seals and pen stands. All these products sell extremely well in China, with demand outstripping supply in the local markets and prices varying wildly from one part of the country to another. One of the Longxi products, for example, a six-inch long, Chinese character-inscribed paper weight which sells for less than 1 *yuan* in the prison's sales office and in the nearby towns, sometimes fetches as much as 30 to 40 *yuan* in shops in the larger cities and in the special economic zones.

Like all other labor-reform units in China, Longxi Prison has in recent years tried to mimic the economic reforms that have been

105

proceeding throughout the rest of society. The main innovation has been the so-called "production responsibility system," which stresses the free market, discourages state subsidies and gives performance-related rewards and penalties to individual workers - in this case, prisoners. In fact, despite the oft-repeated central government policy on labor-reform work of "reform first, production second," there is no doubt that production has nowadays become the primary activity at Longxi Prison. The prison's remoteness from the cities and central government departments, however, renders it less susceptible to any reformist political influences, and the leadership there remains hardline leftist in outlook. The economic reforms at Longxi and most other labor-reform units are little more than opportunist method of maximizing profits, and imply no movement whatever toward political reform or "liberalization."

Prisoners can even, in effect, buy their way out of prison early, thanks to a recently-introduced reform which encourages inmates to use their family members and business contacts outside the prison to secure sales contracts for the prison. The system works like this. If a given prisoner can manage to arrange outside sales of the prison's marble products bringing in a net profit of 8,000 *yuan*, then he will be awarded one so-called "minor merit" point, which in turn amounts to 20 "credit points." For each credit point gained, the prisoner's remaining sentence is reduced by a period of four and one half days. Hence, a "minor merit" wins the prisoner a three-month overall reduction of sentence. Significantly, however, an unwritten rule bars political prisoners from benefitting from this "flexible policy."

Exporting of prison-made goods

I was once present at a mass meeting of the inmates at Longxi Prison during which a prison cadre told us all to encourage our families to undertake sales activities on behalf of the prison. The official stressed in particular that foreign exports of the prison's goods were most ideal, since they yielded the highest profit. (Apparently, many overseas buyers are interested in obtaining marble building goods and handicraft items such as seals and paper weights.) The official even read aloud from a set of rules on the credits and awards that prisoners could earn through their prison-sales efforts and those of their families. Many prisoners then began asking their families and friends to seek buyers for the prison's goods, with a view to earning "minor merits" and getting out of prison

106

early.

I remember one prisoner, a cellmate of mine at one point, who managed to arrange such big overseas sales contracts through his family and friends that he eventually earned profits for the prison to the tune of several hundred thousand *yuan*. The man, whose name was Zeng Qinglin, had previously been an employee of an overseas Chinese import-export corporation based in Shenzhen, and he was serving a 10-year prison term for economic corruption offenses. His business background made it easy for him to fix the deals, but the sheer size of the profits created a problem for the prison leadership, since technically he had earned so much remission on his sentence that he would be due for release almost immediately. So a deal was struck, whereby the prison leadership privately assured Zeng that he would be granted parole once his term of imprisonment reached the fifth year. From then on, he became a highly privileged "guest" of the prison, surpassing all the other inmates in status and even enjoying better living conditions than some of the lower-level officials.

Goods produced by most of the other main prisons in Hunan are also available for export. Yuanjiang, Hengyang and Lingling Prisons, for example, produce vehicles and auto parts which are marketed in various South-East Asian countries. Products from the Changde Diesel Engine Plant are also available for export in small numbers.

While I was imprisoned in Guangdong No.1 Jail, I had to produce various types of handicraft products which, apparently, were mainly for sale overseas. (I was told this by a provincial foreign trade official who had been detained for trying to help pro-democracy activists escape the country.) Later on, during my time at the Changsha No.2 Jail, I had to make packing boxes for a Chinese medical product, a concoction made from snake gallbladder and juice of the pi-pa fruit, which was produced by the Hunan Pharmaceuticals Factory. Changsha No.2 Jail had been contracted to produce the packaging for this medicine, which was shipped for sale overseas in large quantities.

Two of the largest re-education facilities in Changsha, namely the Hunan Switchgear Factory (also known as the Xinkaipu Labor Re-education Center) and the Hunan Silk Factory (also known as the Changsha Women's Re-education Center), export large quantities of their goods abroad. According to a "restricted-circulation" *(neibu)* volume published in Changsha in November 1989, the Hunan Switchgear Factory, whose workshops alone cover 125,000 square meters of floorspace, has since the 1960s been exporting a wide range of its high and low-voltage electrical appliances and products to various countries including Albania, Brazil, Thailand, Yemen and Hong Kong. More recently, the factory has added Tanzania, North Korea, Sri Lanka, Bangladesh and Pakistan to its ever-growing list of international customers. In 1986, according to the confidential volume, the Hunan Commission on Foreign Economic Relations and Trade (which is the provincial counterpart of MOFERT, Beijing's Ministry of Foreign Economic Relations and Trade) awarded the factory the glorious designation of "Advanced Unit in Exporting and Foreign Currency-Earning." The following year, it received the further accolade of "Advanced Unit in Completing Product Tasks for Foreign Aid Purposes."[36]

Similarly, the Hunan Silk Factory, a large production facility with workshops covering 74,500 square meters of floorspace, is said by the same internally published source to have been exporting a wide range of silk cloth products and garments to countries throughout Asia, Africa and Latin America ever since its foundation in 1958. "Since the early 1980s, moreover," continues the source, "the factory, in cooperation with [China's] foreign trade departments, has been exporting its pure-silk and silk-mixture quilt covers, its pure-silk jasmine satin cloth, its printed soft-silk fabric in satin weave and its silk floss taffeta to both the U.S.A. and Japan."

Try as they may, the authorities can offer no convincing denial of the clear fact that goods manufactured by prison labor in China are being exported. If one asks cadres of various Hunan labor-reform establishments at random for their views, they invariably take pride in the

---

[36] *Changsha Sishi Nian: 1949 to 1989* ("Forty Years in Changsha: 1948 to 1989"), compiled and published by the Changsha Municipal Bureau of Statistics, November 1989. The book carries the legend, "Internal Materials - File Carefully," and only 800 copies were printed, each of which carries a two-line form on the inside cover requiring recipient offices or organizations to enter their names and the identifying number of the copy issued to them.

fact that their products are able to find overseas markets. The Chinese government, for its part, does not consider its prison-goods export industry to be in any way reprehensible or a violation of human rights - regardless of the fact that thousands of political prisoners are among those currently being exploited in the Chinese *gulag* for this purpose - and it issues extensive disinformation on the topic as a means of deflecting the growing international criticism of its trade in forced-labor goods.

Forcible employment of time-served prisoners

From the early 1950s onward, the Chinese labor-reform authorities began to apply a policy known as the "forcible retention of time-served prisoners for in-camp employment" *(xingman shifang renyuan de qiangzhixing liuchang jiuye)* - or "forced in-camp employment" for short. Under this policy, millions of former prisoners have, over the past four decades throughout the country, been forced to remain behind after the expiration of their sentences as so-called "workers," usually for the rest of their lives, in the same prison or labor-camp enterprises in which they previously lived as prisoners.

Although blatantly unjust, the use of "forced in-camp employment" is widespread in Hunan Province. Government officials there argue that the policy facilitates the policy of "putting thought-reform in first place" and "allowing prisoners to reform themselves more thoroughly." Holding human rights in utter contempt, the authorities have broken up countless families and created untold numbers of domestic tragedies through this policy. The practice reached a high-point during the 1983 "campaign to crack down on serious crime," and in subsequent years large numbers of prisoners were forcibly retained as workers in prisons and labor camps, especially in northwestern China, after completing their sentences. Most were barred from ever recovering their original urban residency rights or returning to their homes.

After being released on parole in February 1991, I travelled around much of Hunan and was able to learn something about the "forced in-camp employment" situation there. Hunan Provincial No. 2 Prison, for example, is a factory producing heavy-duty trucks. Known outwardly as the "Hengyang Heavy Motor Vehicle Plant," it holds more than 7000 prisoners, organized into around ten different workshops

109

known as brigades *(dadui)*. There is also a small contingent of workers (i.e. non-prisoners) employed in the factory, a minority of whom are the children of prison cadres. The majority of them, however, are "time-served prisoners retained for in-camp employment." A small proportion of such people have remained voluntarily to work in the camp or prison enterprise after completing their sentences, but the great majority have had no say at all in the matter and are simply forced to stay on.

One prisoner I knew who had been forcibly retained as a worker was a man nicknamed "Springtime Pickpocket" *(chun pashou.)* He told me that in 1987 he had completed a 15-year sentence for robbery. As soon as his prison term had ended, however, the authorities canceled his Changsha urban residency permit *(hukou)* and forced him to stay on in the prison factory as a worker. Ostensibly a free citizen, his life remained, in fact, almost identical to that of the prisoners. His daily working hours and production quota were virtually the same as before, as was his daily rest entitlement. The only difference was that he now received a tiny monthly wage and was allowed to take care of his own domestic affairs. In addition, once in a while he was permitted to take a short holiday and go home to visit his family. His overall standard of living had hardly increased at all.

Certainly, his personal dignity was accorded no greater respect than before - the main reason being that, like other "forcibly retained personnel," he had to work in the factory alongside the prison cadres' offspring. Any one of the latter (even if he or she was completely illiterate) enjoyed an unrestricted right to exercise discipline and control over the "released labor-reform personnel." According to "Springtime Pickpocket," his only hope in life lay in somehow gaining personal favor with the prison cadres, so that one of them would eventually be kind enough to release him and allow him to return to Changsha. The great majority of "forcibly retained personnel" all cling to a similar hope. Despite being nominally free and equal citizens, therefore, they would never actually dare to demonstrate or lay claim to any such equality with the cadres.

In Longxi Prison, there was relatively little "forced in-camp employment." Because of its remote and isolated location, the marble plant's productivity was low and it usually ran at a loss. It thus had no great need of even the cheapest additional labor-power. This was also one

110

reason why Longxi had probably the most flexible parole practices of any of the major Hunan prisons. There were, however, a certain number of "forcibly retained personnel" kept in the prison, perhaps as part of a token effort by the cadres to show that they were implementing the "spirit" of the relevant central government documents.

Most of the other main facilities in Hunan Province, including Jianxin Farm, Yuanjiang Prison, the Hunan Diesel Engine Plant and Provincial No. 3 Prison, had larger numbers of "forcibly retained personnel." The average was around 100 persons per prison or labor camp, although some units held more than 200. Among these former prisoners, some undoubtedly were (as the authorities claimed) individuals who had resisted re-education and "failed to reform themselves well." Others were forcibly retained because they had highly-prized technical or professional skills; such people were usually the most wretched and miserable of all those forced to stay on after completion of sentence.

Naturally, these "forcibly retained personnel" feel a constant sense of resentment at the great injustice of their situation, and some do try to escape from time to time. But the authorities usually manage to recapture and bring them back again quite quickly. They rarely punish such people severely (for example by resentencing them), however, and instead usually just hold a criticism meeting within the prison or something similar. The real reason that so few "forcibly retained personnel" try to escape is, rather, because the only point in their doing so would be to return home - and they are all too well aware that if they were ever to return home, they would be caught and returned to the prison enterprise again almost immediately. Their unofficial life sentences would then merely become all the harder to bear.

*****

Tang Boqiao reached the United States in April 1992.

APPENDIX I

Data on Pro-Democracy Prisoners and Ex-Prisoners in Hunan Province

A. Currently Imprisoned

Yuanjiang Prison (Provincial No. 1)

- **Ah Fang** (nickname), 23 years old, originally a student at Changsha University. Home and workplace: the Changsha Nonferrous Metals Design Academy. During the 1989 Democracy Movement, he took part in the Students Autonomous Federation, but withdrew from its activities early on and so was not investigated by the authorities after June 4. In September and October 1989, he set up a private company together with a group of research staff from the Non-Ferrous Metals Design Academy and other institutes. At the end of 1989, the company was closed down by the authorities and branded a "counterrevolutionary organization." Ah Fang was arrested shortly afterwards, and in mid-1990 was tried by the Changsha Intermediate [People's] Court on charges of being "a member of a counterrevolutionary clique" and sentenced to five years' imprisonment. Initially held in Changsha No. 1 and No. 2 Detention Centers, he was later transferred to serve his sentence at Yuanjiang Prison. [5 YRS]

- **Chen Zhixiang**, 34 years old, originally a teacher at the Guangzhou Maritime Transport Academy. He was tried and sentenced on January 11, 1990 by the Guangzhou Intermediate Court to a prison term of ten years. (See *Appendix VIII.A*, below, for full text of the court's verdict on Chen.) During the 1989 Democracy Movement he allegedly organized student demonstrations in Guangzhou and wrote "reactionary articles" with an "extremely bad influence in institutions of higher education." He also had a "reactionary historical background." On June 7, 1989, Chen allegedly painted 20-meter long slogans on the walls along Yanjiang Road Central and Huanshi Road Central in Guangzhou, which according to the authorities, attacked "state, military and Party leaders" and called "for the overthrow of the people's democratic dictatorship." He was arrested shortly thereafter and was eventually convicted on a charge of "counterrevolutionary propaganda and incitement." While Chen is

113

reported to be currently held in Yuanjiang Prison, this cannot be confirmed. Other reports state that Chen is being held in Guangdong Province, although senior provincial officials there have consistently refused either to confirm this or to indicate in which prison or labor-reform camp Chen is currently being held.   [10 YRS]

▪ **Fu Zhaoqin**, peasant from Taojiang County. During the 1989 Democracy Movement he actively participated in the student resistance movement and was accused by the government of "pretending to be a responsible person in the Students' Autonomous Federation, stirring up disturbances, disrupting public order, and humiliating public security cadres." He was arrested in mid-June and held in the Yiyang City Jail. He was subsequently sentenced to four years by a court in Yiyang City on a charge of disrupting social order. (According to the *Hunan Daily* of June 15, "during the period of chaos, the Yiyang City Public Security Bureau arrested a total of over 120 lawless elements who created chaos.")
                            [4 YRS]

▪ **Gao Bingkun**, 37 years old, unemployed, resident of Changsha's Southern District. He was an active participant in the 1989 Democracy Movement. After June 4, he organized a mass lie-in on the railroad tracks and "caused the Number 48 train from Guangzhou to Beijing to stop for over 10 hours." He also shouted "reactionary slogans." On

June 6, he was arrested and held in Changsha's No. 1 Jail. In early 1990 he was sentenced to four years by the Changsha Southern District [Basic-Level People's] Court on a charge of "disrupting traffic order."   [4 YRS]

▪ **Huang Zhenghua**, 54 years old, originally a cadre from a government department in Nan County, Yiyang Prefecture, who had been assigned to work in Changsha. During the 1989 Democracy Movement, he made many public speeches in support of the student movement, and was later accused by the authorities of "inciting hostile feelings among the masses toward the government" and of "conspiring to form an underground organization." He was arrested in early 1990, and in October that year was tried by a district court in Changsha on a charge of "economic criminal activity" and sentenced to six years' imprisonment.   [6 YRS]

▪ **Li Jian**, originally a worker at the Changsha Zhengyuan Engine Parts Factory, 25 years old. During the 1989 Democracy Movement he organized the Workers' Hunger Strike Team which held a hunger strike in front of the provincial government offices together with the students. After martial law was declared in Beijing, he took part in the founding of the Changsha Workers' Autonomous Federation and was its first chairman. On several occasions he organized strikes and demonstrations by the workers. He was arrested after June 4 and held in the Changsha No. 1 Jail. In April of

114

1990 he was sentenced to 3 years by the Changsha City Intermediate Court on a charge of being a member of a "counterrevolutionary group." A person named Li Jian also appears on a November 1991 Chinese government response to a State Department list of detainees, but the character for "Jian" is different. In response to an inquiry from the International Labor Organization, the Chinese government confirmed that Li was arrested around June 16, 1989 and was sentenced to three years for "disturbing the peace." [3 YRS]

■ **Li Weihong,** a worker in the Hunan Fire Extinguishing Equipment General Factory, 26 years old. During the 1989 Democracy Movement he took part in demonstrations. On the evening of April 22, 100,000 people in Changsha took to the streets to demonstrate and shout slogans. They demanded the restoration of Hu Yaobang's good name. Li took the lead in shouting, "Down with the racketeering officials *(daoye)*!" Some radical youths ended up smashing some shops on May 1st Road, and there ensued a "chaotic" incident. Almost 40 shops were smashed and several dozen policemen were injured. That evening Li was arrested on his way home. Shortly after June 4, Li received a suspended death sentence from the Changsha City Intermediate Court on a charge of "hooliganism." (Twenty-seven others involved in the April 22 Incident were sentenced on the same day. In their November 1991 response to a State Department list, the Chinese

government confirmed that Li was sentenced. [SUSP. DEATH]

■ **Li Xiaodong,** 25 years old, originally a worker at the Zhongnan Pharmaceutical Plant in Shaoyang City. During the 1989 Democracy Movement, Li took part in the Shaoyang Workers Autonomous Federation. On the evening of May 19, he led a group of workers to People's Square, the local government offices and elsewhere to demonstrate against the imposition of martial law in Beijing, shouting slogans which allegedly "incited the masses to break into the government headquarters." A clash with the police ensued, and Li was arrested the following day and imprisoned in the Shaoyang Jail. In October 1989, he was tried by the Shaoyang Intermediate Court on charges of "counterrevolutionary propaganda and incitement" and sentenced to 13 years' imprisonment. [13 YRS]

■ **Li Xin,** originally a worker, subsequently resigned, 25 years old. His family lives on Kui'e North Road in Changsha. During the 1989 Democracy Movement he participated in the Changsha Workers' Autonomous Federation and was deputy head of the picket squad. He was arrested in June of 1989 and sentenced in December to a term of 3 years by the Changsha Northern District [Basic-Level People's] Court on a charge of "disturbing social order." [3 YRS]

■ **Liao Zhijun,** 26 years old, a worker

115

at the Changsha Pump Factory. After the student movement was suppressed in Beijing, Liao on June 6 allegedly "blocked traffic in Dongfanghong Square and pretended to be a member of the Students' Autonomous Federation picket squad, inciting some of the masses who didn't understand the true situation to join in. He also forced passing drivers to shout slogans." He was arrested on the spot and held in Changsha's No. 1 Jail. In November 1989, he was sentenced to 10 years by the Changsha Southern District Court on a charge of "robbery." (The story of his arrest was carried in June in the *Hunan Daily*.) [10 YRS]

▪ **Liu Chengwu**, 24 years old, a peasant from Huangtuhang Township, Suining County, Hunan. According to the authorities, "On May 18, 1989, he stirred up the blocking of vehicles in the square of the Changsha Railway Station. When public security cadres tried to get people to stop, he actually took pictures, trying to find some basis on which to stir up even more trouble. He was arrested on the spot." (See the report from mid-June in the *Hunan Daily*.) He was held in Changsha's No. 1 Jail, and at the end of the year sentenced to four years by the Changsha Eastern District Court on a charge of "disrupting social order." [4 YRS]

▪ **Liu Jian'an**, teacher, 40 years old. Formerly a teacher at Changsha's No. 23 Middle School and a graduate of the History Department of Hunan Normal University. During the 1989 Democracy Movement he allegedly started listening to "enemy radio" in Taiwan and wrote 16 "counterrevolutionary letters to Guomindang secret agents", according to the *Hunan Daily*. He was also accused of publishing and distributing "reactionary books." Arrested in June 1989. On December 7, 1989, he was sentenced to 10 years in December by the Changsha Intermediate Court on a charge of "espionage." [10 YRS]

▪ **Lu Zhaixing**, 27, originally a worker in the Changsha Embroidery Factory. He was an important figure in the Changsha Workers' Autonomous Federation. On several occasions he organized worker demonstrations and strikes by the workers of the Embroidery Factory. On June 14, he was arrested at home and held in the Changsha No. 1 Jail. In April of 1990 he was sentenced to three years by the Changsha Eastern District Court on a charge of "disrupting public order." [3 YRS]

▪ **Mao Genhong**, 25 years old, originally a student at the Hunan College of Finance; active to a minor extent during the 1989 Democracy Movement. According to an internal government source, "After graduation, Mao Genhong, together with his younger brother Mao Genwei and others, in mid-1990 set up an underground organization which was broken up by the authorities at the end of 1990." Initially held in the Changsha No. 1 Jail, Mao was in mid-1991 tried on the charge of "forming a counterrevolutionary clique" by the Changsha Intermediate Court and sentenced to three years' imprisonment. He was sent first to Hunan No.3 Prison and then later transferred to Yuanjiang Prison. At least six other people, identities unknown, were detained and eventually tried in connection with the same case. The highest prison sentence imposed was five years. (The other sentences are not known.) [3 YRS]

▪ **Tang Changye**, 29, originally a worker, subsequently resigned. Wears thick glasses. During the 1989 Democracy Movement, he often printed handbills and posted big-character posters. Arrested in October 1989. Sentenced to three years in 1990 by the Changsha Eastern District Court on a charge of "disturbing social order." When he was being held in Cell 15 of the Changsha No. 1 Jail, he suffered a great deal of abuse from fellow prisoners. He was considered mentally ill by the cadres and convicts. [3 YRS]

▪ **Wang Changhuai**, worker, 26 years old. Formerly employed at the Changsha Automobile Factory. Served as Chief of Propaganda Section of Changsha's Workers' Autonomous Federation during the 1989 Democracy Movement. Surrendered to the government on June 15, 1989. Sentenced to three years on December 7, 1989 by the Changsha Intermediate [People's] Court on a charge of "counterrevolutionary propaganda and incitement."[3 YRS]

▪ **Wu Tongfan**, urban resident, 40 years old. His family lives in Fuzhong Alley, Nanyang Street, Changsha. During the 1989 Democracy Movement he had contacts with He Zhaohui, a leader of the Changsha Workers' Autonomous Federation, and others. He was accused of directing things from behind the scenes. He was sentenced (the period of imprisonment is unknown) in mid-1990 by the Changsha Intermediate Court on a charge of "counter-revolutionary propaganda and incitement." [? YRS]

▪ **Xia Changchun**, a worker in the passenger transport section of the Hong Kong Affairs Bureau, 24 years old. He was also arrested on the evening of April 22 and accused of "taking the lead in storming the municipal Public Security Bureau and stirring up chaos." He was held in the Changsha No. 2 Jail. In June, he was sentenced to 15 years by the Changsha City Intermediate Court on a charge of "hooliganism." [15 YRS]

▪ **Yang Xiong**, 25 years old, a resident of Changsha. During the 1989 Democracy Movement, Yang was involved in the Changsha Workers Autonomous Federation. For a time, he was responsible for the federation's picket squad and often organized and led members to go to local factories to urge the workers to go on strike. According to the authorities, "this inflicted upon the Changsha Woollen Mill and other factories economic losses of several hundred thousand *yuan*." On June 8, Yang was in overall

117

charge of the picket squad assigned to keep order at the mass mourning ceremony held that day at the Changsha Railway Station. He was arrested in mid-June, and in early 1990 was tried by the East District Court of Changsha on charges of "disrupting social order" and sentenced to three years' imprisonment. In response to inquiries from the International Labor Organization most recently in January 1992, the Chinese government confirmed the arrest but said he was sentenced to four years.

[3 YRS]

■ **Zhang Jie**, 25 years old, scientific researcher. A graduate of Hefei University, he was formerly employed at the Changsha Nonferrous Metals Design Academy. After the suppression of the 1989 Democracy Movement, he "established a secret underground organization under the cover of setting up a company" and was later arrested. Sentenced to five years in mid-1990 by the Changsha Intermediate Court on a charge of [being a member of a] "counter-revolutionary group." [5 YRS]

■ **Zhang Jingsheng**, 37 years old, worker at the Hunan Shaoguan Electrical Engineering Plant. Originally sentenced to four years in 1981 on a charge of counter-revolutionary propaganda and incitement because he had edited and distributed an underground publication during the Democracy Wall movement and supported a student protest movement at Hunan

Normal University. He was arrested again on May 4, 1989, after giving a speech at a mass pro-democracy meeting at the Changsha Martyrs' Park, calling, among other things, for the release of Democracy Wall activist Wei Jingsheng. Although freed several days later, he then joined the Workers' Autonomous Federation, and was re-arrested on May 28, 1989. In December 1989, he was sentenced to 13 years by the Changsha Intermediate People's Court on a charge of "counterrevolutionary propaganda and incitement." While in jail he wrote a large number of prison songs that are widely popular, and are sung by prisoners throughout Hunan, Hubei, Guangxi, Guizhou and other provinces. [13 YRS]

■ **Zhang Xudong**, worker, 32 years old. Formerly head of the Changsha Elevator Factory (a collective enterprise). His family lives in Chongsheng Alley in Changsha's North District. On May 20, 1989, founded Changsha's Workers' Autonomous Federation with Zhou Yong and others and was a member of its Standing Committee and its Vice Chairman. Several times he organized worker demonstrations and strikes. Arrested in June, 1989. During the entire time he was held at the Changsha No. 1 Jail he wore leg irons and handcuffs. This went on for ten months. (According to the usual practice, only a very small number of criminals who, in the authorities' view, "cannot be allowed to live" are subjected to this sort of treatment.) Sentenced to four years in mid-1990

118

by the Changsha Intermediate Court on a charge of "counterrevolutionary propaganda and incitement." The sentence was confirmed in a Chinese government response to an International Labor Organization inquiry in January 1992, but the government said Zhang was convicted for "disturbing the peace." [4 YRS]

▪ **Zhao Weiguo**, 34 years old, originally a student at one of the universities in Beijing. Expelled from university in early 1987 because of his participation in the student movement of winter 1986-87, he returned to Changde, his hometown in Hunan, and together with eight other students who had also been expelled on account of their pro-democracy involvement, he established a small private business there. During the 1989 Democracy Movement, Zhao gave up his work with the company so that he could provide help to the students in his area. Later on, he travelled specially to Changsha in order to join the SAF and take part in directing and formulating plans for the student movement. In addition, he contributed almost 10,000 *yuan* to the cause. After June 4, 1989, Zhao became a major target of attack by the government, and was arrested in October 1989 and held in Changde City Jail. He was subsequently tried by the Changde Intermediate Court on charges of "counterrevolutionary propaganda and incitement" and sentenced to four years' imprisonment. [4 YRS]

(Two others were arrested at the same time as Zhao Weiguo. Both were originally students from universities in Beijing who had been expelled for their activities during the 1989 movement. One was later released, but nothing is known of the fate of the second.)

▪ **Zhou Min**, worker, 26 years old. Formerly employed at the Changsha Nonferrous Metallurgical Design Academy. Participated in the founding of the Changsha Workers' Autonomous Federation during the 1989 Democracy Movement and was a member of its Standing Committee. Arrested in June 1989. Sentenced to six years in June 1990 by the Changsha Intermediate Court on a charge of "being the leader of a counterrevolutionary group." Sent in September to Yuanjiang Prison to serve his sentence. While held at the Changsha No. 1 Jail, he was frequently subject to corporal punishment and maltreatment. He has become mentally disturbed and his speech is incoherent. [6 YRS]

Hengyang Prison (Provincial No. 2)

▪ **Cheng Cun**, 30, originally a reporter at the Yueyang bureau of the *News Pictorial (xinwen tupian bao)*. From the end of 1988 until June 4, he took part in several large demonstrations in Yueyang and, according to the authorities, contravened Party discipline by privately disseminating pictures of the

119

demonstrations, resulting in an "extremely bad influence." He was arrested after the suppression of the Democracy Movement. In early 1990 he was sentenced to five years by the Yueyang City Intermediate Court on a charge of "counterrevolutionary propaganda and incitement." [5 YRS]

▪ **Guo Yunqiao, Hu Min, Mao Yuejin, Wang Zhaobo, Huang Lixin, Huang Fan, Wan Yuewang, Pan Qiubao,** and **Yuan Shuzhu,** all workers or residents of Yueyang, all between 20 and 35 years old. During the 1989 Democracy Movement they organized the Yueyang Workers' Autonomous Federation and on several occasions organized demonstrations and strikes by the workers. After the June 4 crackdown in Beijing, they marched carrying wreaths and setting off firecrackers. Over 10,000 persons took part in the march. Prior to this they had lain down on the railroad tracks on Yueyang's Baling Railway Bridge to protest the violent acts of the government. When the demonstration reached the offices of the municipal government and the seat of the municipal [Party] committee, to the accompaniment of the shouts of the masses, they took down the sign saying "City Government" and trampled it underfoot, resulting in an "extremely odious influence." On June 9, they were all arrested on the street and held in the Yueyang Jail. In September they were all sentenced by the Yueyang City Intermediate Court on charges of "hooliganism." Guo Yunqiao was given a sentence of death, suspended for two years; Hu

Min and Mao Yuejin were given sentences of 15 years; Wang Zhaobo, Huang Lixin, Huang Fan, Wan Yuewang, Pan Qiubao, and Yuan Shuzhu were given sentences ranging from 7 to 15 years.
[SUSP. DEATH; 7-15 YRS]

▪ **He Aoqiu,** assistant professor in the Chinese department at the Yueyang Teachers' College, 55 years old. During the 1989 Democracy Movement he took part in student demonstrations and meetings and on several occasions made speeches at the meetings. He propagated democratic ideology and exposed the corrupt acts of the local government. He was arrested after June 4 and held in the Yueyang Jail. In March 1990, he was sentenced to three years by the Yueyang City Intermediate Court on a charge of "counterrevolutionary propaganda and incitement." [3 YRS]

▪ **Huang Yaru,** originally a professor in the department of political education at Yueyang Teachers' College, 47 years old. At the end of 1988 he planned to hold an "Academic Conference of the Politics of the Yin Zhenggao Affair," but was prevented from doing so. During the 1989 Democracy Movement he took part on several occasions in demonstrations by the Teachers' College students and wrote "reactionary articles." He was arrested in August, 1989. In March 1990, he was sentenced to five years by the Yueyang City Intermediate Court on a charge of "counterrevolutionary propaganda and incitement." [5 YRS]

- **Li Zimin,** 40 years old, originally a private businessman in Hengyang City, Hunan. He actively participated in the 1989 Democracy Movement and "stirred up trouble everywhere." He also allegedly sent coded intelligence messages to "the enemy" (Taiwan). He was arrested in June 1990. At the end of the year, he was sentenced to 15 years by the Hengyang City Intermediate Court on a charge of "espionage." [15 YRS]

- **Liu Weiguo,** 38 years old, originally a worker in Leiyang City, Hunan. During the 1989 Democracy Movement he allegedly joined a Taiwanese spy organization and "stirred up trouble everywhere," trying to storm the municipal government offices and sabotage his factory's production. In June 1990, he was arrested together with Wang Yusheng. At the end of the year he was sentenced to seven years by the Hengyang City Intermediate Court on a charge of "espionage." Wang's sentence is not known. [7 YRS]

- **Mei Shi,** 40, editor-in-chief of the *Yueyang Evening News* (the first editor of a Party organ in China to be hired for his professional qualifications). Stories about him had appeared several times in the press. During his period of tenure, he published several articles that were quite sharp in tone, exposing the corruption of the CCP. After martial law was declared in Beijing, he still published articles praising the righteous actions of the students. He was arrested after June 4 and held in the Yueyang Jail. In

April 1990 he was sentenced to four years by the Yueyang City Intermediate Court on a charge of "counterrevolutionary propaganda and incitement." [4 YRS]

- **Min Hexun,** approximately 29 years old, originally a teacher in the politics department of Yueyang Teachers Training College. Min supported the student demonstrations in 1989 and wrote a large number of "reactionary articles" urging workers to stage protest strikes. These were later said by the authorities to have "exerted an extremely bad influence." He was arrested in July 1989, and in early 1990 was tried by the Yueyang Intermediate Court on charges of "counterrevolutionary propaganda and incitement" and sentenced to three years' imprisonment. [3 YRS]

- **Qin Hubao,** originally a cadre in the Office of Discussion and Criticism (ODC) in Yueyang City. This was an office established single-handedly by Yin Zhenggao, the vice-mayor of Yueyang which existed solely for the purpose of criticizing cadres. (After it was closed down in late 1988, workers of seven factories demonstrated in protest.) Qin was involved in the same case as Yang Shaoyue, but had other "counterrevolutionary acts." During the 1989 Democracy Movement he went to Beijing and secretly sent back the No. 5, 1989 issue of *Reportage Literature (Baogao wenxue)*. He distributed copies widely in Changsha, Yueyang, and other cities. He was arrested in July of 1989. In December he was sentenced to 10 years by the Yueyang City Intermediate Court on a charge of "counterrevolutionary propaganda and incitement." [10 YRS]

■ **Teacher Mi** (name unknown), originally a teacher in the Chinese department at Yueyang Teachers' College. During the 1989 Democracy Movement he took an active part in student street demonstrations. On several occasions he organized student demonstrations, and often made speeches on campus and wrote "reactionary articles." He had connections with members of the provincial Students' Autonomous Federation. The day after June 4, he took part in a meeting to mourn those who had perished in Beijing. Shortly thereafter he was arrested. In early 1990 he was sentenced to three years by the Yueyang City Intermediate Court on a charge of "counterrevolutionary propaganda and incitement." [3 YRS]

■ **Teacher X** (name unknown), in his thirties, originally a teacher in the linguistics department at Changde Normal University and a graduate of the Chinese department at Hunan Normal University. He had long been involved in pro-democracy activities and joined in at the beginning of the 1989 Democracy Movement, organizing student demonstrations. He wrote a large number of "reactionary articles" and made speeches all over, stirring up the people to demand the restoration of their basic rights. After June 4, at the meeting held in front of the municipal government offices to mourn the perished of Beijing, he called upon the people to rise up to "resist the illegitimate CCP regime" and to carry on an uncompromising struggle. Shortly thereafter he was arrested. At the end of 1989 he was sentenced to 12 years by the Changde City Intermediate Court on a charge of "counterrevolutionary propaganda and incitement" and "being in secret contact with foreign countries" *(litong waiguo)*. [12 YRS]

' **Wang Yusheng** (also seen as Wang Rusheng), an entrepreneur who was then 40, was arrested in June 1990 and accused of being a foreign spy. According to the authorities, he allegedly joined a Guomindang Military Intelligence Bureau in 1985 and returned to the mainland as a spy in October 1986. He was arrested together with Liu Weiguo (see separate entry). Both men "confessed" to the charges against them after authorities seized "incriminating espionage equipment", according to a Hunan Provincial Radio report. [?? YRS]

■ **Wu Weiguo**, 30, originally a cadre in the Yueyang Office of Discussion and Criticism. He was involved in the same case as Yang Shaoyue. He was arrested after June 4 and held in the Yueyang Jail. In December 1989, he was sentenced to five years by the Yueyang City Intermediate Court on a charge of "counterrevolutionary propaganda and incitement." [5 YRS]

• **Xie Yang**, 32 years old, originally the secretary of the Yueyang Communist Youth League. During the 1989 Democracy Movement he publicly declared his support for the patriotic acts of the students. He actively organized and participated in student demonstrations and wrote "reactionary articles." He also went to the Yueyang Teachers' College and other institutes of higher education and gave speeches. After June 4 he was arrested. In early 1990 he was sentenced to three years by the Yueyang City Intermediate Court on a charge of "counterrevolutionary propaganda and incitement."

[3 YRS]

• **Yang Shaoyue**, 36, originally head of the Yueyang City government Office of Discussion and Criticism. He was dismissed after the ODC was closed down in late 1988. During the 1989 Democracy Movement he supported the student movement and wrote "counterrevolutionary articles." In July 1989 he was arrested and held in the Yueyang No. 1 Jail. In December 1989 he was sentenced to five years by the Yueyang City Intermediate Court on a charge of "counterrevolutionary propaganda and incitement." [5 YRS]

• **Zhang Jizhong**, 34, well-known reporter for the *Hunan Daily*. During the 1989 Democracy Movement he supported and participated in student demonstrations and made speeches., urging the broad masses to "overthrow bureaucratism." He was arrested after June 4 and held in the Yueyang Jail. In December 1989, he was sentenced to three years by the Yueyang City Intermediate Court on a charge of "counterrevolutionary propaganda and incitement."

[3 YRS]

• **Zhu Fangming**, 28, a worker in the Hengyang City Flour Factory. He was a vice chairman of the Hengyang City Workers' Autonomous Federation and organized and took part in several demonstrations. He also took part in a sit-in in front of the municipal government offices. After the June 4 tragedy, he led the workers to the [offices of the] municipal government and the municipal Public Security Bureau to demand justice, and a clash with the police occurred. He was arrested shortly thereafter. (According to the Party press, this clash resulted in over 100 policemen being injured.) In December 1989, he was sentenced to life imprisonment by the Hengyang City Intermediate Court on a charge of "hooliganism." [LIFE]

Lingling Prison (Provincial No. 3)

• **Chen Yueming**, 24 years old, a resident of Changsha City, where he ran a motor vehicle spare-parts business. Chen was involved in secret underground pro-democracy work between 1989 and 1990, and was arrested in September 1990. Soon afterwards, he was tried by the Changsha Intermediate Court on a charge of "counterrevolutionary propaganda and incitement" and sentenced to three years' imprisonment. [3 YRS]

■ **Feng Ming**, in his twenties, a resident of Xiangtan City. Feng was arrested for alleged participation in an incident which occurred on May 22, 1989 in which a number of people "burst into the Pingzheng Road Police Station" (a local public security office located in Yuhu District, Xiangtan Municipality.) Feng was arrested on the spot. Later that year, he was tried by the Yuhu District Court of Xiangtan on common criminal charges and sentenced to three years' imprisonment. [3 YRS]

■ **Gong Songlin**, in his twenties, a resident of Xiangtan City. During the 1989 Democracy Movement, he took part in numerous demonstrations and other protest activities, and was subsequently arrested for alleged participation in the "Pingzheng Road Police Station Incident" (see above: case of Feng Ming.) Soon after June 4, he was tried by the Yuhu District Court in Xiangtan on common criminal charges and sentenced to five years' imprisonment. [5 YRS]

■ **Jiang Congzheng**, in his twenties, originally a worker at a Xiangtan factory. During the 1989 Democracy Movement, he took part in demonstrations and urged workers to go on strike. According to the authorities, he "sabotaged normal production activities in the factories," and after June 4 he "forcibly prevented workers from going on their shifts and insulted and intimidated those who chose to do so." Arrested in mid-June, he was tried in early 1990 by a Xiangtan district court on the charge of "gathering a crowd to create disturbances" and sentenced to eight years' imprisonment. [8 YRS]

■ **Liang Jianguo**, 26 years old, originally an employee of a guesthouse run by the Hunan Provincial People's Political Consultative Conference. An active participant in the 1989 Democracy Movement, in early 1990 Liang became involved in secret underground pro-democracy work. He was arrested in June 1990. Soon afterwards, he was tried by the East District Court of Changsha on common criminal charges and sentenced to six years' imprisonment. [6 YRS]

■ **Liu Weihong**, 27 years old, originally a worker at a Changsha factory. During the 1989 Democracy Movement, he allegedly organized workers in his factory to "go on strike and create disturbances," and moreover "made impertinent remarks to the factory leaders." Arrested soon after June 4, 1989, he was brought to trial at the Changsha Intermediate Court in mid-1990 on a charge of "counterrevolutionary propaganda and incitement" and sentenced to four years' imprisonment. [4 YRS]

■ **Peng Aiguo**, 20 years old, a resident of Xiangtan City. During the 1989 Democracy Movement, he was arrested for alleged participation in the "Pingzheng Road Police Station Incident" (see above: case of Feng Ming.) He was tried soon after June 4, 1989 at the Yuhu District Court on a charge of "disturbing public order" and sentenced to six years' imprisonment. [6 YRS]

■ **Qin Dong**, 30 years old, journalist at a Hunan local newspaper and an enthusiastic participant in the 1989 Democracy Movement. Qin was arrested soon after June 4 and accused of having "written reactionary articles." Sometime in 1990, he was tried by Changsha Intermediate Court on a charge of "counter-revolutionary propaganda and incitement" and sentenced to four years' imprisonment. (NB: "Qin Dong" is a pen-name; the journalist's real name is not known.) [4 YRS]

■ **Wang Changhong**, age unknown, a resident of Changsha City and participant in the 1989 Democracy Movement. In early 1990, he established an underground pro-democracy group, and was arrested shortly thereafter on accusations of leaking state secrets. He was tried by the Changsha Intermediate Court in late 1990 on a charge of "forming a counterrevolutionary group" and sentenced to five years' imprisonment. Several other people were arrested and tried in connection with the same case, but no details are known of how they were sentenced. (A different man named Wang Changhong was sentenced in Beijing to 15 years for espionage in January 1990). [5 YRS]

■ **Wu Jianwei**, in his twenties, originally a worker at the Xiangtan Electrical Machinery Plant. During the 1989 Democracy Movement, he allegedly "took part in creating disturbances" and "shouted reactionary slogans." These actions were later said by the authorities to have "led to serious consequences." Arrested soon after June 4, 1989, Wu was tried at the end of that year by the Yuetang District Court, Xiangtan Municipality, on unknown criminal charges and sentenced to 14 years' imprisonment. [14 YRS]

■ **Yan Xuewu**, 26 years old, originally a worker at the Xiangtan Municipal Motor Vehicle Parts Factory. During the 1989 Democracy Movement, he was arrested for alleged participation in the "Pingzheng Road Police Station Incident" (see above: case of Feng Ming.) He was tried soon after June 4, 1989 at the Yuhu District Court on a charge of "disturbing public order" and sentenced to five years' imprisonment. [5 YRS]

■ **Yu Zhijian**, teacher, 27 years old. (Two others involved in the same case are **Yu Dongyue**, the fine arts editor of the *Liuyang News*, and **Lu Decheng**, aged 28, a worker in the Liuyang Public Motorbus Company.) He originally taught in the Tantou Wan Primary School in Dahu Town, Liuyang County, Hunan. During the 1989 Democracy Movement, he gave speeches in Liuyang, Changsha, and other places. On May 19 he went to Beijing with Yu Dongyue and Lu Decheng, and on May 23 the three men defaced the large portrait of Mao Zedong in Tiananmen Square by throwing ink and paint-filled eggs at it. (By defacing the portrait, they meant to denounce "Maoism" and the "proletarian dictatorship.") He was arrested on the spot. On August 11 of the same year he was sentenced to life imprisonment by the Beijing City Intermediate Court on a charge of "counterrevolutionary sabotage and incitement." (Yu Dongyue received a sentence of 20 years and Lu Decheng a sentence of 16 years.) He was later sent back to be held in Hunan Provincial No. 3 Prison. In prison he was put in solitary confinement for six months. [LIFE; 16, 20 YRS]

▪ **Zhong Donglin**, 25 years old, originally a worker at a factory in Shaoyang Municipality. Allegedly a participant in the "May 19" incident in Shaoyang during which some vehicles were set on fire, Zhong was arrested in July 1989. Later that year, he was tried by the Shaoyang Intermediate Court on a charge of arson and sentenced to ten years' imprisonment. [10 YRS]

▪ **Zhou Zhirong**, teacher, 32 years old. Originally a teacher at Xiangtan No. 2 Middle School and a graduate of the Geography Department of Hunan Normal University. During the 1989 Democracy Movement, he gave speeches on several occasions at public gatherings. After June 4, he put on a black woolen coat with the character "sadness" written on the front and the character "mourning" written on the back and conducted a lone sit-in with his eyes closed in front of the Xiangtan municipal government offices. Afterwards he made a speech to an audience of several tens of thousands. In September, 1989 he went of his own accord to the Public Security Department to "surrender" (he does not acknowledge it as "surrender", since he is not guilty of a crime). In December 1989, he was sentenced to seven years by the Xiangtan City Intermediate Court on a charge of "counterrevolutionary propaganda and incitement." The sentence was later changed to five years. When at Longxi Prison, he was accused of organizing "counterrevolutionary meetings," and on the evening of February 12, 1991 was secretly transferred to the Provincial No. 3 Prison (Lingling Prison). [5 YRS]

Longxi Prison
(Provincial No. 6)

▪ **Cai Weixing**, worker, 25 years old. Originally employed at the Changsha Power Machinery Factory. He participated in demonstrations during the 1989 Democracy Movement and was arrested on April 22. His crime, according to the authorities, was "stirring up the masses to beat, smash, and loot." In December 1989, he was sentenced to four years by the Changsha Eastern District Court. [4 YRS]

▪ **Chen Gang**, worker, 25 years old. His family lives in Liberation Village at the Xiangtan Electrical Machinery

Factory. After June 4, he was arrested because he called for justice for his younger brother Chen Ding, a student at the Changsha Railway Academy who had been sentenced to one year on a charge of "counter-revolutionary propaganda and incitement" because he had exhorted workers to strike. At first his crime was said to be "counterrevolutionary propaganda and incitement," but when charges were laid seven days after his arrest, the crime had been changed to "assembling a mob for beating, smashing, and looting." When the public trial was held the next day, the crime had been changed again to "hooliganism." He was sentenced to death by the Xiangtan Intermediate Court. In May 1990 the sentence was changed to death with a 2-year suspension. [SUSP. DEATH]

▪ **Chen Guangliang**, 48 years old, private doctor in Shaoyang City. Some years earlier, he had allegedly joined Liu Chunan's "spy organization" (see below: **Liu Chunan**) and engaged in intelligence collection. During the 1989 Democracy Movement, together with Liu and others, he "went all over the place stirring up chaos in a vain attempt to create even more chaos," according to the authorities. He was arrested together with Liu Chunan in December, 1989. In March 1990 he was sentenced to seven years by the Yueyang City Intermediate Court on a charge of "counterrevolutionary espionage." [7 YRS]

▪ **Deng XX** (nickname: "Shorty"), 23 years old, a resident of Changsha and a small private businessman. Arrested on the evening of April 22, 1989 in connection with the so-called "beating, smashing, looting incident" which occurred there earlier the same day. In mid-June, Deng was tried by the Changsha City East District Court on a charge of robbery and sentenced to four years' imprisonment. [4 YRS]

▪ **Ding Longhua**, in his thirties, a member of the standing committee of the Hengyang Workers Autonomous Federation. During the 1989 Democracy Movement, he made public speeches and organized strikes among the workers. After June 4, 1989, Ding organized a city-wide general strike jointly with the Hengyang Students Autonomous Federation. Arrested shortly thereafter, in February 1990 he was tried by the Hengyang City Intermediate Court on a charge of "counterrevolutionary propaganda and incitement" and sentenced to six years' imprisonment. [6 YRS]

▪ **He Zhaohui**, worker, 24 years old. Originally employed at the Changsha Railway Passenger Transport Section. His family lives in Chenjia Wan in Chenzhou, Hunan. During the 1989 Democracy Movement, he organized strikes by railroad workers and posted slogans, big-character posters, etc. He was also a member of the Standing Committee of the Changsha Workers' Autonomous Federation. He was in the first group of people arrested in June, 1989. In June 1990, he was sentenced to four years by the

Changsha Eastern District Court on a charge of "disturbing social order." The sentence was confirmed in a Chinese government response to an International Labor Organization inquiry. [4 YRS]

■ **Hu Nianyou**, 28 years old, a resident of Guangzhou, Guangdong Province. During the later stages of the 1989 Democracy Movement, Hu went to Changsha and contacted the Workers Autonomous Federation there, and made contingency plans to assist leading members of that organization and of the Students Autonomous Federation to escape from China. In the course of a taxi journey between Changsha and Zhuzhou one day, he and Yao Guisheng and other leading members of the workers federation got into an argument with the taxi driver. After June 4, when the government issued its order for all members of both the autonomous federations to register themselves with the authorities, the taxi driver denounced Hu and the others to the police. Hu was arrested in Zhuzhou shortly afterwards, and in October 1989 he was tried by the Changsha Intermediate Court on charges of "robbery and injury" and sentenced to life imprisonment. [LIFE]

■ **Li Xiaoping**, 28 years old, originally a worker at a factory in Shaoyang. Li participated in the Shaoyang Workers Autonomous federation during the 1989 Democracy Movement, serving as deputy-chief of the organization's picket squad. He took part in many student demonstrations and petition groups, and on May 20 he led a crowd of citizens who pushed their way into the municipal Party Committee and government offices. He was arrested sometime later the following month. In early 1990, he was tried by the Shaoyang Intermediate Court on charges of "hooliganism" and sentenced to six years' imprisonment. [6 YRS]

■ **Liao Zhengxiong**, 24 years old, originally ran a small private business in Changsha city. Arrested in connection with the April 22, 1989 "beating, smashing, looting incident" in Changsha. Liao was tried by the Changsha City South District Court in mid-June, 1989 on a charge of robbery and sentenced to three years' imprisonment. [3 YRS]

■ **Liu Chunan**, 65 years old. He was a retired teacher from Shaoyang City. Some years earlier, he allegedly had joined a Taiwanese spy organization. "During the 1989 Democracy Movement he stirred up the wind and lit fires [apparently only metaphorically (tr.)], created chaos, and radioed information about the chaos to a Taiwanese spy organization." He was arrested in December 1989. In March 1990 he was sentenced to 15 years by the Yueyang City Intermediate Court on a charge of "counterrevolutionary espionage." (see also entry on Chen Guangliang] [15 YRS]

■ **Liu Hui**, 21 years old, an unemployed resident of Changsha city. Arrested on the evening of April 22, 1989 in connection with the so-called "beating, smashing, looting incident" which occurred there earlier on the same day. In mid-June, Liu was tried by the Changsha City East District Court on a charge of robbery and sentenced to five years' imprisonment. [5 YRS]

- **Liu Jian**, worker, 26 years old. He originally worked in the Xiangtan Electrical Machinery Factory. After June 4, because of his righteous indignation, he took part in the burning of expensive furnishings in the home of the head of the factory's public security section. After this he was arrested. In August of the same year, he was sentenced to life imprisonment by the Xiangtan City Intermediate Court on a charge of "hooliganism." He was sent together with Chen Gang to Longxi Prison for labor reform. (Of the 12 persons who participated in this incident, eight are known to have been arrested; of those, six are known to have been sentenced. The circumstances of the four not known to have been arrested are unknown.) [LIFE]

- **Liu Xin**, middle school student, 15 years old. He was in grade 9 *(chu san)* of middle school in Shaoyang City, Hunan. On May 19, 1989, he went out on the streets with his elder sister's husband (the sister's husband was sentenced to life imprisonment; his name is not known) to watch the masses burning an imported car. Liu allegedly supplied some matches. He was arrested in June 1989. In

September 1989, he was sentenced to 15 years by the Shaoyang City Intermediate Court on a charge of "arson." Liu, who is illiterate and of frail health, denies having supplied any matches during the incident, and insists he was merely a spectator.

[15 YRS]

- **Liu Zhihua**, 21 years old, originally a worker at the Xiangtan Electrical Machinery factory, and a supporter of the 1989 student movement. Liu was arrested soon after June 4, 1989 in connection with a public protest against the chief of the public security department of the Xiangtan Electric Machinery Factory, and was accused of inciting anti-government speeches. During the protest, more than 1000 angry workers had gone to the public security chief's home and carried some of his furniture and electrical goods out into the street and set fire to them. At the end of June 1989, Liu was tried by the Xiangtan City Intermediate Court on a charge of "hooliganism" and sentenced to life imprisonment. [LIFE]

- **Lü Zijing**, 30 years old, originally the Shenzhen special representative of Shaoyang's Light Industrial Department. During the 1989 Democracy Movement, he returned on numerous occasions to Shaoyang, allegedly to "spread rumors from Hong Kong and Taiwan." On the evening of May 19, he took part in a large demonstration march around Shaoyang City by students and citizens in protest against Li Peng's imposition of martial law. That evening there occurred a violent clash between police and demonstrators, in which "a police vehicle was burned and several officers were injured." Lü was arrested in early August, after returning to Shaoyang from Shenzhen, and was detained in Shaoyang Jail. In March 1990, he was charged with the crime of "hooliganism" and sentenced to 13 years' imprisonment. He has submitted numerous petitions to the higher authorities, but these have all been rejected.   [13 YRS]

■ **Peng Shi**, 21 or 22 years old, originally a worker at the Xiangtan Electrical Machinery Factory, and a supporter of the 1989 student movement. After June 4, 1989, Peng took part, together with Chen Gang, Liu Zhihua, Liu Xin and others, in a public protest against the chief of the public security department of the Xiangtan Electric Machinery Factory. During this incident, more than 1000 angry workers went to the public security chief's home and carried some of his furniture and electrical goods out into the street and set fire to them. Peng Shi was arrested shortly afterwards and was charged with having led and participated in an arson attack. At the end of June 1989, he was tried by the Xiangtan City Intermediate Court on a charge of "hooliganism" and sentenced to life imprisonment.   [LIFE]

■ **Wu Hepeng, Zhu Zhengying, Liu Jiye** and six others arrested at the same time are workers or residents of Shaoyang City. They were held in the Shaoyang City Jail. During the 1989 Democracy Movement they all actively took part in student demonstrations and meetings. On May 19 the famous "May 19th Incident" took place in Shaoyang. Two imported cars and a police car were burned and three cars were overturned. All nine were present at the time, but only Wu Hepeng took part in the burning of the cars. The other eight were just watching or shouting slogans or helping others. That evening over 10,000 people stormed the Shaoyang municipal government offices, demanding that the city government declare its opposition to the declaration of martial law in Beijing. These nine Democracy Movement activists all took part. After June 4, the public security bureau arrested them all on the basis of videotaped materials. In September 1989, they were sentenced by the Yueyang City Intermediate Court on charges of "arson," "hooliganism," and "counter-revolutionary propaganda and incitement." Wu Heping received a suspended death sentence, Zhu Zhengying received a sentence of life imprisonment, Liu Jiye received a sentence of five years, and the other six all received sentences of upwards of five years. They are all undergoing reform through labor at Longxi Prison.

[SUSP. DEATH; LIFE - 5 YRS]

■ **Xiong Xiaohua**, technician, 25 years old. Originally employed at Xiangtan Power Machinery Factory. He is a graduate of the Xiangtan

Mechanization Special School. His family lives near the Xiangtan Municipal People's Congress Building. During the 1989 Democracy Movement, he organized a group of former classmates to print and distribute propaganda materials, and during the Xiangtan May 29 Incident shouted slogans. He was arrested in July 1989. In November he was sentenced to 13 years by the Xiangtan City Intermediate Court on a charge of "hooliganism." [13 YRS]

▪ **Yang Xiaogang**, worker, 35 years old. His family lives at the [residential quarters of the] Changsha Science [and Technology] Federation. His father is the chairman of the Federation. During the 1989 Democracy Movement, he disseminated news from "enemy [broadcasting] stations" and spread "rumors." He was arrested in May 1989 on a charge of "assembling the masses for beating, smashing, and looting." In September 1989 he was sentenced to 3 years by the Changsha Eastern District Court. In December he was sent to reform through labor at the Longxi Prison. [3 YRS]

▪ **Yao Guisheng**, worker, 26 years old. His family lives in Changsha's South Gate. During the 1989 Democracy Movement he joined the Changsha Workers' Autonomous Federation. After June 4, he was getting ready with two people from Guangzhou (noted elsewhere) to hire a taxi to save Workers' Autonomous Federation leaders and get them out of Changsha. He got into a fight with the driver. Later he was arrested in Zhuzhou. In October 1989, he was sentenced to 15 years by the Changsha Intermediate Court on a charge of "robbery" and "assault." When he was in labor reform at Longxi Prison, he suffered inhuman treatment. He is now mentally ill. [15 YRS]

▪ **Zhang Song**, 24 years old, a resident of Changsha. Zhang was involved in demonstrations during the early part of the 1989 Democracy Movement, and was arrested on charges of "beating, smashing and looting" on the evening of April 22. He was tried in June 1989 on charges of "robbery" and sentenced to five years' imprisonment. [5 YRS]

▪ **Zhang Feilong**, 18 years old, originally a worker at a Shaoyang City factory, and a participant in many protest demonstrations and marches during the 1989 Democracy Movement. On May 19, upon hearing the news of the declaration of martial law in Beijing, a large crowd of Shaoyang residents surged toward the city center and gathered in People's Square to protest against the Li Peng government's attempt to suppress the student movement. The mood of the crowd was very angry and emotional, and several vehicles were set on fire and burned, including a government official's sedan car, a police vehicle and two imported trucks. Zhang Feilong was arrested in mid-June and accused of having participated in the incident. At the end of June, he was tried by the Shaoyang City

Intermediate Court on a charge of arson and sentenced to six years' imprisonment. [6 YRS]

■ **Zhong Hua**, 24 years old, originally a student in the class of 1986 in the environmental engineering department of Hunan University. During the 1989 Democracy Movement he took part in the school's autonomous student union and was the head of its Picket Squad. At the end of May he organized a lie-in by the students on the railway tracks at Changsha Station to block the trains and thereby demonstrate opposition to the government. After June 4, he continued his studies at the university, but fell under suspicion after the Romanian Revolution and in March 1990 was secretly arrested. In July 1990 he was sentenced to three years by the Changsha City Western District Court on a charge of "disrupting traffic order." (Another Hunan University student in the same case, Yao Wei, was held for three months and then released without criminal prosecution.) [3 YRS]

■ **Zhou Wenjie**, in his twenties, originally a worker in a Changsha factory. Arrested in connection with the April 22, 1989 "beating, smashing, looting incident" in Changsha. In mid-June 1989 he was tried by the Changsha City South District Court on a charge of robbery and sentenced to four years' imprisonment. [4 YRS]

Changsha Prison

■ **Chen Bing**, originally a student in the entering class of 1986 in the Hunan Academy of Finance and Economics. He was a radical activist during the 1989 Democracy Movement and advocated no compromise with the government. He opposed all dialogue and links with the government. Later he took part in activities of the Workers' Autonomous Federation and was an important figure in it. After June 4 he was on the run for several months, but was arrested at the end of the year and held in Cell 22 of the Changsha No. 1 Jail. I heard that he was later accused of acts of violence. He has not yet been released. His current circumstances are unknown. [? YRS]

■ **Hou Liang'an**, democratic personage, 35 years old. He was originally the head of the Changsha Soccer Fans' Association and a member of the Changsha branch of the [Chinese People's] Political Consultative Conference (CPPCC). During the 1989 Democracy Movement, he contributed over 2,000 *yuan* to the students in the name of the Soccer Fans' Association, and on several occasions organized deliveries of food by members to students engaged in sit-ins. He was arrested at the end of 1990 on a charge of "extortion." He was held in Changsha's No. 1 Jail. He was sentenced to six months. After he got out of prison, he showed dissatisfaction [with his arrest and

132

sentencing] and petitioned the central and provincial governments. He was later arrested again and accused of establishing an underground organization. He is still being held, but the details of the handling of his case are not known. His influence among the people of Changsha was fairly large. When his father died, he was still in prison. The masses held for his father the grandest mourning ceremony ever held in Changsha in the past several years. Several tens of thousands took part. This was said to be killing two birds with one stone (i.e. both mourning his father and expressing support for Hou in a politically safe way.) [? YRS]

■ **Huang Haizhou**, 28 years old, originally employed at the Hunan People's Publishing House. During the 1989 Democracy Movement he organized a Publishing Industry League in Support of the Students and was a leading figure in it. On several occasions he wrote "reactionary articles" and organized demonstrations by League members. After June 4, he angrily denounced the Li Peng regime, and was arrested. He has been held all along in the Changsha No. 1 Jail. His current circumstances are unknown. [? YRS]

■ **Liu Fuyuan**, 35 years old, originally a small private businessman in Changsha City. During the 1989 Democracy Movement, he organized local residents to donate money to the students. In addition, he participated in the hunger strike and sit-down protest outside the provincial government offices. After June 4, 1989, he allegedly "spread rumors" that "several thousand people were killed by the troops in Beijing." He then went to Thailand for almost a year, but was arrested in Changsha in mid-1990 upon his return. He was held in Cell 13 of the Changsha No. 1 Jail. Liu went on hunger strike many times in prison to protest at his treatment, and later developed a serious gall-stones condition. He is currently still in detention, and it is not known whether he has yet been brought to trial and sentenced.
[? YRS]

■ **Liu Yi**, worker, 24 years old. He was originally employed at the Changsha Power Machinery Factory. During the 1989 Democracy Movement he joined the Changsha Workers' Autonomous Federation and served as its treasurer. He was arrested in June, 1989 and held in Cell 11 of the Changsha No. 1 Jail, next door to Tang Boqiao. He was released in December and arrested again in August, 1990 on a charge of posting "counterrevolutionary slogans." He has not yet been brought to trial. [? YRS]

■ **Yi Yuxin**, 36 years old, originally a cadre at the printing factory of Central-South Industrial University. After the suppression of the 1989 Democracy Movement he continued to engage in underground propaganda activities, printing and distributing propaganda materials. He was exposed and arrested at the end of 1989 and held in the Changsha

No. 1 Jail. His current circumstances are unknown. [? YRS]

Jianxin Labor Reform Camp

- **Teacher Liu** (name unknown), 37 years old. He was originally a teacher in the politics department of Yiyang Teachers' College. During the 1989 Democracy Movement he made speeches in Yiyang, Changsha, and other places and published "reactionary articles." He is an intellectual who took up activity in the Democracy Movement in 1980. He was arrested after June 4. In early 1990 he was sentenced to seven years by the Yiyang City Intermediate Court. He is currently serving his sentence at Jianxin Farm in Yueyang, Hunan. [7 YRS]

Pingtang Labor Reform Camp

- **Tao Sen**, 38 years old, originally a worker at the Changsha City Engine Factory. In his youth he was a student in the Chinese department of Hunan Normal University. In 1980, he had been an important figure in the student movement and the People's Congress elections at the school. In 1981 he was sentenced to five years on a charge of "counterrevolutionary propaganda and incitement." Late in the 1989 student movement he was secretly arrested by the authorities and held in the Changsha No. 1 Prison. In 1990 he was sentenced to five (possibly four) years by the Changsha Eastern District Court on a charge of "economic fraud." He was earlier in the Provincial No. 1 Prison. It is said that he has now been transferred to the Changsha Pingtang Labor Reform Camp. [4/5 YRS]

- **Zhang Xiong**, worker, 24 years old. He originally worked at the Changsha Woolen Mill. His family lives on Liu Zheng Street in Changsha. During the 1989 Democracy Movement, he organized demonstrations and strikes by the mill workers. He also participated in the special picket squad of the Changsha Workers' Autonomous Federation. He was arrested in June 1989 on a charge of harboring Zhou Yong, former head of the Changsha WAF. (Zhou was later acquitted. Zhang's younger brother was also arrested at the same time but later released.) In November he was sentenced to five years by the Changsha Eastern District Court on a charge of "robbery." His former girlfriend reported to the authorities that a small tape player of the Walkman type in his possession might have been obtained from "beating, smashing, and looting". In June 1990, he was sent to undergo reform through labor at the Changsha's Pingtang Labor Reform Camp. [5 YRS]

Other Places of Detention

- **Dong Qi, He Jianming, Dai Dingxiang**, and **Liang Chao**, all workers or residents in Changsha. During the 1989 Democracy Movement they organized the

134

citizenry in support of the students. On the evening of May 20, they heard that the army had entered the city and was heading for Dongfanghong Square. They hurried to the Changsha Railway Station to discuss countermeasures with student leaders. When the public security cadres saw that they were not students, they came up to grill them. A dispute ensued and they were taken away by the public security cadres. During their interrogation at the public security bureau, it was discovered that they were all carrying small knives. (This is common and not evidence of criminal intent.) They were then arrested on a charge of carrying weapons and held in Changsha's No. 1 Jail. In October 1989, they were sentenced respectively to five years, four years, three years and three years by the Changsha Eastern District Court on a charge of "assembling a crowd to create a disturbance." They are currently serving their sentences at a labor reform camp.   [5-3 YRS]

■ **Gao Shuxiang**, around 40 years old, was formerly a cadre in the Hengyang Petroleum Company, where his wife still works. He later became manager of a collective enterprise involved in supplying labor-personnel services, and through his success in running the firm he gained a reputation as a pioneering figure in the economic reforms in Hengyang City. During the 1989 Democracy Movement, Gao went to Beijing, and was first arrested there shortly after June 4. He was then, one month later, either released and returned voluntarily to Hengyang, or was escorted back there in custody. In any event, he was placed under arrest upon his return and charged with embezzling public funds from the company he ran. (The authorities had reportedly tried to pin charges of economic crime on him several times before.) The real reason for the arrest, however, is that the authorities reportedly suspect Gao of involvement in the pro-democracy movement, possibly in connection with provision of funds to the movement. During his interrogation by one Yang Zhanglong, an investigator in the Hengyang South District Procuracy, Gao is said to have been hit so hard that he has lost his hearing in one ear. He has not been given medical treatment, and he remains in incommunicado detention at Wanjiawan Jail, despite repeated rejections of the procuracy's charges by the local court.   [? YRS]

■ **Tang Zhijian**, 31, formerly a worker at the Hengyang Railway Maintenance Department, was arrested in March 1991 by the Hengyang Jiangdong Railway Police for having assisted the brothers Li Lin and Li Zhi (see p.151 for details) to flee China on a train in July 1989. He reportedly confessed, and after one week was freed after paying a fine of 1000 *yuan*. He was then made to sign further confessions, however, and was rearrested in May 1991 and taken to the Baishazhou Detention Center, where he still remains. Tang told Li Zhi, who was held two cells away in the same detention center in mid-1991, that he was being pressured to say that he had received money for helping the Li brothers escape in July 1989. The ostensible charge against Tang is that he had "stolen a tape-recorder on a train." [? YRS]

(NB: Case information on Gao Shuxiang and Tang Zhijian supplied by Li Lin.)

▪ **Wang Luxiang**, in his thirties, originally a producer at Chinese Central Television, and involved in making the controversial television series "River Elegy" *(He Shang)*. During the 1989 Democracy Movement he co-signed, together with other prominent individuals, the "May 16th Declaration" in support of the student movement. He was arrested not long after June 4 and held in a Beijing detention center. During 1990, the authorities announced that several hundred people detained since June 1989 had been released, and they provided a few names including that of Wang Luxiang. According to reliable sources, however, Wang was subsequently rearrested and is reportedly now being held in a prison somewhere in Lianyuan City, Hunan. [? YRS]

▪ **Yang Liu**, 20 years old, a peasant from Xiangyin County in Yueyang Municipality. During the 1989 Democracy Movement, he was working in Changsha as a carpenter and allegedly took part in an incident in which "people burst into a government office." Arrested soon

after June 4, he was tried at the end of 1989 by the South District Court of Changsha on common criminal charges and sentenced to four years' imprisonment. He is now serving his sentence at the Mijiang Tea Farm labor-reform camp in Chaling County. [4 YRS]

Place of Imprisonment Unknown

▪ **Bu Yunhui**, 24 years old, a peasant in Group 6 (a village subdivision) of Tiepuling village, Yiyang County. During the 1989 Democracy Movement he took part in several demonstrations in Yiyang City and Changsha. After June 4, when he was lying down on the railroad tracks in Changsha station, he was threatened by public security cadres and, becoming angry, shouted slogans. He was arrested on the spot and held in Changsha's No. 1 Jail. In early 1990 he was sentenced to three years by the Changsha Eastern District Court on a charge of "disrupting traffic order." (The story of his arrest was carried in June in the *Hunan Daily*.) [3 YRS]

▪ **Hao Mingzhao**, originally a student in the entering class of 1985 in the geology department of Central-South Industrial University. He was the chairman of its [official] student union. In 1988, because he objected to the government's campaign against "bourgeois liberalization," he resolutely went off to Mt. Emei, changed his name, and became a monk. He was later brought back by

136

his school. In mid-April, during the early part of the 1989 Democracy Movement, he was active in many places and planned demonstrations. He was one of the chief organizers of the "May 4th Joint Demonstration." From the time of the founding of the Students' Autonomous Federation he was a member of its Standing Committee. After June 4, he took part in the planning of the June 8 "Mourning Meeting" and made a speech at it. After the provincial government issued its "Registration Order" for the Students' Autonomous Federation, he turned himself in to the Public Security Bureau. He was expelled from his school and shortly thereafter secretly arrested. He was released after several months. He has now disappeared. (Possibly he has been jailed again.)   [? YRS]

▪ **He Jian**, in his thirties, a resident of Hangzhou, Zhejiang Province, where he worked in a state-owned company. During the 1989 Democracy Movement, he allegedly travelled around between several large cities in China and "incited local people to create disturbances." After June 4, 1989, he was arrested in Changsha, Hunan Province, and detained there for several months before being transferred to a detention facility in his native Zhejiang Province. His current circumstances are not known.
[? YRS]

▪ **Jiang Zhiqiang**, 37 years old, from Shaoyang City but original place of work unknown. During the 1989 Democracy Movement he engaged in extensive "incitement" of the local populace, advocating such things as the parliamentary political system and promoting theories against dictatorship. He also posted up a large number of "counter-revolutionary articles," and was involved in secret liaison activities in preparation for the eventual founding of a so-called "counterrevolutionary organization." Jiang was arrested in August 1989 and held in Shaoyang Jail. In early 1990 he was tried by the Shaoyang Intermediate Court on charges of "counterrevolutionary propaganda and incitement" and sentenced to 13 years' imprisonment. He was held thereafter for a while in Longxi Prison, but has since been transferred to another prison (location unknown.)   [13 YRS]

▪ **Li Shaojun**, originally a student in the entering class of 1985 in the physics department of Hunan Normal University. On the eve of the student movement he threw himself into activities for democracy. During the Democracy Movement he served as vice head of the Finance Department of the Students' Autonomous Federation. He took part in all the important actions [of the students] and was one of the chief organizers of the June 8 "Mourning Meeting." In August 1989 he was arrested in Hengyang and held in Cell 23 of the Changsha No. 1 Jail. He was released in December but arrested again in April 1990 at his uncle's home in Guangzhou. He was sent back to Changsha and held for over 2 months before being educated and released.

He has since been arrested again.
[? YRS]

■ **Li Wangyang**, 36 years old, originally a worker at a Shaoyang factory. During the 1989 Democracy Movement, he helped organize the Shaoyang Workers Autonomous Federation, and served as its chairman. On many occasions, he organized strikes and demonstrations among the workers and gave speeches in Shaoyang's People's Square. He was a very influential figure locally. After June 4, he organized the population to carry out strikes at work and to boycott marketplaces. Arrested at the end of June, he was tried in early 1990 by the Shaoyang City Intermediate Court on charges of "counterrevolutionary propaganda and incitement" and sentenced to 13 years' imprisonment. He first underwent reform through labor at Longxi Prison, but was later transferred to another, unknown location.   [13 YRS]

■ **Liu Xingqi**, originally a worker at the Changsha Light Bulb Factory, 24 years old. He was a member of the Changsha Workers' Autonomous Federation. On several occasions he organized strikes and meetings and he took part in organizing the June 8 mass mourning meeting *(zhuidao hui)*. He was arrested shortly thereafter and held in the Changsha No. 1 Jail. According to a recent report submitted by the Chinese government to the *ILO*, Liu was eventually given a three-year sentence.   [3 YRS]

■ **Luo Ziren**, 25 years old, from Guizhou Province. He was originally a temporary [contract] worker at the Changsha Cigarette Factory. During the 1989 Democracy Movement he was a member of the Picket Squad of the Students' Autonomous Federation. He was responsible for the safety of the persons and documents of leaders of the Students' Autonomous Federation. Shortly after June 4, he was arrested at his home town in Guizhou. He was freed in 1990. In November 1991 he was arrested a second time for posting "reactionary handbills." It is not known where he is now held.
[? YRS]

■ **Wen Quanfu**, 38 years old, originally the general manager of the Hunan Province Overseas Chinese Enterprise Company. He supported the students during the 1989 Democracy Movement, but this was later characterized by the authorities as "having encouraged reactionary ideas" within the company and "creating an extremely bad influence among the masses." He was thoroughly investigated after June 4, 1989 and was arrested in September of the same year and held in Changsha No. 1 Jail, in Cell 10. In early 1990, he was transferred to Changsha County Detention Center. There are alleged to be "complex political aspects" to his case, and it is unclear what has happened to him since then. He has definitely not been released, however.   [? YRS]

■ **Xu Yue**, 25 years old, employed in

138

the maintenance workshop of the Tianjin Nail Factory. During the 1989 Democracy Movement he took part in activities in Beijing and later joined the support group from Hong Kong stationed in Beijing where he was responsible for logistics. On June 4, he fled to Guangzhou via Changsha, and on June 8 returned to Changsha to take part in the mourning ceremony organized by the Students' Autonomous Federation. He also took a large number of photographs, which the authorities said he took "with the intention of carrying out additional reactionary propaganda all over the place." On June 13 he was arrested in a hotel in Changsha and held in Changsha's No. 1 Jail. He was transferred out of there in August and his current circumstances are unknown. (The news of his arrest was carried in the *Hunan Daily* of June 17.) [? YRS]

■ **Yang Rong, Wang Hong** and **Tang Yixin**, originally all young employees of the Hunan Province Electrical Battery Plant. During the 1989 Democracy Movement they were all active in the Changsha Workers Autonomous Federation, organizing many factory strikes. Arrested after June 4, they were held for several months at the Changsha No. 1 Jail and then released as innocent. After gaining their freedom, Yang Rong and the other two continued to carry out underground pro-democracy activities, including publishing a journal and a newspaper. In mid-April 1990, they were all rearrested after posting up a slogan banner in public. The government accused them of engaging in counter-revolutionary propaganda activities and of suspected formation of a "counterrevolutionary organization." Their case is still under investigation, but the authorities have apparently instructed that they be given a long sentence. [? YRS]

■ **Zeng Chaohui**, 22 years old, a student at Hengyang Industrial College, class of '87. During the 1989 Democracy Movement he helped organize the Hengyang Students Autonomous Federation and served as its chairman. He took part in organizing many street demonstrations and gatherings, and led a group of students in holding a sit-in protest outside the city government offices which lasted more than 10 days. Zeng was arrested in July the same year, and in early 1990 was tried by the Hengyang Intermediate Court on charges of "counterrevolutionary propaganda and incitement" and sentenced to three years' imprisonment. He was held for a while in Longxi Prison, but his present whereabouts are unclear. (Two other students from the Hengyang Industrial College were also arrested, but their names and present circumstances are not known.) [3 YRS]

■ **Zheng Yaping**, originally a graduate student in the computer science department (Department No. 9) of the National Defense Science and Technology University. Before the 1989 Democracy Movement he had established his own company and engaged in propaganda on democratic ideology. During the Democracy Movement he did not publicly participate in the Students' Autonomous Federation or other organizations. (Discipline is extremely strict at the school because it is the highest educational institution of the Commission on National Defense Science and Industry and is considered of a military nature.) After June 4, he was active for a while in the Students' Autonomous Federation. In the same year he was secretly detained by the military court. His subsequent circumstances are unknown. [? YRS]

▪ **Zheng Yuhua**, teacher, 37 years old. He operated his own private school and had a fairly high understanding of political theory. During the 1989 Democracy Movement, he continually gave advice to the Standing Committee of Hunan's Students' Autonomous Federation. He also organized a think tank. He was arrested in July, 1989. At first he was held in Changsha's No. 1 Jail. Since his transfer out of there in December, his whereabouts are unknown. His family members also have no news of him. [? YRS]

▪ **Zhou Peiqi**, 29 years old, graduate of Central-South Industrial University. He was originally a technician with the Central-South No. 5 Construction Company. Before the 1989 Democracy Movement he had already been involved in the work of publicizing democratic thinking and had taken part in a secret organization. When the Democracy Movement began, he threw himself into it. After May 4, he was in charge of the cash raised by the "Provincial Provisional Committee of Schools of Higher Education." Toward the end of May, he withdrew from the activities of the student organizations. Together with Chen Le (*alias* Liu Zhongtao) and others, he planned to set up a "Democracy Movement Lecture Center," but this came to nothing because of the bloody suppression of the students on June 4. He was arrested at the end of July 1989, and has not yet been tried. His whereabouts are unknown. [? YRS]

Beijing

▪ **Wu Yun**, 23 years old, a student in a Beijing institute of higher education. He was an active participant in the 1989 Democracy Movement. "From June 3 to June 4, he blocked military vehicles in Beijing, beat PLA soldiers with pop bottles, and stole an army helmet." On June 4, he fled to Guangzhou through Changsha, and on June 8 returned to Changsha to take part in a mourning ceremony organized by the Students' Autonomous Federation. On June 13 he was arrested in a hotel. "On his person at the time was a large quantity of reactionary handbills and propaganda materials." He was held in Changsha's No. 1 Jail and later transferred to Beijing. His current whereabouts are unknown. (News of his arrest was carried in the Hunan Daily of June

140

17.)   [? YRS]

• **Xiong Gang,** 23 years old. He was originally a student in the Chinese department of Yuncheng Teacher's College in Shanxi and comes from Hanshou County in Hunan. During the 1989 Democracy Movement he went to Beijing and became the general director of the Federation of Students in Higher Education from Outside Beijing. He went all over spreading reactionary speech. After June 4, he fled back home and was shortly afterwards arrested by the local public security bureau. After being held for several days in Changsha's No. 1 Jail, he was transferred to Beijing, where his circumstances remain unclear. (The report of his arrest was carried in the *Hunan Daily* in June, 1989.)

                        [? YRS]

Shanghai

• **Li Dianyuan,** 26 years old. He was originally a graduate student at Shanghai's Communications University and a Standing Committee member of the Shanghai Students' Autonomous Federation. At the end of May 1989, he went to Changsha and got in touch with the Hunan Students' Autonomous Federation, assisted in its work, and helped organize the June 8th mourning ceremony in Changsha. He was later arrested at his home in Shaoyang. He was first held for several months in Changsha's No. 1 Jail and later transferred to Shanghai. In June 1990 he was sentenced to three years by the Shanghai Intermediate Court on a charge of "counterrevolutionary propaganda and incitement." He is currently serving his sentence.

                        [3 YRS]

B. Executed

• **Chen XX,** age and occupation unknown, a resident of Lian County in Guangdong Province, was arrested together with Yao Guisheng and Hu Nianyou (see above) sometime in mid-June 1989. The three men were accused of having attempted to help WAF members escape from Changsha after the June 4 crackdown. Chen was tried by the Changsha Intermediate Court, in either September or October 1989, and sentenced to death. He was executed on December 26, 1989.

C. Died in Prison

• **Li Maoqiu,** 53 years old, originally a high-level engineer at the Changsha Non-Ferrous Metals Design Academy. In 1986, he went off salary from his unit, while retaining his affiliation. Li began his own breeding business. By the beginning of 1989 he had almost 10,000,000 yuan in assets, including a chicken farm, a dog farm, a salted goods shop, and a roasted snack shop.

141

During the 1989 Democracy Movement he contributed 10,000 yuan to the students. He had no other words or acts. He had, however, "historical problems." His mother's father and his father-in-law had both been students at the Whampoa Military Academy and during the War of Liberation (*i.e.*, the 1945-49 civil war) had been high-ranking Guomindang generals. Not long after June 4, he was arrested. Because no excuse could be found, in mid-1990 he was accused of "economic crime" (fraud). [The government] said that 8,000,000 yuan of his assets had been obtained by fraud and confiscated it all. What with his sadness and anger, in November 1990 Li "exploded to death" in prison. The cause of his death is unclear; the authorities said that he died from a rupturing of the blood vessels of the heart.

D. Re-education through Labor

■ **Boss Wu** (name unknown), about 40, originally the owner of the Wusepan ("Five-Colored Dish") Restaurant on May 1st Road East. The restaurant is situated about 100 meters away from the main entrance to the provincial government offices. During the 1989 Democracy Movement Wu and his family were moved by the righteous actions of the students. They put up a sign which said, "Students eat free." From the time martial law was declared in

Beijing until they were forcibly closed down by the government in early June, they provided almost 60,000 yuan worth of free food to the students. Everyone in Changsha knew about it. After June 4, the government played a trick. On the one hand, they published a notice in the newspapers cancelling the restaurant's business license and wrote a criticism, making it look as if the sanction would only go that far. On the other hand, they secretly arrested Wu and held him for a long time. In 1990 he was sentenced to three years of re-education through labor by the Changsha Eastern District Public Security Bureau. He is currently held in the Changsha Xinkaipu Labor Re-education Center. [3 YRS]

■ **Chen Tianlai**, 24 years old, unemployed, high school graduate, resident of Dongan County in Hunan. During the 1989 Democracy Movement he "infiltrated the ranks of the students" and took to the streets to create disturbances. Moreover, he spread "rumors" and "superstitions" all over the place. He was later arrested. In November 1989 he was sent to three years of re-education through labor by the Lingling Prefecture Public Security Bureau. [3 YRS]

■ **Deng Liming**, worker, 29 years old. He originally worked in Shaoyang City, Hunan. During the 1989 Democracy Movement he "created disturbances" in Shaoyang City. He disseminated "reactionary speech," posted big-character posters, and stirred up the masses to "wreck." He was arrested in July 1989, and in December was sent to 3 years of re-education through labor by the Shaoyang City Public Security Bureau. [3 YRS]

■ **Deng Yuanguo**, 32 years old, originally a teacher at the Huaihua No. 1 Middle School. During the 1989 Democracy Movement he appealed publicly on behalf of the student cause, and was placed under "shelter and investigation" for a period after the June 4 suppression. In 1990, following the failure of the August 19 coup in the Soviet Union, Deng made statements calling for the Soviet Communist Party to step down from power, and was promptly arrested a second time. Soon afterwards, he was sentenced to two years' re-education through labor. [2 YRS]

■ **Duan Ping**, 32 years old, from Yongzhou City, Hunan; originally a teacher in Qiyang No.1 Middle School. During the 1989 Democracy Movement he allegedly made secret link-ups and stirred up "disturbances." He was sent to two years of re-education through labor. He was released this year. Upon his release, Duan opened an electronic game parlor. After the failure of the coup in the Soviet Union, he was arrested again, apparently for having made statements welcoming the coup's failure. He was again sent to the Xinkaipu Labor Re-education Center for three years of re-education through labor. [2+3 YRS]

■ **Fu Guangrong**, unemployed youth *(shehui qingnian)*, 27 years old, resident of Zhuzhou City, Hunan. During the 1989 Democracy Movement he spread "rumors" all over the place and directed the students to "create disturbances." He also helped the students hide. After his activities were exposed he was arrested. In early 1990 he was sent to 3 years of re-education through labor by the Zhuzhou City Public Security Bureau. [3 YRS]

■ **Hu Junda**, teacher, 35 years old. He was originally a lecturer at the Xiangtan Electrical Machinery Specialized School. During the 1989 Democracy Movement, he wrote "counterrevolutionary articles," encouraged the students to create disturbances, and stirred up the workers to go on strike. After June 4, he fled to Shenzhen, and swam into Hong Kong from Shekou. Later he returned voluntarily to the mainland and was arrested. After being locked up in the Xiangtan Jail for 10 months, he was sent to three years of re-education through labor by the Xiangtan City Public Security Bureau. [3 YRS]

■ **Jiang Fengshan**, teacher, 37 years old. He originally taught in the philosophy department of Xiangtan University. During the 1989 Democracy Movement he gave public speeches on several occasions. He supported the students in "creating a disturbance" and after June 4 stirred up the workers to go on strike and block traffic. He was arrested in July

1989 and held in the Xiangtan City Jail. In early 1990 he was sent to three years of re-education through labor by the Xiangtan City Public Security Bureau. [3 YRS]

- **Liu Jianwei**, 30 years old, originally a worker in the Vehicle Section of the Passenger Transport Department of Changsha's Railway Bureau. During the 1989 Democracy Movement he took part in the Changsha Workers' Autonomous Federation. In mid-June of 1989 he secretly got several leaders of the provincial Students' Autonomous Federation out of the city on trains. He was arrested in September 1989. In early 1990 he was sentenced to three years of re-education through labor by the Changsha Railway Public Security Bureau. He is being held in the Changsha City Xinkaipu Labor Re-education Center.) [3 YRS]

- **Long Xiaohu**, 30 years old, cadre. He originally worked in the Hunan Provincial Foreign Affairs Office and is a graduate of People's University. (He is said to be the grandson of the Guomindang governor-general of Yunnan, Long Yun.) During the 1989 Democracy Movement he did liaison work for the students. After June 4, he left China legally. In May 1990 he returned to China at the invitation of the PRC Asian Games Committee in order to attend the opening ceremonies of the Asian Games, having received an invitation from the State Physical Education Commission. He was then accused of hiding four blank passports and

almost HK$100,000 for the purpose of "rescuing student leaders." He was arrested on the evening of June 3 and held at the public security branch station in Changsha's Eastern District. He was later secretly sent to 2 years of re-education through labor. [2 YRS]

- **Ma Heping**, 29 years old, unemployed youth, resident of Hengyang City. During the 1989 Democracy Movement he allegedly "created disturbances" in many places, "sneaked into" the ranks of the students to take part in demonstrations and "cursed" the public security authorities. He was arrested in June, 1989, and in November was sent to three years of re-education through labor by the Hengyang City Public Security Bureau. [3 YRS]

- **Peng Liangkun**, 25 years old, worker. He originally worked in a large factory in Xiangxiang County, Hunan. During the 1989 Democracy Movement he went to many places, according to the authorities, to "stir up the wind and light a fire," wishing to "bring chaos" to society. He also disseminated news from "enemy stations" (i.e. VoA and BBC.) He was arrested after June 4, and in November 1989 was sent to three years of re-education through labor by the Xiangxiang County Public Security Bureau. [3 YRS]

- **Qian Lizhu** (the surname may be incorrect,) 26 years old, peasant, resident of Yueyang City, Hunan. During the 1989 Democracy

144

Movement he came to the city allegedly to "create rumors," attacked the Party and the government, and took part in "making disturbances." He was arrested after June 4. In October 1989, he was sent to three years of re-education through labor by the Yueyang City Public Security Bureau. [3 YRS]

■ **Wu Changgui**, worker, 30 years old. During the 1989 Democracy Movement he helped organize the Xiangtan Workers' Autonomous Federation and was a member of its Standing Committee. On several occasions he organized demonstrations, sit-ins, and strikes by the workers. He was arrested in June, 1989, and in early 1990 was sent to 3 years of re-education through labor by the Xiangtan City Public Security Bureau. [3 YRS]

■ **Wu Wei**, **Deng Jun**, **Xiong Jianjun**, and **Fu Guanghui**, all workers in the Changde City Water Supply Plant, all between 20 and 30 years old. During the 1989 Democracy Movement they organized a "Workers' Autonomous Organization" and agitated for strikes, leading to a brief shutoff of Changde's water supply. All four were arrested after June 4. In November 1989 they were sent variously to two to three years of re-education through labor by the Changde City Public Security Bureau. They may now be free, but Asia Watch has no confirmation of their release. [2-3 YRS]

■ **Xia Kuanqun**, cadre, 34 years old. He was originally employed in a government organ in Changde City. During the 1989 Democracy Movement he got the cadres in his unit to go out into the streets to support the students. He also donated several hundred *yuan* to the students. He was later ferreted out during investigations. In November, 1989 he was sent to three years of re-education through labor by the Changde City Public Security Bureau. [3 YRS]

■ **Xiao Shenhe**, 32 years old, a peasant from Ningxiang County, Hunan. He was quite active in the 1989 Democracy Movement and on several occasions took part in demonstrations and meetings. He also planned to set up an "Anti-Corruption Action Group." He was arrested after June 4 and held in the Changsha County Jail. At the end of 1989 he was sent to three years of re-education through labor at the Changsha City Xinkaipu Labor Re-education Center. [3 YRS]

■ **Zhong Minghui**, 30 years old, teacher. He originally taught in a middle school in Jinshi City, Changde Prefecture, Hunan. During the 1989 Democracy Movement he wrote "reactionary articles" and spread "rumors," creating a very "bad influence." He was detained after June 4, and at the end of 1989 was sent to three years of re-education through labor by the Jinshi City Public Security Bureau. [3 YRS]

E. Psychiatric Incarceration

■ **Peng Yuzhang**, professor, over 70 years old. Originally a professor at Hunan University; since retired. During the 1989 Democracy Movement he firmly supported the students from beginning to end. He took part in sit-ins and hunger strikes and moved many of the masses. Arrested in June, 1989. Held in Cell 24 of Changsha No. 1 Jail. He protested and all day long would shout demands that he be released. As a result he was punished by being placed on the "shackle board" *(menbanliao)* for several months. (See Chapter 5 for explanation.) After this he was released on the grounds of "mental illness." (I heard this directly from a cadre.) Only after I got out of jail did I learn that he had been locked up in a "mental hospital." His family is not permitted to visit him.

■ See also: **Tang Changye, Yao Guisheng, Zhou Min**, above.

146

F. Released

Confirmed Releases

Cai Feng, originally a student in the entering class of 1986 in Central-South Industrial University, possibly in the physics department. He attended the "Conference on the 70th Anniversary of the May 4 Movement" held by "China Youth" magazine. His speech was very radical. He advocated "immediately taking to the streets," before the student movement had broken out. During the Democracy Movement, he was active mainly in his school's autonomous student union. He was not arrested immediately after June 4, but only in early 1990, after a "counter-revolutionary student organization" in which he had participated was broken up [by the police]. He was released after being held for several months. (Some other important members received prison sentences; their cases are related elsewhere.)

Cai Jinxuan, originally a worker at the Changsha Textile Mill, 24 years old. He was a member of the Changsha Workers' Autonomous Federation. On several occasions he organized worker strikes and printed propaganda materials. On June 15 he surrendered and was held in the Changsha No. 1 Jail. He was released in April 1990.

Chen Ding, originally a student in the entering class of 1987 at the Changsha Railway Academy. He was an active participant in the 1989 Democracy Movement. After June 4, he returned home and with a group of his fellow students mobilized the workers at a local factory, the Xiangtan Electrical Machinery Factory (a large provincial factory with several tens of thousands of employees) to go on strike in opposition to the government's violence. His arm was broken by a group of factory security men led by the factory's security section chief. After this the factory's workers spontaneously went to the home of the security section chief, carried off expensive furnishings, and burned them. This was a very serious matter, and as a result he, his elder brother Chen Gang, and six or seven workers were arrested. Seven days later he was indicted by the Xiangtan City Intermediate [People's] Procuracy on a charge of "counter-revolutionary propaganda and incitement." Trial was held the next day and he was sentenced to one year. His elder brother Chen Gang received a death sentence, later changed to a suspended death sentence. The other workers (see entry under Peng Shi for names) received sentences ranging from five years to life. After being released in mid-1990, Chen Ding returned to his school to continue his studies. (After June 4, his school expelled over 20 students, but later allowed them all back.)

Chen Guangke, in his forties, originally a cadre at one of the Hunan daily newspaper offices. During the 1989 Democracy

147

Movement, he enthusiastically participated in protest activities and wrote several articles for his newspaper in support of the student movement. He was arrested after June 4, held for almost a year and then released in mid-1990.

Chen Guojin, 22 years old, originally a student at Loudi Teachers Training College. During the 1989 Democracy Movement, Chen was an office-holder in the college's Students Autonomous Federation, and organized many student demonstrations and petitioning activities. He also carried out liaison work with students from other provinces. After June 4, he convened a large mourning ceremony on the college campus for the dead of Beijing and gave a speech in which he condemned the communist government. He was arrested shortly afterwards, detained in Loudi Jail and then released in May 1990.

Chen Le (also known as Liu Zhongtao), originally an auditor in the history department at Hunan Normal University and a worker at the Hunan Rubber Factory. On the eve of the 1989 Democracy Movement he took part in the activities of the "Democracy Salon." On May 4, he took part in organizing the Provisional Committee with representatives of various schools. Later he was relieved of his post because his status was "not genuine" (i.e. he was not a real student.) After the Students' Autonomous Federation was established he served as special assistant to the chairman. (The Students' Autonomous Federation had 2 chairmen; each had a special assistant.) After June 4, he planned the establishment of a "Democracy Movement Lecture Center." In August 1989, the affair was exposed and he was arrested and held in Cell 17 of the Changsha No. 1 Jail. While he in he went on a hunger strike. He was released in early 1990.

Chen Shuai, 26 years old, originally a worker at Changsha's No. 1 Xinhua Factory. After the Beijing students began their hunger strike, Chen and several other local workers organized the Changsha Workers Autonomous Federation. He early on served as spokesman for the federation and played a prominent role in its work. Subsequently, he withdrew from any public activities. He was arrested after June 4, and in 1990 was tried by the Changsha Intermediate Court on charges of "counterrevolutionary propaganda and incitement" and sentenced to two years' imprisonment. Now released.

Dai Shangqi, 35 years old, originally a teacher at Shaoyang Teachers Training College. He joined the 1989 Democracy Movement during its early stages, supporting the just protest actions of the students. After the students in Beijing began their hunger strike, Dai led a group of students to hold a sit-in before the main gate of the Shaoyang government offices. He also wrote a large number of so-called "reactionary articles" asserting that the government had forfeited its own legal status through its actions; these articles were provocative and very influential. He was arrested and imprisoned after June 4. In 1990 he was tried by the Shaoyang Intermediate Court on charges of "counterrevolutionary propaganda and incitement" and sentenced to three years of "criminal control" (guanzhi).

Deng Keming, temporary worker, 21 years old, Sichuanese. He formerly worked at the Changsha Measuring Instruments Factory and other units. During the 1989 Democracy Movement he was an active participant. He was arrested the evening of the April 22 Incident. In July of the same year he was sentenced to two years by the Changsha Eastern District [Basic-Level People's] Court on a charge of "beating, smashing, and looting." He was later sent to Longxi Prison to undergo labor reform. While laboring in prison, his wrist was broken. He has now been released. He currently wanders from place to place.

Fan Zhong, originally a student in the entering class of 1986 in Central-South Industrial University. Before the 1989 Democracy Movement he was the chairman of his school's student union and the vice chairman of the Hunan Students' Union (all government-approved posts). Midway through the student movement he began to change his views and participated in the founding of the Hunan Students' Autonomous Federation, taking a leading role.

After the reorganization of the Students' Autonomous Federation he was a general director along with Tang Boqiao. He was in charge of the sit-in in front of the provincial government offices. After June 4 he took part in organizing the June 8th mourning meeting, but because of traffic problems was unable to attend it. On June 29 he was arrested and held in Cell 6 of the Changsha No. 1 Jail. He suffered a great deal in prison, and on several occasions was manacled to the "shackle board" (menbanliao) for several months. He was also subject to electric shocks. He was later accused of the crime of "disrupting social order." He was held until December of 1991, when he was "exempted from criminal sanctions" and released by the Changsha City Western District Court.

Gong Yanming, 38 years old, originally general manager of the Yinhai Company, a subsidiary of Hunan Province General Import-Export Corporation. During the 1989 Democracy Movement, he supported the righteous protest actions of the students, and encouraged cadres and officials of his company to take to the streets and participate in protest demonstrations. Placed under investigation after June 4, he was arrested in July 1989. The authorities accused him of economic impropriety, and he was later charged with the crime of corruption. He was released as innocent, however, at the end of 1990. In May 1991, an extraordinary article appeared in China Youth Daily (Zhongguo Qingnian Bao) asserting that

149

"political scores" should not be settled against people under the guise of accusing them of "economic offenses," and appealing against the injustice done to Gong Yanming.

He Nan, 34 years old, originally a cadre in a Changsha municipal construction firm. During the 1989 Democracy Movement, according to the authorities, he "spread rumors all over the place," and later on he "reproduced and distributed videotapes which had been made overseas and smuggled into China concerning the June 4 incident." Arrested in late 1989, He Nan was "released on bail for medical treatment" in August 1990 after developing kidney stones.

Hu Hao, originally a student in the entering class of 1985 in Hunan Medical University. During the 1989 Democracy Movement he was a member of the Standing Committee of the Students' Autonomous Federation and director of its secretariat. He took part in all the important activities of the student movement. After June 4 he escaped to the countryside and was later arrested and held in Cell 19 of the Changsha No. 1 Jail. He was released in early 1990.

Hu Xuedong, 26 years old, originally a student at the Central-South Industrial University During the 1989 Democracy Movement, Hu was responsible for secret liaison work in the Hunan SAF. Although not investigated or detained for some time after the June 1989 crackdown, he was denounced and exposed by someone to the authorities in March 1990. He was subsequently arrested and detained in Changsha No. 1 Jail for nine months, before being released as innocent in December 1990.

Huang Zheng, 23 years old, originally a cadre at a provincial import-export corporation. Huang was arrested in early 1990 for alleged "political offenses" believed to be related to the pro-democracy movement (although details are not known), and detained in Changsha Municipal No.1 Jail. Sometime in 1991 he became ill and was "released on bail for medical treatment." His case has not yet been formally concluded, however, and like other pro-democracy prisoners allowed out for medical treatment he could be redetained and brought to trial at any time.

Lei Shaojun, teacher, 30 years old. He originally taught in the department of social sciences of Central-South Industrial University. He was "the most popular teacher in 1988" (CSIU). After the suppression of the 1989 Democracy Movement, Lei announced at a meeting at the school to mourn "the perished of Beijing" that he was resigning from the Party. He was arrested in December, 1989, and detained in secret. In June, 1990, he was sentenced to two years of control *(guanzhi)* by the Changsha Intermediate Court on a charge of

150

"counterrevolutionary propaganda and incitement." Since then he has been at the school subject to control and supervision (*jianguan*).

Li Jie, 27, originally a worker in Dept. 416 of the Ministry of Aeronautics. He was a member of the Changsha Workers' Autonomous Federation. He took part in hunger strikes and sit-ins, and on several occasions organized demonstrations and strikes. After June 4 he surrendered and was held in the Changsha No. 1 Jail. He was released in June 1990.

Li Lin and **Li Zhi**, two brothers who were involved in the 1989 Democracy Movement in Hunan Province, were released from prison in Hengyang City on July 15, 1991 following a campaign of international pressure on their behalf. Both men had fled to Hong Kong in July 1989 to evade arrest; Li Lin found work there as a motor mechanic, and Li Zhi, his younger brother, worked in a cosmetics firm. In February 1991, however, following public statements by Chinese leaders guaranteeing safety for pro-democracy activists who had gone overseas, the two returned openly to China. They were arrested almost immediately and placed in incommunicado detention. Li Lin, formerly a steel worker in Hengyang City and a member of the Hengyang Workers Autonomous federation in May-June 1989, had publicly renounced his Party membership following the June 4 massacre in Beijing. Li Zhi, a rock musician, had

been active in the pro-democracy protests in Changsha, the provincial capital. Following news of their secret arrests in February 1991, President Jimmy Carter wrote to the Chinese leadership requesting the brothers' release, and Hong Kong businessman and human-rights activist John Kamm lobbied vigorously to the same end within the Chinese governmental and judicial elite. On July 9, 1991, the Lis were brought to trial and sentenced to five-and-one-half months' imprisonment - backdated to February 15, the date of their arrests - on charges of "illegally crossing the border." Shortly after their release, they were allowed to return to Hong Kong, and they now live in the United States. Li Lin's wife and young child remain in China.

Li Yuhua, 21 years old, originally a student in the Chinese department at Changde Teachers' College. During the 1989 Democracy Movement he was vice chairman of the Changde Autonomous Union of [Students in] Institutions of Higher Education. On several occasions he organized student demonstrations and he conducted a sit-in for almost 20 days in front of the municipal government offices. On June 5 he organized a traffic blockage by students and city residents, "creating great economic losses." He was arrested in July 1989. In January 1990 he was sentenced to two years' imprisonment by the Changde City Intermediate Court on a charge of "counterrevolutionary propaganda and incitement." In April he was sent

151

to Longxi Prison in Hunan to serve his sentence. He has since been released.

Liu Mianli, 32 years old, originally a teacher at the Loudi Teachers Training College. During the 1989 Democracy Movement, Liu wrote so-called "reactionary articles," gave numerous public speeches and called upon the students to take a confrontational stance toward the government. In his view, this was the only way to "win back justice." Several days after June 4, he took to the streets with some students and shouted out slogans such as "Down with Li Peng," creating a great stir. Arrested in July 1989, he was held for more than two years in Loudi Jail. He was only recently released.

Liu Jianhua, originally a student in the entering class of 1985 in the agricultural machinery department of the Hunan Agricultural Academy. On the eve of the student movement he was admitted to the graduate school of Fudan University. During the 1989 Democracy Movement he was the chairman of his school's autonomous student union. On several occasions he organized demonstrations in which students from campuses several dozens of *li* away [one *li* is about a third of a mile] in the suburbs marched to the provincial government offices. He was fairly influential among students at his school. His school was responsible for arranging the set-up of the June 8 "Mourning Meeting." He was arrested in September 1989 and held in the

Changsha No. 1 Jail and the Changsha County Jail. He was released in early 1990 and at that time expelled from his school. His student status has since been restored (as is the case with all students expelled from that school).

Long Jianhua, originally a student in the entering class of 1986 in the foreign languages department of Hunan Normal University. He took part in the early activities of the Democracy Salon and was in the front line from start to finish in the 1989 Democracy Movement. He took an important part in the planning of the May 4 Joint Demonstration, the organization of the Joint Action Provisional Committee of [Hunan] Institutions of Higher Education, and the establishment of the Hunan Students' Autonomous Federation. He was also the vice chairman of the school's autonomous student union. He wrote a large number of posters, banners, and other propaganda materials. After June 4 he fled back to his native place in the Xiangxi Autonomous Prefecture, Hunan, and was arrested there in mid-September. He was held in Cell 3 of the Changsha No. 1 Jail and released as innocent in December 1990. He returned to his school to continue his studies. In March 1990 he was arrested again because he had made up his bed to look like a coffin and had hung form it a portrait of Hu Yaobang edged in black silk. After six months he was released after being educated. He is currently teaching at a middle school in a village in

152

Xiangxi.

Long Xianping, teacher (female), 35 years old. Originally a teacher at Xiangtan University. During the 1989 Democracy Movement she gave several speeches, and after June 4 she organized mourning activities by the students at Xiangtan University. She was arrested in September 1989 and sentenced to three years in mid-1990 by the Xiangtan City Intermediate Court on a charge of "counter-revolutionary propaganda and incitement." She was released after serving two years in Changsha Prison (this prison holds mostly female prisoners).

Lu Shengqun, 37 years old, originally a sales and marketing official at the Hunan Province Light Industrial Institute. He played no important political role during the 1989 Democracy Movement, but after June 4 he helped leaders of the Hunan SAF, including Tang Boqiao, escape to Guangzhou and other places; in addition, he found a place for Tang Boqiao to hide temporarily. He was arrested in early July 1989, and held for several months before being released.

Manager Zhang (given name not known), in his forties, originally a manager of the Changsha Municipal Heavy Machinery Plant. During the 1989 Democracy Movement, Zhang supported the idea of the students and workers staging strike activities, and, according to the authorities, he "on several occasions gave banquets for students and local residents who had come to the factory to make disturbances, which had an extremely bad effect." Arrested soon after June 4, 1989, he was detained for several months and then released. He is presently unemployed.

Mao Genwei, 22 years old, occupation unknown. He was arrested at the end of 1990 on suspicion of involvement in the underground group allegedly set up by his brother, Mao Genhong (who was later sentenced to three years' imprisonment) and others, and was detained for almost a year at the Changsha No. 1 Jail. In mid-1991, he was put on trial but then exempted by the court from criminal punishment and released.

Mao Yongke (female), in her thirties, originally a teacher at a school in Xiangtan. A Christian, she was arrested sometime prior to the 1989 Democracy Movement (probably in 1987) on charges of "using religion as a cloak for political activities" (i.e. pro-democracy activities.) She was sentenced to four years' imprisonment and held in Changsha No. 1 Jail. She was recently released. She has a daughter and is currently unemployed.

Mo Lihua, teacher (female), 34 years old. Originally a teacher at Shaoyang Teacher's College in Hunan. During the 1989 Democracy Movement, she supported the student demonstrations. After June 4, she made a speech at a mass meeting in the Shaoyang People's Square. The

153

response was unprecedented in warmth; she became a well known figure in Shaoyang. On June 14, she was arrested. On December 24, she was sentenced to three years by the Shaoyang City Intermediate Court on a charge of "counterrevolutionary propaganda and incitement" and was sent to Changsha Prison. She has since been released.

Pan Mingdong, private businessman, 40 years old. He was formerly a boxing coach with the provincial Physical Education Commission. He has been in prison several times for political reasons. During the 1989 Democracy Movement, he expressed sympathy for the righteous actions of the students and gave them assistance. He was arrested in October 1989 on a charge of "drafting a declaration of Hunan self-government." He was later sent to two years of re-education through labor because the accusation lacked an evidentiary basis. He was held in Changsha's Xinkaipu Labor Re-education Center.

Tang Hua, in his thirties, originally the deputy editor of *Young People*, a magazine published by the Hunan Provincial Communist Youth League. During the 1989 Democracy Movement, he often sought out the student leaders and helped them to work out strategies for the movement. He was later accused by the authorities of "spreading rumors" during the movement "to attack the Party and government" and of having published articles in *Young People*

magazine "championing democracy and science." Arrested after June 4, 1989, he was held and investigated for more than one and a half years before eventually being released.

Tan Li, student (female), 20 years old. She was in the entering class of 1986 in the foreign languages department of Hunan Normal University. During the 1989 Democracy Movement, together with another female student named Zhang Xiaoyan, Tan Li wrote and posted on a wall on campus a big-character poster. Because the poster said "Down with the Communist Party," she was arrested in November 1989 after being thoroughly investigated. (Zhang was locked up in the same cell as Tan for almost a year before being excused from criminal sanction.) In June 1990 she was sentenced to one year by the Changsha Intermediate Court on a charge of "counter-revolutionary propaganda and incitement." She was then sent to Changsha Prison and has now been released.

Tan Liliang, teacher, 28 years old, graduate of the education department of Hunan Normal University. While at university he was named a "model 3-good student" four years in a row, a major honor when only one student per department is so named. (The "3 goods" are virtue, *(de)*, knowledge *(zhi)*, and physical fitness *(ti)*.) Tan taught at Hunan's Loudi Teachers' College. During the 1989 Democracy Movement he organized class boycotts and demonstrations by the students.

154

He also planned a "long-term resistance struggle" with Hunan Normal University students who had come to make link-ups. He was arrested in July, 1989. In early 1990, he was sentenced to two years by the Loudi Prefecture Intermediate Court on a charge of "counterrevolutionary propaganda and incitement." He was then sent to Longxi Prison for reform through labor, and has since been released.

Tang Boqiao, originally a student from the entering class of 1986 in the politics department at Hunan Normal University. On the eve of the 1989 Democracy Movement he helped organize a "Democracy Salon." Its activities were first within Hunan Normal University, but it later extended to all institutions of higher education in Changsha. After the outbreak of the 1989 student movement, he took part in late April in the Committee to Prepare Demonstrations and Meetings in Commemoration of the 70th Anniversary of the May 4 Movement. Its key members were from Hunan Normal University, Hunan University, and Central-South Industrial University. After the demonstration and rally on May 4, together with representatives from institutions of higher education in Changsha, he founded the Joint Action Provisional Committee of Hunan Institutions of Higher Education and served as provisional chairman. On May 14 he went to Beijing to observe and participate in the Beijing student movement,

returning on the evening of May 19. On May 22 he took part in the reorganization of the Students' Autonomous Federation and served as chairman. On May 24 he directed a city-wide protest demonstration. On May 28 he drafted a "pledge of loyalty" for the students. That evening the Students' Autonomous Federation declared that the students would return to their campuses and held a collective oath-taking ceremony. On June 8, Tang and Zhang Lixin presided over a meeting of 140,000 persons to mourn the dead of Beijing. On June 27, 28 and 29, Hunan television repeatedly broadcast a province-wide "wanted notice" for him. In the early morning of July 13, he was arrested in Jiangmen City in Guangdong. On July 17, 1990, he was tried by the Changsha City Intermediate Court and sentenced to three years' imprisonment, with subsequent deprivation of political rights for two years, on a charge of "counterrevolutionary propaganda and incitement." In November 1989, he was sent to Hunan's Longxi Prison to undergo reform through labor. He was paroled on February 12, 1991. He subsequently escaped abroad, and was admitted to the United States as a political refugee in April 1992.

Tang Zhibin, 30 years old, originally a reporter for *Young People*, the journal of the provincial Communist Youth League. During the 1989 Democracy Movement, he joined with the students to take part in demonstrations and sit-down protests. According to the authorities,

155

he was "appointed as an adviser" by the students and "his ideology went into reverse." Tang was arrested at the end of 1989, and released in mid-1990. He was sacked from his official post, however, and is now unemployed.

Wang Jisheng, student, 22 years old. He originally studied in the Yueyang Engineering Academy. During the 1989 Democracy Movement he organized the Yueyang Students' Autonomous Federation and served as a member of its Standing Committee. On several occasions he organized student street demonstrations. He also held a sit-in in front of the offices of the Yueyang city government. He was arrested in July, 1989. In November 1989, he was sentenced to one year by the Yueyang City Intermediate Court on a charge of "disrupting social order." In 1990, having served his sentence, he was released from Longxi Prison.

Wang Yongfa, 38 years old, teacher, university graduate. He originally taught at the No. 1 Middle School of Lanshan County, Lingling Prefecture, Hunan. During the 1989 Democracy Movement, he distributed handbills and organized street demonstrations by the students. He was arrested in October 1989. Although declared innocent and ordered to be freed by the court at his trial in February 1990, Wang was nonetheless sent to undergo two to three years' re-education through labor by the Lanshan County Public Security Bureau. (See Appendix VIII.D) He was freed in February 1992.   [3 YRS]

Wei Nan, originally a self-financed student in the construction department of Hunan University. He had been expelled from Beijing University at the time of the 1987 student movement. During the 1989 Democracy Movement he was a leader of the Hunan University autonomous student union. In general he had relatively few public activities. He was arrested after June 4 and held in the Changsha No. 1 Jail. He was released in December and arrested again in April 1990. He was held almost three months. He is now a student at Changsha's Communications Academy.

Wu Fangli, 21 years old, originally a student at Hunan's Xiangtan University. He became actively involved in the student protest movement only during its later stages, becoming head of the college's student propaganda section. He often led the students in street demonstrations, giving speeches and going around factories urging the workers to go on strike. After June 4, Wu went to the Xiangtan Iron and Steel Plant and other large-scale local enterprises to provide accurate news about the massacre in Beijing and called upon the workers to stage a total strike. He was arrested later that month and held until the end 1989, when he was released.

Wu Xinghua, around 50 years old, originally a senior journalist at the

156

Hunan branch office of *Xinhua* (New China) News Agency. During the 1989 Democracy Movement, according to the authorities, "Wu wavered in his political stance, and after the suppression of the counter-revolutionary rebellion he came out in clear opposition to the Party, with extremely adverse consequences." He was secretly arrested in July 1989 and detained for over a year. Eventually he was "released on bail for medical treatment."

Xiao Feng, 55 years old, originally general manager of the Hunan Province General Import-Export Corporation. After June 4, 1989, he was accused of having "donated company funds to the students" during the Democracy Movement and of subsequently helping the students to conceal the money. He was suspended from work and placed under investigation, then arrested in early 1990. Later that year, he was released on bail for medical treatment, and is currently unemployed.

Xie Changfa, cadre, 35 years old. He formerly worked in succession at the Changsha Steel Factory, the Changsha city government, and as a township head in Liuyang County. During the 1989 Democracy Movement he gave speeches on several occasions in Liuyang, Ningxiang, Wangcheng, Changsha, and other places. One speech in particular that he delivered in Liuyang County had a "particularly bad influence." He was arrested in

July 1989 and held in Cell 13 of the Changsha No. 1 Jail. In early 1990 he was sent to two years of re-education through labor by the Changsha City Public Security Bureau.

Yang Chang, 24 years old, a resident of Guangzhou, Guangdong Province, and originally a student at Jinan University. During the 1989 Democracy Movement, he carried out liaison activities between the students autonomous associations of various colleges and universities in the interior of China, including those in Changsha. After June 4, 1989 he was extremely active in helping students escape arrest and go into hiding, and he was himself arrested in August that year. Held first in Guangzhou and then in Changsha, he was released in mid-1990.

Yi Gai, originally a student in the music department at Hunan Normal University. In 1988 he served as the head of the "Hunan Cultural Delegation to Express Greetings to the Laoshan Front Line." During the 1989 Democracy Movement he served as head of the Students' Autonomous Federation Liaison Department, being responsible for liaison between the autonomous student unions of the various schools. It was also known as the "Internal Liaison Department." He also wrote a "Report of an Investigation into the Hunan Student Movement." [*Hunan xueyun kaocha baogao*]: the title deliberately mimics the wording of Mao's famous "Report of an Investigation into the Hunan Peasant Movement."] When he was serving in the army he had been jailed for eight months by a military court for political reasons. He was arrested after June 4 and held in the Changsha No. 1 Jail. This time, too, he was held for eight months. He was released in March 1990, and has now become an unemployed vagabond.

Yu Chaohui, originally a student in the entering class of 1985 in the department of general medicine of Hunan Medical University. He was a fairly frequent participant during the latter part of the 1989 Democracy Movement and served as special assistant to the chairman of the Students' Autonomous Federation. On June 14 he fled with Tang Boqiao and others to Guangzhou, Xinhui County [in Guangdong], and other places. He was later arrested after returning to Changsha and held in Cell 27 of the Changsha No. 1 Jail. Because he "informed and established merit" while in jail, he was released in November 1989.

Yue Weipeng, originally a student in the entering class of 1985 in the Chinese department of Hunan Hydraulic Power Normal University. He took part in the later period of the activities of the Democracy Salon, and on May 4 took part in the founding of the Provisional Committee. After the founding of the Students' Autonomous Federation he was a member of its Standing Committee. He was a leader of the student movement at his school. He was arrested after June 4 and held in Cell 24 of the Changsha No. 1 Jail.

He was released in December 1989 and assigned to be a teacher in a remote county in Gansu.

Zeng Ming, teacher, 29 years old. He originally taught at Central-South Industrial University. During the 1989 Democracy Movement, he connected up secretly with the students. After June 4, he angrily denounced the government and demanded that Li Peng be punished. He fell under government suspicion after the Romanian Revolution and was arrested in December 1989. In May 1990, he was sentenced to half a year by the Changsha Intermediate Court on a charge of "counter-revolutionary propaganda and incitement." He has already been released.

Zhang Lixin, 25 years old. He was originally a student at Beijing Normal University and the leader of a Beijing Students' Autonomous Federation propaganda team that went to the south. He was also a member of the Standing Committee of the Beijing Students' Autonomous Federation and the leader of its picket squad. In early June, 1989, he went from Shanghai to Changsha and got in touch with the Hunan Students' Autonomous Federation. On June 8, together with Tang Boqiao, a leader of the Hunan Students' Autonomous Federation, he presided over a mourning ceremony held at the Changsha Railway Station. At the end of June he was arrested at a friend's house in Xiangtan City. Also arrested at the same time were 3 Beijing

University students. He was held at the Changsha No. 1 Jail and later transferred to Beijing. In mid-1990 he was released.

Zhang Xiaoyan, 21 years old, originally a student in the foreign languages department of Hunan Normal University. During the 1989 Democracy Movement she took part in her department's (unofficial) Democratic Propaganda Team. On several occasions she gave speeches both on and off the campus. She also wrote "reactionary articles and wall posters." She was arrested in late 1989 and held in the Changsha No. 1 Prison. In June 1990 she was exempted from criminal sanctions on a charge of "counterrevolutionary propaganda and incitement" by the Changsha City Intermediate Court.

Zhou Liwu, teacher, 27 years old, graduate of the philosophy department of Xiangtan University. He taught at the Hunan No. 2 School of Light Industry. During the 1989 Democracy Movement he wrote "reactionary articles" and planned student demonstrations. He also made speeches in public attacking the Party and the government. He was arrested after June 4. In early 1990 he was sentenced to 2 years by the Changsha Intermediate Court on a charge of "counterrevolutionary propaganda and incitement" and was sent to Longxi Prison to undergo labor reform. He never admitted any guilt.

Zhou Shuilong, 39 years old, originally a worker at the Changsha

North Station of the Changsha Branch of the Railway Bureau. During the 1989 Democracy Movement he joined the Changsha Workers' Autonomous Federation and served as vice head of the Picket Squad. On several occasions he organized demonstrations and strikes and posted up numerous handbills. He was arrested in mid-August 1989. At the end of 1989 he was sentenced to two years of re-education through labor by the Changsha Railway Public Security Bureau, and was sent to serve his sentence at the Changsha City Xinkaipu Labor Re-education Center.

Zhou Yong, 30 years old, originally a worker at the Changsha No. 2 Ventilator Equipment Plant. During the 1989 Democracy Movement, he organized the Changsha Workers Autonomous Federation and served as its chairman. He led the workers to carry out hunger strikes, sit-in protests and demonstration marches, and frequently sent members of the workers federation to visit the various factories in the city and mobilize workers to go on strike. During a several-day period after June 4, several dozen factories in the Changsha area came out on strike. "In the Changsha Cigarette Factory alone, this caused more than 1 million *yuan* in economic losses." Arrested in mid-June, 1989, Zhou was released in early 1990 for having "performed meritorious service."

Presumed Released after Prison Terms

He Bowei, 22 years old, a student in the Chinese department at Hunan Normal University. During the 1989 Democracy Movement he threw himself into the student movement and organized a Dare-to-Die squad at his school, swearing to carry the democracy movement through to the end. The Dare-to-Die squad later changed its name to the Blood Song squad, and He served as the squad leader. The activities of the Blood Song squad among the students had a very great influence. He was arrested in July 1989. In April 1990, he was sentenced to two years by the Changsha Western District [Basic-Level People's] Court on a charge of "disrupting social order."

Xiao Ming, teacher, 35 years old. He originally taught in the philosophy department of Xiangtan University. During the 1989 Democracy Movement, he wrote a great number of "reactionary articles" and stirred up the students to go out into the streets to demonstrate. After June 4 he also gave several speeches "viciously attacking the Party and the government" and was arrested in July. In mid-1990 he was sentenced to 2 years by the Xiangtan City Intermediate Court on a charge of "counterrevolutionary propaganda and incitement." He was later sent to labor reform at Yuanjiang Prison.

Zhang Xiaojun, teacher, 24 years old. He was formerly the Secretary of the Young Communist League at Taoyuan County Teacher's College in Hunan. During the 1989 Democracy Movement, he organized student demonstrations and turned a deaf ear to the government's calls to desist. He was arrested in October 1989. In April 1990, he was sentenced to 2 years by the Changde City Intermediate Court on a charge of "counterrevolutionary propaganda and incitement." In July he was sent to Longxi Prison for reform through labor.

Presumed Released after Re-education

Chen Xiangping, cadre, 31 years old. He originally worked in a department of the Changde city government in Hunan. During the 1989 Democracy Movement his steadfastness wavered, his thinking went over to the other side, and he showed dissatisfaction with the Party. He was later investigated. In November 1989 he was sent to two years of re-education through labor by the Changde City Public Security Bureau.

Fan Yuntie, peasant, 32 years old, resident of Jinshi City, Hunan. During the 1989 Democracy Movement he "infiltrated the ranks of the students" and created opportunities to "make disturbances." After June 4 he also hid "reactionary elements." In November 1989, after his arrest, he was sent to two years of re-education through labor by the

Jinshi City Public Security Bureau.

Liang Wang, worker, 24 years old. He was originally employed at the Changsha Woolen Mill. He was exceptionally active during the 1989 Democracy Movement. He made link-ups, stirred up strikes, and got together with the students to "make disturbances." He was later arrested, but because of lack of evidence was sent to two years of re-education through labor by the Changsha City Public Security Bureau.

Liu Wei, 25 years old, originally a worker at a Changsha municipal factory. During the 1989 Democracy Movement, he joined the Changsha Workers Autonomous Federation and served as a member of its picket squad. He participated in several protest demonstrations and marches, and encouraged the workers to go on strike. Arrested in July 1989, he was sent by the Changsha public security bureau in November of the same year to two years of re-education through labor.

Qing X, teacher, 30 years old, graduate of technical college. Originally taught at the No. 1 Middle School of Yongzhou City in Lingling, Hunan. With Zheng Jinhe (see below), he committed serious political errors during the 1989 Democracy Movement. He wrote "articles of counterrevolutionary propaganda" and organized street demonstrations by the students. He was arrested in September 1989. In December, he was sent to two years of re-education

through labor by the Yongzhou City Public Security Bureau.

Xiao Huidu, teacher, graduate of Hunan Normal University, 34 years old. He formerly taught at the No. 1 Middle School of Huaihua County, Hunan. During the 1989 Democracy Movement, he connected up with students from outside the area and helped the students "make chaos" [dongluan]. In addition, he wrote "reactionary slogans." In October 1989 he was arrested, and in early 1990 he was sent to 2 years of re-education through labor by the Huaihua City Public Security Bureau.

Xiong Xiangwen, worker, 28 years old. He was originally employed in a factory in Linli County. During the 1989 Democracy Movement he stirred up the workers to go on strike and disseminated all kinds of "rumors" and "reactionary speech," "trying to create chaos." He was arrested after June 4, and in November 1989 was sent to two and one-half years of re-education through labor by the Changde City Public Security Bureau.

Yan Fangbo, student, 17 years old. He formerly attended middle school in Longshan County in the Xiangxi Autonomous Prefecture, Hunan. During the 1989 Democracy Movement he organized street demonstrations by middle school students and had contacts with Hunan Normal University students who came to Longshan County to make link-ups. He also posted "reactionary slogans." He was arrested fairly late in

161

1989. In early 1990 he was sent to two years of re-education through labor by the Xiangxi Autonomous Prefecture Public Security Bureau.

Zhang Guohan, unemployed youth, 32 years old. He is a resident of Changsha and lives on Shuyuan Road in Changsha's Southern District. During the 1989 Democracy Movement he actively supported the students and collected money on their behalf. He also got the individual businessmen *(geti hu)* to make contributions to the students. After June 4 he continued to have contacts with student leaders. He was arrested in August, 1989. In December he was sent to two years of re-education through labor by the Changsha City Public Security Bureau.

Zhang Ronghe, student, 17 years old. He originally attended middle school in Linfeng County, Changde, Hunan. During the 1989 Democracy Movement he posted big-character posters and disseminated reactionary speech. He also organized street demonstrations by students. He was arrested after June 4. At the end of 1989 he was sent to two years of re-education through labor by the Linfeng County Public Security Bureau.

Zhao Muyu, teacher, 28 years old. He originally taught in the No. 1 Middle School of Jinshi City, Changde Prefecture, Hunan. During the 1989 Democracy Movement he stirred up the students to go out into the streets and demonstrate and wrote articles attacking the government. He was arrested after June 4 and in December 1989 was sent to two years of re-education through labor by the Jinshi City Public Security Bureau.

Zheng Jinhe, teacher, university graduate. He was formerly the Communist Youth League Committee Secretary at the No. 1 Middle School of Yongzhou City, Lingling Prefecture, Hunan. He was influential in his work with youth. During the 1989 Democracy Movement, he took the side of the students and secretly supported them in joint demonstrations with the Lingling Teacher's College. He was subsequently arrested, and in December 1989 was sent to two years of re-education through labor by the Yongzhou City Public Security Bureau on the grounds of "counter-revolutionary error."

***

APPENDIX II

GLOSSARY OF CHINESE NAMES
(WITH OCCUPATION + CURRENT STATUS)

NAME		OCCUPATION	STATUS
Ah Fang	阿 方	Worker	5 yrs
Boss Wu	吴老板	Businessman	3 yrs [*]
Bu Yunhui	卜云辉	Peasant	3 yrs
Cai Feng	蔡 峰	Student	X [R]
Cai Jinxuan	蔡瑾璇	Worker	X [R]
Cai Weixing	蔡卫星	Worker	4 yrs
Chen XX	陈某某	Worker	Executed
Chen Bing	陈 兵	Student	? yrs
Chen Ding	陈 锭	Student	1 yr [R]
Chen Gang	陈 钢	Worker	Death w/r
Chen Guangke	陈光科	Cadre	X [R]
Chen Guangliang	陈光亮	Doctor	7 yrs
Chen Guojin	陈国金	Student	X [R]
Chen Le	陈 乐	Worker	X [R]
Chen Shuai	陈 帅	Worker	2 yrs [R]
Chen Tianlai	陈田莱	Unemployed	3 yrs [*]
Chen Xiangping	陈湘平	Cadre	2 yrs [*] [R]

KEY:

"yrs"	=	length of prison/labor-reform sentence
"yrs [*]"	=	length of re-education through labor sentence
"?"	=	length of sentence not known
"X"	=	detained without trial
"death w/r"	=	death sentence with two-year reprieve
"(F)"	=	female
"[R]"	=	released

163

Chen Yueming	陈月明	Businessman	3 yrs
Chen Zhixiang	陈志祥	Teacher	18 yrs
Cheng Cun	城村	Journalist	5 yrs
Dai Dingxiang	戴定湘	Worker	3 yrs
Dai Shangqi	戴商起	Teacher	X [R]
Deng Jun	邓军	Worker	2-3 yrs (?)
Deng Keming	邓克明	worker	2 yrs [R]
Deng Liming	邓黎明	Worker	3 yrs
Deng XX	邓某某	Businessman	4 yrs
Deng Yuanguo	邓园国	Teacher	2 yrs [*]
Ding Longhua	丁龙华	Worker	6 yrs
Dong Qi	董奇	Worker	5 yrs
Duan Ping	段平	Teacher	2 + 3 yrs [*]
Fan Yuntie	范运铁	Peasant	2 yrs [*] [R]
Fan Zhong	范中	Student	X [R]
Feng Ming	冯明	Worker	3 yrs
Fu Guanghui	付光辉	Worker	2-3 yrs [*]
Fu Guangrong	付光荣	Unemployed	3 yrs [*]
Fu Zhaoqin	付兆钦	Peasant	4 yrs
Gao Bingkun	高炳坤	Worker	4 yrs
Gong Songlin	龚松林	Worker	5 yrs
Gong Yanming	龚雁鸣	Manager	X [R]
Guo Yunqiao	郭云桥	Worker	Death w/r
Hao Mingzhao	郝铭钊	Student	? yrs
He Aoqiu	合敖秋	Professor	3 yrs
He Bowei	何博伟	Student	2 yrs [R]
He Jian	何健	Worker	? yrs
He Jianming	何俭明	Worker	4 yrs
He Nan	何南	Cadre	X [R]
He Zhaohui	何翻辉	Worker	4 yrs
Hou Liang'an	侯亮安	Intellectual	? yrs
Hu Hao	胡浩	Student	X [R]
Hu Junda	胡俊达	Teacher	3 yrs [*]
Hu Min	胡敏	Worker	15 yrs
Hu Nianyou	胡年有	Worker	Life
Wu Xinghua	吴兴华	Journalist	X [R]

164

Hu Xuedong	胡学栋	Student	X [R]
Huang Fan	黄 凡	Worker	7-15 yrs
Huang Haizhou	黄海舟	Journalist [?]	? yrs
Huang Lixin	黄立新	Worker	7-15 yrs
Huang Yaru	黄雅如	Professor	5 yrs
Huang Zheng	黄 峥	Cadre	X [R]
Huang Zhenghua	黄正华	Cadre	6 yrs
Jiang Congzheng	蒋从政	Worker	8 yrs
Jiang Fengshan	蒋风山	Teacher	3 yrs [*]
Jiang Zhiqiang	蒋志强	Worker	13 yrs
Lei Shaojun	雷少军	Professor	X [R]
Li Dianyuan	李典元	Student	3 yrs
Li Jian	李 枧	Worker	3 yrs
Li Jie	李 杰	Worker	X [R]
Li Maoqiu	李茂秋	Engineer	Died in prison
Li Shaojun	李少军	Student	? yrs
Li Wangyang	李旺阳	Worker	13 yrs
Li Weihong	李卫红	Worker	Death w/r
Li Xiaodong	李小东	Worker	13 yrs
Li Xiaoping	李小平	Worker	6 yrs
Li Xin	李 新	Worker	3 yrs
Li Yuhua	李玉华	Student	2 yrs [*]
Li Zimin	李子民	Businessman	15 yrs
Liang Chao	梁 超	Worker	3 yrs
Liang Jianguo	梁建国	Worker	6 yrs
Liang Wang	梁 王	Worker	2 yrs [*] [R]
Liao Zhengxiong	廖正雄	Businessman	3 yrs
Liao Zhijun	廖志军	Worker	18 yrs
Liu Chengwu	刘成武	Peasant	4 yrs
Liu Chunan	刘楚南	Teacher	15 yrs
Liu Fuyuan	刘福元	Businessman	? yrs
Liu Hui	刘 晖	Unemployed	5 yrs
Liu Jian	刘 健	Worker	Life
Liu Jian'an	刘建安	Teacher	18 yrs
Liu Jianhua	刘建华	Student	X [R]
Liu Jianwei	刘建伟	Worker	3 yrs

Liu Jiye	刘继业	Worker	5 yrs
Liu Mianli	刘面立	Teacher	X [R]
Liu Wei	刘 伟	Worker	2 yrs [*] [R]
Liu Weiguo	刘伟国	Worker	7 yrs
Liu Weihong	刘卫红	Worker	4 yrs
Liu Xin	刘 新	High-school student	15 yrs
Liu Xingqi	柳星期	Worker	X [R]
Liu Yi	柳 毅	Worker	7 yrs
Liu Zhihua	刘志华	Worker	Life
Long Jianhua	龙建华	Student	X [R]
Long Xianping	龙献萍	Teacher (F)	2-3 yrs [R]
Long Xiaohu	龙小虎	Cadre	2 yrs [*]
Lu Decheng	鲁德成	Worker	16 yrs
Lu Shengqun	卢胜群	Salesperson	X [R]
Lu Zhaixing	卢摘星	Worker	3 yrs
Lü Zijing	吕自晶	Cadre	13 yrs
Luo Ziren	罗子任	Worker	7 yrs
Ma Heping	马和平	Unemployed	3 yrs [*]
Manager Zhang	张厂长	Manager	X [R]
Mao Genhong	毛跟红	Student	3 yrs
Mao Genwei	毛跟卫	Worker	X [R]
Mao Yongke	毛永科	Teacher (F)	4 yrs [R]
Mao Yuejin	毛岳津	Worker	15 yrs
Mei Shi	梅 实	Editor	4 yrs
Min Hexun	闵和迅	Teacher	3 yrs
Mo Lihua	莫莉花	Teacher (F)	3 yrs [R]
Pan Mingdong	潘明栋	Businessman	2 yrs [*] [R]
Pan Qiubao	潘秋宝	Worker	7-15 yrs
Peng Aiguo	彭爱国	Worker	6 yrs
Peng Liangkun	彭良坤	Worker	3 yrs [*]
Peng Shi	彭 实	Worker	Life
Peng Yuzhang	彭玉璋	Professor	X [R]
Qian Lizhu	千里柱[?]	Peasant	3 yrs [*]
Qin Dong	綦 冬	Journalist	4 yrs
Qin Hubao	綦护保	Cadre	10 yrs
Qing X	卿 某	Teacher	2 yrs [*] [R]

Tan Li	潭 丽	Student (F)	1 yr [R]
Tan Liliang	谭力量	Teacher	2 yrs [R]
Tang Boqiao	唐柏桥	Student	3 yrs [R]
Tang Changye	唐长业	Worker	3 yrs
Tang Hua	唐 华	Editor	X [R]
Tang Yixin	汤一心	Worker	? yrs
Tang Zhibin	唐致彬	Journalist	X [R]
Tao Sen	陶 森	Worker	4-5 yrs
Teacher Liu	刘老师	Teacher	7 yrs
Teacher Mi	米老师	Teacher	3 yrs
Teacher X	某老师	Teacher	12 yrs
Wan Yuewang	万岳望	Worker	7-15 yrs
Wang Changhong	王长宏	Worker	5 yrs
Wang Changhuai	王长淮	Worker	3 yrs
Wang Hong	王 虹	Worker	? yrs
Wang Jisheng	王吉生	Student	1 yr [R]
Wang Luxiang	王鲁湘	TV producer	? yrs
Wang Rusheng	王如生	Worker	? yrs
Wang Yongfa	王勇法	Teacher	3 yrs [*] [R]
Wang Zhaobo	王兆波	Worker	7-15 yrs
Wei Nan	魏 楠	Student	X [R]
Wen Quanfu	文全福	Manager	? yrs
Wu Changgui	巫长贵	Worker	3 yrs [*]
Wu Fangli	吴芳丽	Student	X [R]
Wu Hepeng	吴鹤鹏	Worker	Death w/r
Wu Jianwei	伍建伟	Worker	14 yrs
Wu Tongfan	吴同凡	Worker	? yrs
Wu Wei	吴 伟	Worker	2-3 yrs [*]
Wu Weiguo	吴卫国	Cadre	5 yrs
Wu Yun	武 云	Student	? yrs
Xia Changchun	夏长春	Worker	15 yrs
Xia Kuanqun	夏宽群	Cadre	3 yrs [*]
Xiao Feng	肖 峰	Manager	X [R]
Xiao Huidu	肖会渡	Teacher	2 yrs [*] [R]
Xiao Ming	肖 明	Professor	2 yrs [R]
Xiao Shenhe	肖申和	Peasant	3 yrs [*]

167

Xie Changfa	谢长发	Cadre	2 yrs [*] [R]
Xie Yang	谢阳	Cadre	3 yrs
Xiong Gang	熊刚	Student	? yrs
Xiong JianJun	熊建军	Worker	2-3 yrs [*]
Xiong Xiangwen	熊湘文	Worker	2.5 yrs [*] [R]
Xiong Xiaohua	熊晓华	Technician	13 yrs
Xu Yue	徐岳	Worker	? yrs
Yan Fangbo	严方波	Student	2 yrs [*] [R]
Yan Xuewu	言学武	Worker	5 yrs
Yang Chang	杨昌	Worker	X [R]
Yang Liu	杨柳	Peasant	4 yrs
Yang Rong	杨荣	Worker	? yrs
Yang Shaoyue	杨绍岳	Cadre	5 yrs
Yang Xiaogang	杨晓刚	Worker	3 yrs
Yang Xiong	杨雄	Worker	3 yrs
Yao Guisheng	姚桂生	Worker	15 yrs
Yao Wei	姚为	Student	X [R]
Yi Gai	易改	Student	X [R]
Yi Yuxin	易于新	Cadre	7 yrs
Yin Zhenggao	殷正高	Official	Sacked
Yu Chaohui	虞朝晖	Student	X [R]
Yu Dongyue	俞东岳	Editor	20 yrs
Yu ZhiJian	余志坚	Teacher	Life
Yuan Shuzhu	袁树柱	Worker	7-15 yrs
Yue Weipeng	岳维鹏	Student	X [R]
Zeng Chaohui	曾朝晖	Student	3 yrs
Zeng Ming	曾明	Professor	8.5 yrs [R]
Zhang Guohan	张国汉	Unemployed	2 yrs [*] [R]
Zhang Jie	张捷	Scientist	5 yrs
Zhang Jingsheng	张京生	Worker	13 yrs
Zhang Jizhong	张继忠	Journalist	3 yrs
Zhang Lixin	张立新	Student	X [R]
Zhang Ronghe	张荣和	Student	2 yrs [*] [R]
Zhang Song	张硕	Worker	5 yrs
Zhang XiaoJun	张晓军	Professor	2 yrs [R]
Zhang Xiaoyan	张小燕	Student (F)	X [R]

168

Zhang Xiong	张 雄	Worker	5 yrs
Zhang Xudong	张旭东	Worker	4 yrs
Zhang Fei long	张飞龙	Worker	6 yrs
Zhao Muyu	赵牧羽	Teacher	2 yrs [*] [R]
Zhao Weiguo	赵卫国	Businessman	4 yrs
Zheng Jinhe	郑进和	Teacher	2 yrs [*] [R]
Zheng Yaping	郑亚平	Student	? yrs
Zheng Yuhua	郑玉华	Teacher	X yrs
Zhong Donglin	钟冬林	[?]	[?]
Zhong Hua	钟 华	Student	3 yrs
Zhong Minghui	钟明辉	Teacher	3 yrs [*]
Zhou Liwu	周礼武	Teacher	2 yrs [R]
Zhou Min	周 敏	Worker	6 yrs
Zhou Peiqi	周沛旗	Technician	? yrs
Zhou Shuilong	周水龙	Worker	2 yrs [*] [R]
Zhou Wenjie	周文杰	Worker	4 yrs
Zhou Yong	周 勇	Worker	X [R]
Zhou Zhirong	周志荣	Teacher	5 yrs
Zhu Fangming	朱芳鸣	Worker	Life
Zhu Zhengying	朱正英	Worker	Life
Gao Shuxiang	高树祥	Businessman	X
Li Lin	李 林	Worker	5.5 mths. [R]
Li Zhi	李 智	Musician	5.5 mths. [R]
Tang Zhijian	汤之健	Worker	X

169

APPENDIX III

Lists of Key Members of the Hunan SAF and Hunan WAF

A. Hunan Students' Autonomous Federation

Name	Institution	Position in SAF	Current status
Chen Kehao	Hunan University	Vice General Director of Sit-Ins	Expelled from university
Chen Le (Liu Zhongtao)	Hunan Normal University	Special assistant to chairman	Detained several months; now released
Fan Zhong	Central-South Industrial University	Co-chairman; General Director of Sit-Ins	Detained 1½ years; now released
Hao Mingzhao	Central-South Industrial University	Standing Committee member	Arrested in 1990; current status unknown
He Bowei	Hunan Normal University	Head of school Dare-to-Die Squad	Sentenced to 2 years
Hu Hao	Hunan Medical University	Standing Committee member	Detained several months; now released

170

Li Shaojun	Hunan Normal University	Head of Finance Department	Detained 3 times; still in detention
Li Wei	Hunan University	Vice Chairman of school Autonomous Student Union (ASU)	Punished administratively by university
Li Zheng	Hunan College of Finance and Economics	Standing Committee member	Expelled from university
Liu Chaohui	Hunan Normal University	Representative of school ASU	Punished administratively by university
Liu Jianhua	Hunan University of Agriculture	Chairman of school ASU	Detained for several months; now released
Liu Wei	Changsha Railway College	Standing Committee member	In France
Long Jianhua	Hunan Normal University	Standing Committee member	Detained twice for a total of 7 months
Lu Siqing	Central-South Industrial University	Standing Committee member	Surrendered; expelled from university
Shen Yong	Hunan University	Representative of school ASU	Punished administratively by university
Shui Li	Hunan University	Standing Committee member	Punished administratively by university

Tang Bing	Hunan College of Finance and Economics	Head of school picket squad	Sentenced to unknown term
Tang Boqiao	Hunan Normal University	Chairman	Sentenced to 3 years, then paroled; escaped and now in U.S.
Wei Nan	Hunan University	Vice Chairman of school ASU	Detained twice for a total of several months; released
Xia Siqing	Hunan Normal University	Representative of school ASU	Punished administratively by university
Yi Gai	Hunan Normal University	Head of Liaison Department	Detained; current status unknown
Yu Chaohui	Hunan Medical University	Special assistant	Detained several months; released
Yuan Ningwu	Central-South Industrial University	Head of Propaganda Department	Punished administratively by university
Yue Weipeng	Hunan Hydraulic Normal University	Standing Committee member	Detained 5 months; now released
Zhang Guangsheng	Central-South Industrial University	Head of Planning Department	Punished administratively by university
Zheng Yan	Hunan Normal University	Representative of school ASU	Punished administratively by university

Zhong Hua	Hunan University	Head of school picket squad	Sentenced to 3 years
Zhu Jianwen	Hunan Normal University	Standing Committee member	Punished administratively by university

B. Workers Autonomous Federations

Name	Work Unit	Role in WAF	Current status
Changsha WAF:			
Cai Jinxuan	Changsha Textile Mill	Standing Committee member	Held for eight months; now released
Chen Bing	Student, Hunan College of Finance and Economics	Activist	Still in detention; not known if tried
Chen Shuai	Changsha No.1 Xinhua Factory	Spokesman	Sentenced to 2 years; now released
Chen XX	Resident of Lian County, Guangdong Province [?]	Assisted escape network	Sentenced to death and executed
He Zhaohui	Changsha Railway Passenger Transport Section	Vice Chairman	Sentenced to 4 years
Hu Nianyou	Resident of Lian County, Guangdong Province [?]	Assisted escape network	Sentenced to life imprisonment
Li Jian	Dongyuan Engine Parts Factory	General director	Sentenced to unknown term
Li Jie	Dept. 416, Ministry of Aeronautics	Standing Committee member	Held for one year, now released

Li Xin	Resigned from original unit	Vice Head of Picket Squad	Sentenced to 3 years
Liu Jianwei	Passenger Vehicle Section, Changsha Railway Bureau	Activist	Sentenced to 3 years' labor re-education
Liu Wei	A Changsha factory	Picket	2 years' labor re-education; now released
Liu Xingqi	Changsha Light Bulb Factory	Standing Committee member	Held for six months, then released
Liu Yi	Changsha Engine Factory	Head of Finance Department	Sentenced to unknown term
Lu Zhaixing	Changsha Embroidery Factory	Standing Committee member	Sentenced to 3 years
Pan Mingdong	Private businessman (restaurant owner)	Standing Committee member	Sentenced to 2 years of re-education through labor
Peng Yuzhang	Hunan University teacher	Advisor	Sent to mental hospital
Tang Yixin	Hunan Electrical Battery Plant	Activist	Not yet sentenced
Wang Changhuai	Changsha Automobile Factory	Standing Committee member	Sentenced to 3 years
Wang Hong	Hunan Electrical Battery Plant	Activist	Not yet sentenced

Wu Tongfan	Resigned from original unit	Advisor	Sentenced to unknown term
Yang Rong	Hunan Electrical Battery Plant	Activist	Not yet sentenced
Yao Guisheng	Hunan Woolen Mill (detached from unit at no salary)	Head of Picket Squad	Sentenced to 15 years
Zhang Jingsheng	Changsha Shaoguang Machinery Factory	Standing Committee member	Sentenced to 13 years
Zhang Xiong	Hunan Woolen Mill	Head of Special Picket Squad	Sentenced to 5 years
Zhang Xudong	Changsha Hongqiang Electrical Machine Factory	Vice Chairman	Sentenced to 4 years
Zheng Yuhua	Detached from unit at no salary	Advisor	Still in detention; not yet sentenced
Zhou Min	Changsha Non-Ferrous Metals Design Academy	Vice Chairman	Sentenced to 6 years
Zhou Shuilong	Changsha North Station, Changsha Railway Bureau	Vice Head of Picket Squad	2 years' labor-re-education; now released
Zhou Yong	Changsha No.2 Fan Factory	Chairman	Released

Shaoyang WAF:

Li Wangyang	Shaoyang factory	Chairman, Shaoyang WAF	Sentenced to 13 years
Li Xiaodong	Zhongnan Pharmaceutical Plant, Shaoyang City	Activist	Sentenced to 13 years
Li Xiaoping	Shaoyang factory	Vice Head of Picket Squad	Sentenced to 6 years

Xiangtan WAF:

| Wu Changgui | Xiangtan factory | Standing Committee member | Sentenced to 3 years' labor re-education |

Hengyang WAF:

Ding Longhua	Hengyang factory	Standing Committee member	Sentenced to 6 years
Li Lin	Hengyang steel worker	Activist	Escaped, then returned to China and was arrested; freed July 1991, lives in USA
Zhu Fangming	Hengyang Flour Factory	Vice Chairman	Sentenced to life imprisonment

Yueyang WAF:

NB: Nine members of the Yueyang WAF are known to have been arrested and heavily sentenced, but none of the factory affiliations or WAF positions of the nine are known. Their names and prison terms (most of which are only approximately known) are as follows:

Guo Yunqiao:	death with reprieve	**Hu Min**:	15 years
Huang Fan:	7-15 years	**Huang Lixin**:	7-15 years
Mao Yuejin:	15 years	**Pan Qiubao**:	7-15 years
Wan Yuewang:	7-15 years	**Wang Zhaobo**:	7-15 years
Yuan Shuzhu:	7-15 years		

APPENDIX IV

Tang Boqiao: From Student Leader to "Counterrevolutionary"[37]

Flight from Changsha

On June 4, 1989, the sound of gunfire on Tiananmen Square shattered the nation's illusions. As the terrifying crackdown unfolded, the students fled in fear and trepidation in all directions. After co-hosting the "Oath-Taking Rally in Memory of the Martyrs in Beijing" in Changsha,[38] I myself escaped to Guangdong Province on June 14 and went into hiding in Guangzhou, Xinhui, Foshan, and Jiangmen. Thanks to the generous help and protection I received from many different people, I remained safe for many days.

As the head of Hunan's student pro-democracy movement, however, I felt I could not put my own safety first and so gave up any thoughts of escaping abroad. On July 4, I decided to "enter the jaws of the tiger" and go back to Hunan in order to distribute among other pro-democracy fugitives some of the donations that I had received from people overseas to help me escape. The remainder I would keep behind as a reserve fund for the future democratic movement.

I discovered, however, there was no way I could enter Changsha as copies of an arrest warrant for me had been posted up on the entrances and exits of all the railway stations in Hunan Province, and passengers getting on and off the trains all had to go through security

---

[37] An earlier version of this autobiographical account appeared in the Hong Kong monthly *Kaifang* in October 1991, pp. 60-65.

[38] Zhang Lixin, head of the Beijing Students Autonomous Federation delegation touring southern China, and I hosted this rally, which was held at Changsha railway station on June 8 with 140,000 people (including overseas media) in attendance.

checks. So I left the train at Hengyang, one stop before Changsha, and got on another train back to Guangzhou. During the journey (in an incident that was as suspense-filled as the movies), I just managed to evade detection by public security officers who came on to the train to carry out a search.

Upon arrival back in Guangzhou, I went to Xinhui that night and hid out in the home of a peasant family (relatives of a friend of mine), not leaving the house for several days. At about 11 p.m. on July 11, just as I was going upstairs to sleep, I suddenly heard knocks on the door and a middle-aged man came in and said something to my host in a loud, gutteral voice before quickly leaving. Running up the stairs, my host told me in poor Mandarin: "Pack your stuff and leave here with me now. That village cadre just told me that the public security men are here to get you." My heart missed a beat and I had a premonition that I would not be able to get away this time. I hardly remember anything of our departure from the village apart from the ghostly howls and barking of dogs. That night, the peasant, whom I will never forget for the rest of my life, and I trudged along in the wilds, breathless with anxiety, for nearly 40 kilometers.

The trap closes

The next day, we took refuge at someone's home in Jiangmen City. The nerve-wracking escape of the previous night had exhausted me and I fell into a deep sleep right there in the sitting room. In the early hours of July 13, I was suddenly awakened by the clatter of loud knocking on the front foor, and before I had time to react, a swarm of heavily armed public security personnel and officers of the People's Armed Police swarmed into the room like a pack of mad dogs. "This is Tang Boqiao," snapped one of them. I made a futile attempt to defend myself, asking "Why are you arresting me?", but the next thing I felt was a series of hard objects clamping down on my throat, and my whole body, upside down, being hoisted into the air. Fists and cudgels (probably electric batons) rained down on me, and I felt as if I was dying.

As they pushed me out of the house and I looked around me, I felt a sense of deep and tragic solemnity welling up within me. There before me stood a vast array of over 100 military police, all armed to the teeth, and a row of police cars glowing with a steely, cold light. The

180

police were all scurrying around as if in some rapid-deployment military exercise against an enemy army - and at that moment, I realized with great clarity my own value and the strength of democracy. We had made the butchers of the people frightened!

I was taken to the Jiangmen City No. 1 Jail in Guangdong Province, where, for the first few days, I came down with a high fever of 39.6°C. My internal organs had been badly injured in the beating and I could neither eat nor sleep for days and I passed a lot of blood in my stool. (I have still not fully recovered even today.) Because I was a "criminal awaiting trial," the cadres informed me that I was not entitled to any medical expenses and so no treatment could be given to me - not even medicine. I could do nothing but clench my teeth and try to get through the suffering on my own. My fellow inmates were outraged at this injustice.

A few days later, a four-member security team set up specially by the Hunan and Changsha public security departments came to Jiangmen and took me back to Changsha. En route, I was kept in the Guangdong Provincial No. 1 Jail in Guangzhou City for a week, and again I was given no medical treatment.

On the train journey back to Changsha, two incidents impressed me in particular. One was that the security forces lied to the train crew, telling them that we were all cadres from the Changsha municipal Party committee. We were put in the train's special soft-berth compartment, a privilege normally enjoyed only by cadres at or above the level of provincial bureau chief. My police escorts warned me not to greet any acquaintances on the way and to report to them if I happened to see any.

The second such incident was that upon our arrival at Changsha Station, a whole crowd of pot-bellied government VIPs were there "cordially awaiting" us. No one was allowed to watch us or take pictures, and some Hong Kong businessmen from the same train who tried to do so were roughly pushed aside. A Toyota Corolla Supersaloon raced up to the platform, and in a matter of minutes, I was bundled into the car and driven out of the station through an underground passageway direct to the Changsha City No. 1 Jail.

It was clear from these two incidents just how nervous the

security forces accompanying me felt about their own role, and how much fear they had toward the general public. I also got some insight into the overall efficiency of their repressive operations. All the high-ranking government cadres turned out to watch me being sent into custody, as if to make the point that I really was some kind of "arch criminal".

The interrogations

Once inside the jail, I found that almost all the prisoners there already knew my name and were familiar with the details of my case. Apparently, the jail commandant had earlier briefed them on my background and instructed them to actively inform the jail authorities of any "counterrevolutionary statements" I might make and to keep a close eye on my behavior so as to prevent me from attempting to escape or commit suicide. While I knew that any such happenings would have created headaches for the authorities, I had never expected that the government would be quite so worried about us "turmoil elements."

The came the endless interrogation sessions. According to law, interrogations are meant to be carried out humanely. But in rule-by-man China, where - especially since the June 4 incident - the law counts for little, my experience was anything but humane.

I was interrogated by three cadres of section-chief level from the pre-trial investigation division of the Changsha City public security bureau. All three were Party officials who had made it through the Cultural Revolution and had picked up some special tricks and techniques for dealing with political prisoners. After establishing that I was a "diehard element" who would not bow to simple coercion, they then started using some of their "brilliant tricks" on me instead.

The first thing they tried was the so-called "interrogation by shifts" technique, in which one is kept under constant questioning for many hours per day. This grueling ordeal lasted from morning till night and continued for at least four months. Sometimes, the interrogations lasted as long 20 hours a day. The aim was to break down my resistance and get me so exhausted that I would finally answer whatever questions they put to me. At one stage, for example, they tried to make me admit that I had contacted Wang Dan, the Beijing student leader, by cipher telegram. The charge was based on two things: that I had been in Beijing during the mass student hunger strike there; and someone had informed against me. The interrogators grilled me on this matter for over ten hours a day for more than 20 days, but got nothing from me.

They even grilled me on my alleged relationships with a whole bunch of people of whom I had absolutely no knowledge, including senior Party and government officials, certain foreigners and also some leading members of the Hong Kong Alliance in Support of the Patriotic Democratic Movement in China. They also questioned me about my "contacts" with Liang Heng, a former student from my own college who had left China for the United States 10 years earlier and whom I had never even met. They made up endless ludicrous stories about my supposed nefarious activities with all these people. During the four months of my interrogation, five volumes of case records were compiled, each of over 400 pages and full of sheer rubbish.

The second technique they employed was to plant a spy in my cell - something I was entirely unprepared for. The person assigned to this task was a serious and well-educated looking man in his 40s, who introduced himself to me as being a former adviser to the Changsha City Worker's Autonomous Federation. Within a few days of joining our cell, he managed to insinuate himself into my trust and confidence, and I revealed to him many of my secret thoughts and also some confidential information about the movement, including details of the large sum of money that I'd been given to help me escape. As I later discovered, all this information went straight into the hands of the public security authorities, and once they had got what they needed the man was conveniently "released." Some time afterwards, he reappeared in another cell where Chen Yi, the main suspect in Changsha's biggest murder case of 1989, was being held. The stooge quickly became Chen's "good friend," and one month later the case was cracked and Chen was tried and executed.

Gang beatings

They also tried simple thug tactics to extort a confession from me. Their main method was to instigate the other prisoners in my cell to gang up on me, and since I would not easily submit to this I often ended up being attacked by all of them at once. Although several of my cellmates supported me, they never dared to stand up and protect me, for

183

fear of offending the cadres. On one occasion, in which seven or eight of the toughest inmates - two of whom were murderers famed throughout Changsha - all suddenly turned on me, I was so badly beaten up that I could scarcely move for a whole week. Even to this day, I shudder to recall the incident. When I complained to the authorities about the beatings, their response was merely to transfer me to an adjoining cell and instruct the prisoners there to continue my "treatment." In order not to go against my conscience, I endured all the torture without confessing anything. I fell ill again several times, and they continued to refuse me medical help on the grounds that I had not yet repented my crimes.

On December 29, 1989, I was formally placed under arrest. (Prior to then I had been held as a mere "detainee" and the process of interrogation had gone by the fine-sounding name of "performing one's duty as a citizen.") The charges levelled against me were "counter-revolutionary propaganda and incitement" and "treason and defection to the enemy" - the grounds for the latter charge being that I had had contact with a few college students from Hong Kong and had at one point considered "fleeing the country." Upon hearing the word "treason," I felt overwhelmed with anger and shouted, "Get out, you bunch of gangsters and crooks! You won't get away with this!" Surprisingly enough, they stayed quite calm and simply noted down what I had said - as evidence of my "bad attitude" - and then left. That night, however, war broke out in my cell, as the other inmates suddenly fell upon me all at once. The blows that rained down on my body, however, elicited only one response from me: "Cowardly beasts!"

For the next six months, no one paid much attention to me, and my life revolved around the daily ritual of making match-boxes (all the prisoners had to do this), eating and sleeping. There were usually around 20 other prisoners in my cell, although the number rose to more than 30 during the 1990 "anti-crime campaign." Since the cell was about 18 square meters in area, this meant less than one square meter per person at the best of times. At night, one had to lie on one's side on the communal sleeping platform, jammed up against the other prisoners, so everybody became infected with skin diseases. The monthly subsistence allowance from the government was only 24 *yuan* per prisoner, and each meal consisted of some sour-pickle soup with a little winter melon, pumpkin, and seaweed thrown in. The reward for a full day's work was either two cigarettes, or - if one failed to complete the day's quota (which was often the case since the quotas were set so high) - a dose of the electric baton.

Because I was not "obedient" and was thought to be "up to instigation" in prison, they kept transferring me to different cells in the hope each time that the new "cell boss" would be able to subdue me and deter me from "speaking wild thoughts." The result was that I suffered more than I might otherwise have done, but many more people got to know the true face of the government.

My "public" trial

Finally, after I'd spent more than a year in detention (far longer than the legally permissable limit), my case was brought to trial. On that day - July 17, 1990 - I was pronounced to be a sinner against the people and a "counterrevolutionary" (fortunately, the charge of "traitor to the motherland" had been dropped) and was sentenced to three year's imprisonment.

What happened then is still fresh in my memory. As I was escorted into the Changsha Intermediate Courthouse, I saw three judges, two procurators, and a lawyer sitting there primly on the rostrum. My own appointed lawyer had failed to turn up, but when I raised a protest about this it was ignored. (The hearing, according to the rules of due process, should have been invalidated on this ground alone.) The audience consisted only of my two sisters (one of whom worked in the public security bureau) and some of their colleagues. Even they had only learned of the trial through "internal" sources and had had to rush to the courthouse at the last minute. None of my fellow students from Hunan Normal University who had promised to come and testify on my behalf were allowed to attend the hearing.

Once the judges and procurators had finished their routine questions and answers, they asked me whether I had anything to say. I asked them why they had not let my fellow students come as visitors and witnesses. They looked puzzled and replied, "Let your campus-mates come? Why, that would never do!" After a brief adjournment, the chief judge announced the sentence: three years in prison, with two years' subsequent deprivation of political rights. The entire hearing had taken less than two hours.

Afterwards, a kind-hearted cadre quietly told me that the hearing was just a facade, since my guilt and the length of my sentence had been pre-determined by the higher-level authorities a full month before. This was why the court had refused to admit any of my fellow-students to the trial; moreover, they had deliberately postponed the hearing until after the start of the college summer vacation. Before leaving, the cadre also told me, "Don't expect too much or you'll only suffer more." I vowed silently to my campus mates, "See you all in 1992!"

Life under the "proletarian dictatorship"

From then on I was formally a convict, no different from countless murderers, robbers, rapists and thieves. (The Chinese government does not admit that it holds any political prisoners.) The authorities then removed their hypocritical mask and began to exercise "proletarian dictatorship" over me. For the first two months, I was held in the Changsha No. 2 Jail and given intensive "ideological education for criminals." In early November, 1990, I was shuttled between several other jails and then sent to Longxi Prison to undergo labor-reform. Because the winter there brings a piercing cold wind, the local cadres call this prison "Siberia" (Xiboliya). Publicly, it is known as the "Shaoyang Marble Factory," since it specializes in the production of marble goods, including for export.

Upon arrival, I was placed in a "prison induction team" to learn the regulations and undergo preliminary disciplining. Because I was the last of the "1989 counterrevolutionary criminals" to be sent to Longxi, however, I was effectively exempted from the special "political study classes" that all the others had had to go through. (This was the only good thing that had happened to me since my initial detention over a year before.)

There were two things that I found particularly intolerable about prison life. One was that we were forced each day to sing three songs in chorus: "Without the Communist Party, There Would be No New China", Socialism is Good" and "Learn from the Good Example of Lei Fang". The warden would then shout out three questions, to which we had to shout out the answers in unison:

Q: "Who are you?"   A: "Criminals!"

186

Q: "Where are you?"   A: "In prison!"
Q: "Why are you here?" A: "To reform ourselves through labor!"

At the beginning I tried to act dumb, but I soon found out it wasn't worth trying to resist them on this. From then on, I used to sing the songs as loudly as I could, and I answered all the questions with a yell. Each time I would clench my teeth in hatred.

The second ordeal was the daily parade drill, or "military training" as they called it. This was purely and simply an opportunity for the wardens to play around with us and humiliate us. Because I often used to show resistance, I ended up being put into fetters and handcuffs and being placed in solitary confinement. (Somehow, I found that such punishment only helped me to maintain my mental equilibrium better.)

At one point, I was assigned to be a teacher in the prison's education section - probably the best "job" that could be hoped for. But before I could give my first class, I was thrown into the "strict regime" unit - a prison-within-the-prison. The reason for this was that I had apparently participated in organizing a "counterrevolutionary rally." (Actually, it had been little more than a chat between a group of 17 of the political prisoners.) Seven of us were accused of having instigated and led the "rally" and were consigned to the strict regime unit as punishment. The incident caused quite a stir among the other prisoners and received close attention from the higher-level authorities.

For the first three days of this punishment, we had to sit motionless for an average of 10 hours per day performing so-called "introspection." This is actually one of the most oppressive forms of ill-treatment imaginable. One is made to sit on a tiny stool less than 20 cm in height on a raised platform of about 90 square cm, with back held bolt-upright, both feet flat on the floor and hands placed neatly on one's lap. Throughout, one has to look directly at the wall just ahead, and if for any reason such as a momentary lapse of attention one happens to slouch forward slightly or bend one's head, one will be hit by the guard with an iron rod or handcuffed to the door. At night, one is locked up alone in a small room less than two square meters in area, in which the only bed is a cement slab of about 30 cm in width.

The time when we were given this punishment was the coldest

187

part of winter, and we were unable to get any sleep at all. After three days, we could stand it no more and decided to go on a collective hunger strike as a means of protest. On the seventh day, miraculously enough, we were all "rehabilitated" by the authorities and sent back to the normal cells. (I still have a letter I wrote to the prison governor during the hunger strike - luckily for me, I never actually sent it.)

Released on parole

To my astonishment, almost the first thing that greeted me after I was released from the strict regime unit was an official "notice of parole." This was an unprecedented event in Longxi Prison history, and I was at a complete loss as to what the reason for it might have been. Only later did I discover that the prison authorities had had little choice but to issue the release order, since an internal document had just been issued by the central authorities requiring the local judicial authorities to review cases of certain relatively prominent pro-democracy figures who had been sentenced too heavily.[39] This clearly was largely due to the strong international and domestic pressure then being put on the Chinese government over the human rights issue. Another factor in my case was that certain enlightened figures in the higher levels of the Hunan provincial government apparently disagreed with the hardliners' policy and had intervened on my behalf.

During the 18 months I was behind bars, I was imprisoned in altogether 16 cells of seven jails and prisons in five different places. I was interrogated by agents of at least 10 different public security or screening organs, including security personnel from Beijing, Shanghai, Wuhan, Chongqing, Guangzhou, Yueyang, Hengyang, Changsha, Jiangmen and

---

[39] The main reason for this appears to have been the relatively lenient sentence of four years' imprisonment handed down to Beijing student leader Wang Dan in January 1991. While this sentence was intended to appease international pressure over the human rights violations, it also left the problem of glaring discrepancies between the Wang Dan sentence and the much higher sentences given to many other leading pro-democracy figures in other parts of the country, particularly workers. There is no evidence to suggest that this readjustment policy lasted for more than a few weeks, however, and the only beneficiaries of it seem to have been a few student leaders, including myself.

Xinhui. According to information disclosed to me by an internal source, my case cost the goverment more than 140,000 *yuan*. The Ministry of State Security alone sent its personnel to Hong Kong for investigation purposes at least twice. Dozens of people were involved as suspects in my case, including my relatives, my father's colleagues, the cadres of the provincial public security department, a few leaders of my university and also people from the various households that had given shelter to me while I was on the run. When I reflect on this, all sorts of emotions well up in my mind.

Just prior to my release, I was summoned before the prison authorities and told, "Remember, you are only on parole, and you can be sent back here at any time if your performance is poor!" In addition, they said, I was on no account to leave my hometown, have any contact with other "turmoil elements" or make any inflammatory remarks (so-called "counterrevolutionary instigation") when talking to people. I had been looking forward to having a few drinks together with two other released "counterrevolutionaries" after getting out. Now, I had to drop this plan.

The news of my father's death

One rainy day just before Chinese New Year's Eve, in February 1991, I appeared before my family again at last, shaven-headed and drenched from head to foot. How they both cried and smiled at me, with a mixture of sorrow and happiness! My mother, however, looked ten years older than before, and my sisters also showed signs of deep sadness. Then came the news: I had lost my beloved father! The day after he received his copy of the arrest warrant for me, with its twin charges of "counterrevolution" and "treason", he had been knocked down and killed in a traffic accident - the copy of the arrest warrant still in his pocket at the time. I was the only man left in my family, and I was devastated.

My father was only 54 years old when he died. He worked diligently for China in the field of education all his life. He underwent innumerable hardships and scored remarkable achievements. A man of strong integrity, he was much respected by the people in my town. But he left the world in despair. This was a story that could move Heaven itself to tears. I vowed then that I would record all the stories of suffering I had learned in prison, in everlasting memory of my dad.

On hearing the news of my release, all the neighbors came over. They took my hands and said tearfully: "You've suffered...", "You're back at long last...", "It's all right now..." and "Heaven is just..!" They then related to me many touching incidents that had occurred while I was away. For example, a former county magistrate had come to my home, with the help of a walking stick, soon after I was arrested and had said to my father, "Your son is an excellent student and always won the "three outstandings" award (*san hao*: academics, sports and ethics) for our locality. He must be feeling very sad now. You should comfort him and cook something nice for him whenever you can to keep up his health. You just tell him, "Your Uncle X says you are a good young man!" After the June 4 massacre, the people of my hometown heard a rumor that I had been killed in Tiananmen Square, so they held a memorial meeting for me. On the Festival of the Dead in 1990, moreover, some leading provincial cadres, who did not leave their names, rolled up in their sedan cars to pay their respects at my father's grave. All these touching stories gave me much comfort, and I was deeply grateful to my folks. They understood me.

A conflict between filial duty and loyalty to the cause

Once I realized that my own "parole" and the releases or reduced sentences of some other democratic activists, especially the students, had been a result of the people's silent resistance, my own convictions grew stronger. I quietly took an oath: I would share weal and woe with the nation throughout my life and dedicate all that I had to my motherland and the people who supported me.

Soon after the Spring Festival, I paid a brief visit to where my father's soul rested and then started on my journey. I left home and went to Changsha, where I immediately reestablished contacts with my former comrades and restarted pro-democracy activities, using the several hundred *yuan* that my mother had been saving up month after month through her own thrift and plain living.

My student status and urban residency rights had been cancelled by the government, and I could expect no help from them in finding a job. On several occasions, I tried to start up a business partnership with some private enterprises, only to encounter groundless interference and obstruction from the government. The authorities clearly intended to

190

keep me in a state of limbo, wretched and impotent, while all the time telling the people how "very lenient" they had been with us students!

After four months of extensive travel and liaison, some new prospects began to open up. During this time, I returned home only once. I visited my father's grave and stayed with my mother for only three days. I knew that she was still as anxious over me as she had been in 1989. She had only one wish: that I would stay with her, right there at home by her side. For more than a year when I was in prison, she had travelled hundreds of kilometers every month just to visit me - though she was never actually permitted to see me. One time, the bus she was on turned over and two of her ribs were broken, leaving her bedridden for over a month. What a parental heart! Seeing her face growing thinner day by day, I could only say this silently in my heart: "I'm sorry, my good mother. Your son cannot be loyal to his cause and filial to you at the same time." Wiping away my tears, I left home, with head bent low.

The government continued to regard me as a constant scourge and took a series of measures to monitor and threaten me. They knew wherever I went almost immediately and approached all those with whom I had contact, including my former girlfriend, warning them not to have anything to do with me as I was a "very dangerous person." Public security officials went to my home and told my mother that they were going to make me "repeat" what I had gone through before. I knew they had no evidence against me and that it was nothing more than a bluff. But on the second anniversary of the June 4 crackdown, when a series of wall posters appeared in Changsha and a small protest rally was staged, the authorities became convinced that I was the mastermind, and a secret order was issued for my re-arrest. (An internal source alerted me to this.)

I had no choice but to go into exile. It had been more than two years since the last time I had had to flee. After hiding out for a month in a friend's place in one of the cities, I realized I had very little time left before the net closed in on me. So I made my bid for freedom, and on July 28 I finally got out of the country. I was left with one lasting regret, however: that I had finally became worthy of the charge of "treason". Yes, I had betrayed that country held in the grip of the communist party dictatorship, and I deserved the name of "traitor to the country."

Two years earlier, my comrades abroad had strongly urged me

to flee the country. But I carried an unswerving sentiment for the land that had given birth to me and brought me up, and I did not have the heart to leave behind all those relatives, friends, and compatriots with whom I had a shared destiny. I did not see clearly, moreover, the true face of the government, and I believed in the idea of letting fate take its course. I became, as a result, a "criminal guilty of counterrevolution."

Today, however, I have a deeper appreciation of the peril facing China and of the sufferings undergone by its people, and I have a stronger love than ever for that profoundly nurturing land. I abandoned my country simply because I had no choice. As I look now at the colorful world on this side, I can only sigh at the striking contrast and try to strengthen my resolve.

APPENDIX V

In Mourning for the Perished of the Nation

[Oration delivered at the June 8, 1989 Mass Mourning Meeting in Changsha]

Was it the indignant, still-beckoning spirit of Qu Yuan from more than two thousand years ago that took you away? Was it the heroic spirits of seventy years ago that called to you? Was it the loving heart of your numberless predecessors before the Monument to the People's Heroes that moved you so? You have suddenly gone, suddenly gone. You have left behind only a river of fresh blood, you have left behind only a deep love, and a deep hate. You have gone. Spirits of Beijing, where do you rest? Oh where do you rest? The mountains and rivers weep, the sad wind whirls. Before the evil gun muzzles, before the ugly face of fascism, before my people in suffering, and before the calm, smiling face on your death mask, I can do no more than make this offering to your spirits with vibrant, leonine nerve.

You are gone! Today, two thousand years ago, Qu Yuan, his heart afire with loyal ardor, leapt into the pitiless Miluo River: "I submit to the crystal-clear depths - Oh Death, come now!" Today, two thousand years later, you, our loyal brothers and sisters, fell under the guns of the so-called "people's own soldiers," you fell under the tanks of "the most cherished ones."

Yes, you are gone! The tears in your eyes, the blood flowing now from your chests, all have become a river, a downpour. June 4: no Chinese of true heart will ever forget this day. June 4, June 4, 1989: every common man and woman who seeks freedom, democracy, and peace will forever remember. June 4: China's national day of everlasting

193

shame. China's eternal day of national disaster![40]

In Tiananmen Square, revered by all the people of China, three thousand lives were wiped out in a single night. In but a few short days, a myriad beating hearts were smashed into stillness. In those few days, the souls of all the people of China were ripped and torn into shreds, and the nerves of the people of the whole world were stretched and broken. Three thousand living, breathing, vibrant people who a few days before had flesh and blood and ideals and feelings were erased in a single night.

A myriad different lives, a myriad different stories, reduced in an instant to the [government's] single trite judgment: "suppressed thugs." But did they need tanks to crush them - those thugs? Did they need to engulf them in flames? Did they need to unleash dumdum bullets - banned worldwide - on the thugs? They called you thugs, and now your eyes cannot close in peaceful death. Your innocent, pained, and indignant eyes turn skyward and cry: "Oh Heaven! We are not thugs!"

You were the sons and daughters of loving parents, you were the students of proud teachers. You were brothers, sisters, friends, sometimes even enemies. But how many dreams you still had to dream! How many poems you still had to discover! You would have been fathers and mothers, you who still had so many new roads to travel down.

On that day, when you knelt before the Great Hall of the People, you became the sufferers who, wide awake, smashed their way out of the iron cell. You loved life; and so you knelt, seeking basic rights and honesty in the name of the nation and the state. How could you who had made so many poems accept the label of "chaos" for your acts? In past days you had been vibrant and active on your green campuses, painting in the broad brushstrokes of a life based upon ideals. Strolling among the flowers under the moon, you poured out all your most tender feelings. How beautiful it was!

---

[40] The original text says "June 3" here and elsewhere, since it was late that night that the killing began. In the period immediately after the massacre, it was symbolized in China by the date "June 3" and only later came to be known as the "June 4" massacre.

Then later, you cried out - with the voice of the whole people you cried out, and took to the streets with demonstrations, sit-ins, and hunger strikes. How could you who had dreamed so many dreams have imagined that unarmed and defenseless, struggling with only a loving heart and your own life for the right to a beautiful life, you would be so cruelly cut down and slaughtered by the fascist government? What was your crime? Oh what was your crime?

You have gone! The smile on your death mask is still before us. We bend our ears to listen, but we will never hear your voices again. We reach out to touch your face but can touch you no more. We call out "Brother," we call out "Sister," but you will never hear us again, Oh never again. We reach out to touch you, we stubbornly try to take your hand. But we cannot touch even a handful of your ashes.

You have gone, you youth have gone forever. You had time still to love, but you had no more time to live. So that those who lived on might live better, so that those who loved on might love better, you rose up from your place of kneeling, and embarked upon the road of no return. And then suddenly you fell, cut down from your proud place of standing. Although your heads were torn from your bodies, your souls could not be killed. China weeps now, mourning for its broken backbone. You are gone forever, and a generation of heroic outcries are lost to the nation.

The Goddess of Democracy has fallen. But you, who were cut down in your prime and yet shall live always in our hearts, you are the eternal Goddesses of Democracy. You shall always be in our dreams, in our memories. You shall live eternally in history. Fearless and proud, you died standing up, you died standing up. Look now: those who escaped with their lives from the bloody rain and the fetid wind have already stood forward. They are your brothers, fathers, teachers, friends -- in their own hearts, they have stood up.

Who has ever seen thugs with such thick glasses! Who has ever seen such a "People's Government" and a "People's Army," where the gun-wielders outnumber the pen-wielders. Those who knelt before have now, finally, stood up. No more do they weep, no more do they hope in vain, no more do they hesitate. No more do they worry only about themselves and their families. You will be proud of us! Your blood was not shed in

195

vain! Your tears did not flow in vain!

The salt of your blood adds a bitter strength to the life of the era. And the sun of life from your blood, the scarlet banner, now lights up the flames of love and hate. We, the living Descendants of the Yellow Emperor,[41] citizens for freedom and peace, have burst forth to exchange our warm blood for freedom, to wash away the dust with our warm tears, to make today's outcry remembered tomorrow, to show to the world the wounds of history! As long as the truth is in our hearts, we do not fear to shed our blood. We hereby vow: we shall never be deflected from our goal!

Hang Li Peng! Send Li, Deng [Xiaoping] and Yang [Shangkun] to the sacrificial altar!

Pray for the souls of Beijing, for the perished of the nation!

Rest in peace, Oh brave souls!

---

[41] A rhetorical term for the Chinese people.

APPENDIX VI

Hunan Daily on Arrests and Trials of Workers

Counterrevolutionary criminals
Zhang Jingsheng, Liu Jian'an and Wang Changhuai
are Sentenced to Prison Terms[42]

This paper learned that on December 8, the Intermediate People's Court of the City of Changsha called a special mass rally to pronounce judgment on and punish counterrevolutionary criminals. At that rally, the court publicly convicted three criminals who engaged in counterrevolutionary activities during the turmoil of last spring and summer. In accordance with the law, the court sentenced counterrevolutionary criminal Zhang Jingsheng to a fixed term of thirteen years' imprisonment, with three years' subsequent deprivation of political rights; it sentenced counterrevolutionary criminal Liu Jian'an to a fixed term of ten years' imprisonment, with two years' subsequent deprivation of political rights. Counterrevolutionary criminal Wang Changhuai was sentenced to a fixed term of three years' imprisonment, with one year's subsequent deprivation of political rights.

Zhang Jingsheng, pen-name Han Xing, male, 35, was formerly a casual worker of the Hunan Shaoguang Electrical Factory. He was sentenced to a fixed term of four years' imprisonment, with three years'

---

[42] "The City of Changsha publicly convicts criminals who engaged in counterrevolutionary activities during the turmoil," *Hunan Daily*, December [?], 1989. (Taken from undated press clipping.) Note that the article describes three cases, two of which - Zhang Jingsheng and Wang Changhuai - are related while the third, that of Liu Jian'an, bears no relation whatever to the other two. The paragraph on Liu, who is alleged to have been a spy, was even inserted between those on Zhang and Wang - for no other apparent reason than that the *Hunan Daily*, which had so little damning to write about Zhang and Wang, felt it needed to tar them "by association" with the spy case.

subsequent deprivation of political rights on charges of counterrevolutionary propaganda and incitement. He was released after serving his term. But he was unrepentant, and remained hostile to the people. On May 4 of this year, he made speeches to student demonstrators at Hunan University and the Hunan Martyrs' Park, clamoring for "democracy," "freedom" and a "multi-party system." He also complained and called for redress on behalf of the counterrevolutionary Wei Jingsheng. On May 21, he joined, on his own initiative, the illegal organization, the Workers Autonomous Federation. He incited the workers to go on strike and the students to boycott classes. What was especially abominable was that, after the counterrevolutionary rebellion broke out in Beijing, he wrote an extremely reactionary "Urgent Appeal," which was mimeographed by the Workers Autonomous Federation and hundreds of copies were distributed throughout the city. In that "appeal," he wildly pledged to fight the people's government in a bloody battle to the death. His counterrevolutionary bluster was extremely arrogant. As Zhang was a counterrevolutionary recidivist, he was sentenced severely according to law to a long prison term.

Liu Jian'an, male, 38, was formerly a teacher at Changsha's No. 25 Middle School. From May 1989 on, he secretly tuned in to broadcasts by enemy radio stations. He covertly planned to establish contacts with enemy secret services. Between July 2 and 14, he sent sixteen letters to Guomindang (Nationalist) secret services in Taiwan, Hong Kong and Japan, trying to establish a liaison. He used such aliases as Li Shiji, Li Ji and a dozen others, and mailed the letters from Changsha, Yiyang, Yueyang and Wuhan. In those letters, he described himself and his status to enemy secret services and applied to join them. He indicated his counterrevolutionary determination and vainly tried to establish secret organizations to conduct underground activities. He also wrote items for broadcast by the *Voice of Free China*, and organized the publication of reactionary manuscripts. He asked enemy secret services to send agents to get in touch with him, specifying the places and methods for rendezvous, and asked for assignment.

Wang Changhuai, alias Huang Feng, male, 25, was formerly a worker at the Changsha Automobile Engine Plant. On May 22 of this year, Wang joined the illegal Workers Autonomous Federation and became its chief of organization, standing committee member, and chief of propaganda successively. During that time, he was in charge of the federation's seal, banner, letters of recommendation and membership cards. He designed the organization chart for the Workers Autonomous Federation. When the counterrevolutionary rebellion broke out in Beijing, Wang became extraordinarily active, running around on sinister errands. He himself wrote a call to strike, mimeographed it and distributed, posted and broadcast it throughout the city. He also signed the "Urgent Appeal" written by Zhang Jingsheng, and mimeographed and distributed it all over the city. That appeal viciously attacked the party and government, fabricated rumors to mislead the people, and called on the people to get organized and go on strike. On June 15, 1989, awed by the power of government policy and the law, he went to the Public Security Bureau of his own accord and gave himself up. He was given lenient sentence according to law.

APPENDIX VII

Declaration of Hunan Autonomy[43]

Hunan Should Lead the Way and
Practice Patriotic Self-Government

Hunan is bounded on the north by water and hemmed in on three other sides by mountains. Hengshan, the Mountain of the South, sits astride the alluvial plain drained by the Xiang River, which flows right through the province. Like a "magic gourd," it collects all that is best in China.

As the sayings go, "Lake Dongting, measuring 800 *li* all around, is rich in fish and rice." "When the harvests are in from Hunan and Hubei, the whole country is well-fed." Hunan is known throughout the world for its rich resources.

Hunan controls the approaches to both the north and the south. It can respond to both the east and the west. It can attack and advance, or retreat and defend.

When we advance by cutting off supplies, Guangdong has to submit. When we move east down the Yangtze, we capture Shanghai, and Hubei, Jiangxi and Fujian will come to us. Divide our troops, we launch our northern expedition. Shandong and Shanxi will beat the drums and help us. Beijing and Tianjin will act from inside in coordination with our forces attacking from outside. We shall capture the bandit chieftain at one fell swoop. Then, we shall pacify the northwest, the southwest, the northeast, Tibet and Inner Mongolia, unifying the country with ourselves at the center.

---

[43] This document was drafted by a radical group in Hunan, comprised partly of PLA officers, and was printed up as a flyer and distributed around the province shortly after the crackdown began.

Retreat and we evacuate Changsha to lure the enemy in. We then break the dikes to drown the enemy. With small detachments in the mountains of Liuyang and Pingjiang in eastern Hunan, we will wage guerrilla warfare to tie the enemy down, and wait for our main force from the high mountains in western Hunan to come from the direction of Changde to surround the enemy. Then, our crack troops in Shaoyang and Hengyang will rush out, attacking the enemy from both the north and the south like bolting the door and beating the dog. The powerful invading enemy can only surrender or be annihilated.

The people of Hunan, being the offspring of centuries of intermarriage between northerners and southerners, are genetically advantaged and possess very high intelligence. In addition, the geographic environment gives the people of Hunan the advanced knowledge of the big cities as well as the toughness and determination of the mountain people. The legend of "outstanding personality from the land of wonders" and "only Hunan produces exceptional talent" is not just bragging.

Historical evidence abounds. The Mongols of the Yuan Dynasty ran rampant all over Eurasia. But when they advanced on Changsha, Hunan Province, "people heard the northerners sing: the walls of Tanzhou is iron-clad." The brutes of the Eight Banners of the Manchus could not have entered Changsha had they not bribed the traitors to hand over the city. The Japanese invaders were arrogant. But they had to enter and leave Changsha no less than seven times and lost 40,000 crack troops of the Guandong Army. And finally they surrendered in Hunan. Everyone knows what happened to the Taiping Heavenly Kingdom and the Communist Party.

Today, the reactionary dictatorial rulers face retribution for a life of crime. The people will triumph!

It is fitting that the banner of "democracy and rule of law" will first fly high over Hunan.

Preparatory Committee for Patriotic
Self-Governance by the People of Hunan

June 8, 1989

APPENDIX VIII

Court Verdicts and Re-Education Decisions

A. Case of Chen Zhixiang[44]

Criminal Verdict
of the Intermediate People's Court
of Guangzhou Municipality, Guangdong Province

Guangzhou/Court/Criminal No.262 (89)

Public Prosecutor:
Lan Jinping, Procurator acting on behalf of Guangzhou Municipal People's Procuratorate

Defendant:
Chen Zhixiang, male, 26, Han nationality, born in Nantong City, Jiangsu Province. Education: college graduate, former teacher at Guangzhou Maritime College. Residence: Room 205, 15 Pangui Street, New Port Road, Guangzhou. Taken into custody on July 4, 1989 and arrested on August 12, 1989. [The defendant is] currently in custody.

Defender:
Zheng Jinghao, Attorney, Guangzhou Municipal Legal Affairs Office.

Guangzhou People's Procuratorate brought an indictment in this

---

[44] Chen Zhixiang is currently reported to be held in Yuanjiang Prison, but Asia Watch cannot definitely confirm this. He may in fact be held in Guangdong Province, immediately to the south of Hunan. For further details, see p.113.

court against the defendant Chen Zhixiang who was charged with conducting counterrevolutionary propaganda and incitement. This court formed a collegial panel in accordance with law and on December 4, 1989 opened a court session and conducted a public hearing of the case. The public prosecutor appeared in court to support the prosecution. The defender appeared in court to defend the accused.

This court has, in the course of the public hearing, ascertained that the defendant, Chen Zhixiang, following the suppression of the counterrevolutionary rebellion in Beijing, carried with him paint and a brush on June 7, 1989 to the construction site of the former "Sails of the Pearl River" on Yanjiangzhong Road, Guangzhou and wrote on the wall there a reactionary slogan measuring more than 20 meters in length. It read: "Avenge the young people who died in Beijing. Hang the executioners Deng [Xiaoping], Yang [Shangkun] and Li [Peng] and execute the running-dog Chen[45] and all the other accomplices." Around three o'clock in the afternoon of the same day, the defendant Chen Zhixiang went to the east side of the Guiyuan Hotel on Huanshizhong Road, Guangzhou, and wrote on the wall a reactionary slogan also more than 20 meters long, which read: "Wipe out the Four Pests on behalf of the people. Hang Deng, Yang and Li, who butchered the common people, and execute the running-dog Chen and all the other accomplices."

The above-mentioned facts have been attested to by witnesses' testimony and written evidence; verified by criminal science and various technical devices; and admitted to by the defendant. The evidence is complete and sufficient to prove the case.

In the opinion of this court, the defendant Chen Zhixiang, harboring a counterrevolutionary motive, openly wrote large-scale reactionary slogans at public thoroughfares, maliciously attacking and slandering Party, government and military leaders and attempting to incite the people to overthrow the political power of the people's democratic dictatorship. His actions constituted the crime of conducting counterrevolutionary propaganda and incitement. The way in which the crime was committed was vile, and the crime itself is serious and must be

---

[45] This is probably a reference to Chen Xitong, the hardline-leftist Mayor of Beijing.

punished severely according to law. Taking the law of the land seriously in order to protect the political power of the people's democratic dictatorship and the socialist system, the trial panel of this court made a decision on December 24 after discussions and, in accordance with Articles 102 and 52 of the Criminal Law of the People's Republic of China, renders the following verdict:

The defendant Chen Zhixiang committed the crime of conducting counterrevolutionary propaganda and incitement and is hereby sentenced to a fixed-term period of 10 years' imprisonment (the period of imprisonment to be calculated starting from the date of this judgment's execution, and with a one-day reduction of sentence for each day spent in custody prior to execution of the judgment, that is, the imprisonment shall end on July 3, 1999), with three years' subsequent deprivation of political rights.

If the defendant does not submit to this judgment, he may, within a 10-day period starting from the day following receipt of the judgment, lodge with this court a petition, plus one duplicate copy, as an appeal to the Guangdong Provincial High People's Court.

The First Criminal Panel of the
Guangzhou Intermediate People's Court

Chief Judge: Li Jiangpei
Judge: Yang Liangan
Acting Judge: Deng Ganhua

[Seal of the Guangzhou Intermediate People's Court]

January 3, 1990
Clerk: Chen Weimin

APPENDIX VIII.B

Case of Tang Boqiao

Indictment
of the Changsha People's Procuratorate
(Hunan Province)
Chang/Proc./Crim.Ind. (1990) No.8

Defendant: **Tang Boqiao**, male, 22, Han nationality, born in the municipality of Lengshuitan, Hunan Province, college educated, a student of section two of the class of '86, the department of political science, Hunan Normal University.

Residence: school for the children of employees of the factory producing equipment for hydro-electric power plants in the municipality of Lengshuitan.

He was taken in on July 13, 1989 for the case in question and was officially arrested by the Public Security Bureau of Changsha on July 29.

Investigation of the case of defendant Tang Boqiao engaging in counterrevolutionary propaganda and incitement was concluded by the Changsha Public Security Bureau. The case was forwarded to this procuratorate for indictment on January 18, 1990. Later, however, it was returned to the Public Security Bureau on March 3, 1990 for further investigation. That was completed by the Changsha Public Security Bureau on April 10, and was forwarded again to this procuratorate for examination and indictment. Our examination shows that:

Defendant Tang Boqiao was chief leader of the illegal organization, Hunan Students Autonomous Federation. From May 1989 on, he organized and participated in illegal rallies and demonstrations on many occasions. After the quelling of the counterrevolutionary rebellion in Beijing, defendant Tang Boqiao attended, in the evening of June 7, a meeting called by Fan Zhong, Zhang Lixin and others. At that meeting,

205

they plotted to hold a memorial meeting on June 8 for the counterrevolutionary thugs suppressed in Beijing. Defendant Tang Boqiao instructed Li XX, a student in the department of Chinese of Hunan Normal University, to draft a "memorial speech." That speech invented the story of our martial law troops having massacred students, workers and citizens and of having killed thousands of them. It was most pernicious. On June 8 of the same year, defendant Tang Boqiao co-chaired, with Zhang Lixin, the "memorial meeting" held on the square in front of the Changsha railway station. Liu Wei, Lu Siqing, Zhou Ming and Zhang Lixin (all prosecuted in separate cases) spoke at the meeting. They venomously attacked the party and government and incited antagonism. On June 12, 1989, the People's Government of the City of Changsha issued a public notice outlawing the Hunan Students Autonomous Federation and the Changsha Workers Autonomous Federation. Defendant Tang Boqiao refused to register with the authorities. On June 15, together with Yu Zhaohui and others, he absconded to Guangzhou and Xinghua and made telephone contacts with people outside the country. They accepted 92,500 *yuan* and HK$4,500.00, as well as a book of secret codes for communication sent from Hong Kong. Tang Boqiao passed out his calling cards, bearing the title of Executive Director of the Hunan Students Autonomous Federation, and copies of the memorial speech delivered at the "June 8" memorial meeting, to people outside the country. At the same time, defendant Tang Boqiao absconded to Muzhou township in Xinghui County, attempting to cross the border at Zhuhai and sneak into Macao.

The above-mentioned facts of his crime are attested to by witnesses' testimony, criminal scientific technique as well as by photographs, telephone receipts and evidence of confiscated booty. The defendant also admitted as much in his recorded confessions. The facts are clear and the evidence solid, complete and sufficient to prove the case.

In the opinion of the procuratorate, defendant Tang Boqiao planned and organized illegal demonstrations and presided over the "June 8" memorial meeting. His activities violated Article 102 of the *Criminal Code of the People's Republic of China* and constituted the crime of counterrevolutionary propaganda and incitement. In order to consolidate China's political power of the people's democratic dictatorship, defend the socialist system and punish counterrevolutionary crimes, and in accordance with Article 100 of the *Criminal Procedure Law of the People's Republic of China*, we indict the defendant and request that your court judge him according to law.

To the Intermediate People's Court,
the City of Changsha, Hunan Province

Luo Jingjian,
Procurator acting on behalf of
the Procuratorate of the City
of Changsha [Seal]
April 17, 1990

N.B.

1. The defendant Tang Boqiao is being held at the No.1 Jail of the Changsha Public Security Bureau.
2. Enclosed are case materials in three books and four volumes; and
3. Two books and two volumes of diaries as evidence.

Certificate of Release

(91) No.70

Tang Boqiao, male, 22, of Hunan Normal University, was sentenced on August 9, 1990 on charges of counterrevolutionary propaganda and incitement by the Intermediate People's Court of the City of Changsha to a fixed term of three years' imprisonment with two years' subsequent deprivation of political rights (from February 12, 1991 to February 11, 1993). This is to certify that he is being released on parole.

Longxi Prison
February 12, 1991

(This copy to be issued to the released individual.)

APPENDIX VIII.C

Case of Mo Lihua

Verdict
on the Criminal Case of Mo Lihua
Returned by
the Intermediate People's Court of the City of Shaoyang
Hunan Province
(1989 Crim-Pre.No.150)

Prosecutors:
Lu Kuiquan, prosecutor, People's Procuratorate of the City of Shaoyang

Wang Jianjun, acting prosecutor, People's Procuratorate of the City of Shaoyang

Defendant:
Pen name: **Mo Li**
Mo Lihua, female, 35, born in Shaodong County, Han nationality, was formerly a teacher of the department of education, Shaoyang Normal College.

Residence: Building No.6-1-1, staff dormitory, Shaoyang Normal College.

Taken in on June 14, 1989 on charges of counterrevolutionary propaganda and incitement. Formally arrested on September 10 of the same year. She is being held in the jailhouse of the Shaoyang City Public Security Bureau.
Defense attorney:

Chen Qiuming, attorney, No.1 Law Office of the City of Shaoyang.

On November 25, 1989, the People's Procuratorate of the City of Shaoyang, Hunan Province, in its (1989) Criminal Indictment No. 108, brought before this court the suit against defendant Mo Lihua on charges of counterrevolutionary propaganda and incitement. This court organized a collegiate bench of judges according to law and held a public trial. It has been ascertained that:

Defendant Mo Lihua, together with Huang XX and Zhou X, students of Shaoyang Normal College, left Shaoyang on May 26, 1989 for Beijing to find out about the disturbances there. They collected some information about those disturbances. After they returned to Shaoyang, Mo addressed an audience of more than eighty people in the evening of June 3, in the training section classroom of Shaoyang Normal College. She talked about ten major issues in "Understanding the Beijing Student Movement." She attacked and slandered Li Peng as "creating disturbances and threatening the people with army troops," claiming that "the people will have instant peace the moment Li Peng is removed." She also clamored for "establishing democratic politics - the parliamentary system and a political design institute in China," etc. In the evening of June 6, Mo again addressed all teaching staff and students of Shaoyang Normal College through the college's public address system. She repeated those reactionary remarks mentioned above.

In the night of June 3 and early morning of June 4, the counterrevolutionary rebellion was suppressed in Beijing. Defendant Mo Lihua spoke at the "memorial meeting" held in the evening of June 4 at Shaoyang Normal College by Li XX and a few others to honor the handful of thugs. She also spoke at the People's Square of Shaoyang in the evening of June 5. She viciously attacked and slandered the suppression of the counterrevolutionary rebellion by our party and government as a "bloody suppression of the people by a fascist government." She arrogantly clamored for the building of a "still taller and still more beautiful goddess of democracy" to honor the handful of counterrevolutionary thugs. She called for overthrowing the Central People's Government as a memorial ceremony for the "courageous spirits" of the thugs, and so on and so forth.

The above facts have been attested to by witnesses, oral and written testimonies and recorded depositions. The defendant's confessions are also on record. The facts are clear-cut and the evidence is solid and sufficient to prove the case.

In the opinion of this court, defendant Mo Lihua made public speeches at a time when our party and state won a decisive victory in curbing the disturbances and suppressing the rebellion, voicing grievances on behalf of and praising the counterrevolutionary thugs in Beijing. She attached party and state leaders and viciously attacked the decision and measures taken by the Central Committee of the Party and the State Council to put an end to the disturbance and suppress the rebellion. She incited the masses to rise up and oppose the authorities in a vain attempt to achieve her objectives of overthrowing the political power of the dictatorship of the proletariat and the socialist system. Her activities constitute the crime of counterrevolutionary propaganda and incitement. In accordance with Articles 102 and 152 of the *Criminal Law of the People's Republic of China*, this court renders the verdict as follows:

Defendant Mo Lihua committed the crime of counterrevolutionary propaganda and incitement, and is sentenced to a fixed term of three years' imprisonment, with a one year subsequent deprivation of political rights.

This prison term begins with the execution of the sentence; one day in custody before the execution of the sentence will be counted for one day in prison.

If the defendant refuses to accept the verdict, she may, within ten days from the second day after receiving this verdict, submit her appeal and two copies thereof to this court, to appeal to the Higher People's Court of Hunan Province.

> The First Criminal Trial Court of the
> Intermediate People's Court of the City
> of Shaoyang, Hunan Province (Seal)

Judge: Zhou Houhui
Acting judge: Xu Zhongyi
Acting judge: Xu Hong
December 24, 1989
Clerk of the court: Shen Zhiyong

Document of Shaoyang City Personnel Bureau
Shao/Personnel (1991) No.07

Written reply
Concerning punishing Mo Lihua by
discharging her from public employment

Shaoyang Normal College:

Your report asking for instructions concerning discharging Mo Lihua from public employment has been received.

Mo Lihua was sentenced to a fixed term of three years imprisonment by the Intermediate People's Court of the City of Shaoyang on December 24, 1989 (verdict Crim-Pre. No.150) on charges of conducting counterrevolutionary propaganda and incitement during the disturbances of 1989. In accordance with the spirit of Document No.160 of 1982 issued by the Ministry of Labor and Personnel, and after deliberations, Mo Lihua shall be punished by discharging her from public employment.

Personnel Bureau of the City of Shaoyang
April 5, 1991

Report to: the Personnel Office of Hunan Province
Send to: the Office of the City Committee of the Party, Office of the City Government, Organization Department of the City Committee of the Party, City Discipline Committee
Issue to: Mo Lihua

APPENDIX VIII.D

Case of Wang Yongfa

[NB: In the following case, the defendant was sent to undergo re-education through labor despite a clear verdict of not guilty and an order of immediate release having been issued by the court. (Asia Watch)]

Lingling Sub-Procuratorate of the
Hunan Province People's Procuratorate

Decision Not to Prosecute
Hunan Proc/Ling Sub-proc/No Ind. (1990) No.01

Defendant: **Wang Yongfa**, male, 37, Han nationality, born in Lanshan County, Hunan Province, college educated, teacher of political studies, member of the Chinese Communist Party.

Residence: dormitory of the No. 1 Middle School, Lanshan County.

Taken into custody on October 23 (?), 1989 by the Public Security Bureau of Lanshan County on charges of counterrevolutionary propaganda and incitement. Arrested on January 7, 1990 by the Public Security Bureau of Lanshan County with the approval of the People's Procuratorate of Lanshan County given on December 26, 1989.

Investigations into the case of defendant Wang Yongfa, charged with counterrevolutionary propaganda and incitement, were completed by the Lanshan County Public Security Bureau, and the case was forwarded to the Lanshan County People's Procuratorate on January 8, 1990 for examination and indictment. Having examined the case, the Lanshan County People's Procuratorate, in accordance with Article 15 of the *Criminal Procedure Law of the People's Republic of China*, submitted the

213

case to this sub-procuratorate on January 13 for examination and indictment. It has been ascertained that:

In early June 1989, when the counterrevolutionary rebellion was being crushed in Beijing, defendant Wang Yongfa tuned in to enemy radio broadcasts and believed the rumors he heard. In the morning of June 5, when Wang Yongfa was making preparations for his class in the teaching and research group office, the chief political instructor, Fan Yucai, remarked: "The TV reported the killing of a People's Liberation Army man by the thugs. It was horrible." Wang retorted: "You are looking at it in a one-sided way. You only saw the death of one PLA man. Do you know that up to one thousand students and workers also died?" Later, he spread the story that "thousands of students and workers were either killed or injured. Hordes of PLA men rushed the students and machine-gunned them down." When he was criticized by other teachers, he added: "The Central TV has no credibility." Then, in the afternoon of June 6, when defendant Wang Yongfa was lecturing on political studies for classes of 38 and 39, he was asked by students to talk about the situation. He spread the rumor to students in those two classes that "the martial law troops in Beijing got into a fight with the students and citizens. Many died on both sides. The PLA suppressed the students and citizens. They used machine guns, tanks and armored cars to suppress groups of students and citizens." He added that Wang Dan was bayoneted to death by PLA men. He also said, "On Tiananmen Square, three college co-eds knelt before PLA men, imploring the latter not to shoot them. Yet the PLA men opened fire, killing two of them; the third was seriously hurt and was interviewed by a VOA reporter in the hospital." At the same time, he recited for the students some doggerel and made provocative statements. All this confused the students and was most pernicious.

The above-mentioned facts are attested to by the witnesses' testimony, by the written evidence and the recorded partial confessions of the defendant. They are sufficient for passing a judgement.

In the firm opinion of this sub-procuratorate, defendant Wang Yongfa has long neglected the remolding of his world outlook. He tuned in to enemy broadcasts during the counterrevolutionary rebellion and publicly spread sayings of incitement, causing confusion among teachers and students. His activities were of a serious nature. But the remarks defendant Wang Yongfa made during the quelling of the counterrevolutionary rebellion were mainly rumors he had heard, believed and spread. They constituted a serious political mistake. In accordance with Article 10 of the *Criminal Code of the People's Republic of China* and Section 1 of Article 11 and Article 204 of the *Code of Criminal Procedure of the People's Republic of China*, and after deliberations by the procuratorate committee of this sub-procuratorate, Wang Yongfa is not to be indicted and is hereby released.

Chief procurator: Li Shengqing
        [signature]

[Seal of the Lingling Sub-
Procuratorate of the Hunan
Province People's Procuratorate]
February 20, 1990

Certificate of Release
from Re-education Through Labor

This is to certify that:

Wang Yongfa, male, 39, of the No. 1 Middle School of Lanshan County, Hunan Province, was committed for re-education through labor on October 27, 1989.[46] Due to shortening of his term by exactly one month, he is being released from re-education through labor.

(Official seal of the Administration of Re-education Through Labor, Xinkaipu, Hunan Province) February [?], 1992

Notes:

1. The holder of this certificate should go to the public security and food authorities of his domicile to register for residence and food rations.

2. (illegible)

Food to be supplied up to the end of February [?]: (illegible)

---

[46] This is incorrect. In fact, Wang was held in a detention center from the time of his initial arrest in October 1989 until February 20, 1990, when the procuracy formally decided not to prosecute him. He was only then - and quite in violation of the procuracy's decision, which also stated that he was "hereby released" - transferred to a labor re-education camp to serve out a 2½-year term of re-education. The document's mention of October 27, 1989 as the date of first committal for re-education is thus a cosmetic sleight-of-hand, albeit one which defers to the rule that time spent in pre-hearing detention should be deducted from the eventual length of sentence.

APPENDIX VIII.E

Case of Xie Changfa

People's Government of the City of Changsha
Administrative Committee on Re-education Through Labor

Decision on Re-education Through Labor

Chang/Re-ed/Labor (1990) No. 180

Xie Changfa, alias Fang Feiyu, male, 38, Han nationality, born in Pingtang Township, Wangcheng County, college educated, currently employed as a technician at the Changsha Steel Mill. Residence: No.501, the Huobashan Dormitory of the Refrigerated Warehouse for Foreign Trade of Hunan Province, the City of Changsha.

During the period of the disturbances at the end of spring and beginning of summer, 1989, Xie actively took part in those disturbances and engaged in counterrevolutionary propaganda and incitement activities. On June 4, Xie sneaked into the No.1 and No.4 Middle Schools of Liuyang County and made speeches to more than 100 students of those two schools. "I hope you students will actively participate in this movement and strive to become vanguards of democracy." he said. He added, "I have a mother and a loving wife and child. But I would not hesitate to give everything I have...for the revolution." Incited by Xie, some students wrote slogans and posters and planned to take to the streets the following day. On June 6, Xie wrote an "Appeal to All the Policemen and Fellow Citizens," and gave it to Fan Zhong, a leader of the Hunan Students Autonomous Federation, to be broadcast. Early in the morning of June 9, Xie made a speech in front of the provincial government compound. He proposed to those present to form a Citizen's Dare-to-Die Corps to "protect the students and the democratic movement..." He then took paper and pen from He Kede and called on those present to sign up. On that same day, Xie left Changsha for Liuyang, carrying with him ten copies of the reactionary journal, *Da Gong Bao*, [with the lead story] entitled "The bloody suppression continues in

217

Beijing; The number of dead and injured exceeds 10,000; The Public Indignant," and gave them to Jiang Shiruo, Tan Shaocheng and Wei Qiusheng, all township cadres. On June 10, Xie gave five copies of *Da Gong Bao* to Xiao Yu, Liu Jiangming, Deng Xihua and Liu Boming, all students of the No. 4 Middle School of Liuyang County. On June 11, he gave five copies of *Da Gong Bao* to Xun Chunling, Li Chunlan and Yao Zuoping and asked them to distribute the journal among their fellow students.

As described above, Xie Changfa travelled to and from Liuyang and Changsha, making speeches, writing reactionary articles and distributing reactionary journals during the disturbances. His activities constituted the crime of counterrevolutionary propaganda and incitement. In accordance with the *Provisional Regulations Governing Re-education Through Labor* transmitted by the State Council, it is hereby decided that Xie Changfa is to be taken in for re-education through labor for two years.

[Official Seal of the Administrative Committee on Re-education Through Labor, the City of Changsha]

March 23, 1990

Record of Search

December 20, 1990

Luo Haijiao, a member of the Sub Office of the Public Security Bureau of the City of Changsha, Hunan Province, with search warrant No.24 issued by the Public Security Bureau of the City of Changsha on December 9, 1989, and with Kong Songbo as witness, searched the body, residence and other relevant places of **Xie Changfa**, a resident in the local government of the Township of Guandu.

In the course of the search (give brief description of the search):

[BLANK SPACE]

The opinion of the party searched on the search was as follows:

[BLANK SPACE]

A copy of this search record (together with a list of confiscated items) has been issued to [BLANK SPACE] for his record.

The searched party: Xie Changfa (signed)
The witness: Kong Songbo (signed)
The searcher: Luo Haijiao (signed)

219

APPENDIX VIII.F

Case of Zhou Shuilong

[NB: In the following case, the defendant was unlawfully sentenced to re-education through labor by order of an office of the Public Security Bureau. According to official regulations, such sentences may only be imposed by so-called Labor Re-education Administrative Committees. (Asia Watch)][47]

Sub-Office of the Public Security Department
Guangzhou Railway Bureau

Decision on Re-education Through Labor
Chang/Rail/Public/Sub/RL (89)No. 16

Zhou Shuilong, male, 39, Han nationality, born in Hengshan County, Hunan Province, finished junior-middle school, currently employed as boilerman at Changsha North Station of the Changsha Railway Sub-Bureau

Residence: B4, Guangu Lane, Shuyuan Road, South District, the City of Changsha.

---

[47] The *Labor Re-education Administrative Committees* (LRACs) are supposed to be tripartite bodies comprising representatives of the Civil Affairs, Labor and Personnel, and Public Security ministries. Set up in the early 1980s, the ostensible purpose of the LRACs was to take away from the public security authorities the sole power to impose punishments of labor re-education, in order to reduce the latter's blatant misuse of this power. The reform failed, however, and public security officials have continued to impose labor re-education sentences entirely on their own authority. According to official press accounts, the LRACs meet only "once per year" and are "little more than old folks' homes".

Taken into custody for investigation by this Sub-Office on August 17, 1989 on charges of stirring up trouble and disturbing public order.

It has been ascertained that Zhou Shuilong violated the law, and the facts are as follows:

In mid-May 1989, he joined the Workers Autonomous Federation on the recommendation of He Zhaohui, vice-chairman of that illegal organization in Changsha. In late May, he became deputy leader of the Workers Autonomous Federation pickets, and received a card bearing the number "Changsha Workers Autonomous Federation Picket No. G0027." He assisted the illegal organization Hunan Students Autonomous Federation and served as picket for students staging a sit-down protest in the provincial government compound.

In the afternoon of May 24, the Hunan Students Autonomous Federation and the Workers Autonomous Federation organized an illegal demonstration. Zhou Shuilong served as a picket, carrying an iron rod about two feet long.

One morning toward the end of May, some members of the Hunan Students Autonomous Federation gave speeches at the Changsha Automobile Electrical Appliances Plant and clashed with the plant administration. Zhou Shuilong, holding a banner of the Autonomous Federation of Changsha Railway Workers, followed Zhou Yong, a leader of the Workers Autonomous Federation, and others, to give support to the members of the Hunan Students Autonomous Federation.

In the morning of June 4, Zhou Shuilong took part in blocking the crossroad at May First Road, disrupting railway and May First Road traffic.

On June 8, the Hunan Students Autonomous Federation and the Workers Autonomous Federation organized and convened a "memorial meeting" to honor the thugs killed during the suppression of the rebellion in Beijing. Zhou Shuilong was responsible for moving the wreaths from the provincial government compound to the memorial meeting held on the square in front of the Changsha Railway Station. He also served as a picket.

Between mid-May and early June, Zhou Shuilong, together with members of the Hunan Students Autonomous Federation, posted hundreds of illegal posters, "proclaiming strikes" and "appealing to compatriots," at the Changsha Cigarette Factory, the meatpacking plant, the aluminum plant, the Hunan Switchgear Factory, the machine tool plant and on the main thoroughfares in the South District of Changsha.

What was still more serious was that on June 7, Zhou Shuilong, together with Zhang Zhihui and others from the Jingwanzi team of Red Star Village of Yuhuating Township on the outskirts of Changsha, went to post "strike notices" at the Changsha Cigarette Factory. They clashed with the economic police of the factory who had tried to stop them. Zhou falsely accused the policemen of beating up people, and declared he would call in reinforcements to block the factory entrance. Early the following morning, Zhang Xudong, Commander-in-Chief of the Workers Autonomous Federation, sent people to block the gate of the Changsha Cigarette Factory. Zhou Shuilong arrived there later and incited the people gathered there, causing a day-long work stoppage which resulted in losses to the tune of 1,231,031.38 *yuan*.

In accordance with Section 4 of Article 10 of the *Provisional Regulations Governing Re-education Through Labor* of the Ministry of Public Security, transmitted by the State Council on January 21, 1982, it is decided that Zhou Shuilong is to be re-educated through labor for two years, beginning on August 17, 1989 and ending August 16, 1991.

(Official seal of the sub-office of the Public Security Department of Guangshou Railway Bureau)

December 19, 1989

APPENDIX IX

Prison Songs by Zhang Jingsheng

It's Not that I Want to Leave You

不是我願意离开你　我亲爱的媽媽

不 是 我 願 意 离 开 你 我 亲 愛 的 媽
It's not that I want to leave you, dear mother,

媽 孩 儿 的 命 运 不 能 和 你 相 連 在 一
But your son's fate cannot stay woven with

起 只 恨 那 罪 恶 的 命 运 把 母 子 俩 分 离
yours. How I wish that cruel destiny had not torn us apart,

不 知 道 何 年 何 月 相 聚 在 一 起
For I know not when we might be reunited.

心 中 的 痛 苦 和 悲 伤 有 誰 能 知 道
Who can ever know the pain and sadness I feel,

孤 独 的 我 一 人 不 知 走 何 走 何 何
As solitary and lonely I stare at an empty future,

方 漫 长 的 人 生 道 路 何 处 是 好
The road of life stretching endlessly ahead, no refuge in

宿 我 怀 着 一 颗 破 碎 的 心 站 在 了 十 字
sight, I hold my shattered heart at a crossroads.

路
路

秋 天 的 沙 啊 送 住 了 我 的 双 眼
As autumn sandbirds fill the sky and obscure the horizon,

少 年 的 壮 志 失 去 了 我 哭 断 了
I shed bitter tears for the lost proud confidence of my

肠 得 不 到 亲 人 的 温 暖 我 离 开 了 故
youth, The loving warmth of family and home is now a thing of the

past, And all roads lead only to my old familiar prison cell.

In lonely anguish, I wander lost at this bleak crossroads,

The sun's evening rays lighting up the land all around,

For my heart is filled only with cold and emptiness,

And an endless pitch- dark

night.

Song of Changqiao Prison

長橋之歌

年青的我 呀 被孤进了 牢 房 親人呀親
When I was young, I was thrown into prison, But don't grieve for

人 你不要悲 伤 如今的 社 会
me, my dearest one. For society's just that

就是 这 样 有痛苦 有 烦 惱
way nowadays, Nothing but pain and

还 有 悲 伤
trouble and sadness.

我站 在牢房 里手捧暑三丽 米还有 一碗
I stand here in my cell, a ball of rice in my hand, and a bowl of

当 好 湯 这就是 長桥 的生 活
want-to-go-home soup. That's all there is to life in Chang qiao,

226

情切切 泪汪 汪 只当下 憾
An aching heart and tears of remorse. 娘

天空的 小 鸟在 自由地飞 翔 飞回了我
Little bird flying so high in the sky, You spiral

那 美丽的家 乡 带去我深情
so gaily and free. Carry my thoughts on

亲切的问 候 祝福我爹 娘
back to my hometown, And bring health and good luck

身体健 康
to my loved ones.

LIST OF 142 PRISONS, LABOR CAMPS, RE-EDUCATION
CENTERS AND JAILS IN HUNAN PROVINCE

| INTERNAL NAME | EXTERNAL NAME | LOCATION |
| [+ NOS. HELD] | [+ PRODUCTS] | [+ SOURCE REFS.] |

A. PRISONS

1. 省第一监狱
YUANJIANG PRISON
(Provincial No.1)
[>6000]

[?]
[Automobile parts]

沅江市南咀新沅路
YuanJiang City,
Nanzui, Xinyuan Road
[B125/C79/D131]
Zip: 413104

2. 省第二监狱
HENGYANG PRISON
(Provincial No.2)
[>7000]

湖南重型汽车制造厂
Hunan Heavy Motor
Vehicle Factory
[Automobiles]

衡阳市同心路
Hengyang City,
Tongxin Road
[A313/B300/E140]
Tel: 23161

3. 省第三监狱
LINGLING PRISON
(Provincial No.3)
[4000]

省劳动汽车配件厂
Provincial Laodong
Vehicle Parts Factory
[Automobile parts]

零陵地区永州市
何家坪 Lingling
Prefecture, Yongzhou
City, HeJiaping
[A604/B413] Tel: 2692
Zip: 425000

KEY:
"A" = Hunan Province Telephone Directory 《湖南省电话号簿》, Hunan 1990
"B" = Hunan Province Zipcode Manual 《湖南省邮政编码实用手册》, Changsha 1990
"C" = Atlas of Hunan Province 《湖南省地图册》, Hunan 1990
"D" = Zipcode Atlas of China 《中国邮政编码图集》, Harbin 1989
"E" = China Urban Zipcode Atlas 《中国城市邮政编码地图集》, Harbin 1991

4. 省第四监狱　　　　　　[?]　　　　　　　　怀化市
HUAIHUA PRISON　　　　　　　　　　　　　　Huaihua City
(Provincial No.4)
[>2000]

5. 省第五监狱　　　　　　[?]　　　　　　　　郴州地区
CHENZHOU PRISON　　　　　Prison has "office"　　Chenzhou Prefecture
(Provincial No.5)　　　　listed at Wulidui,　　[A364/B383/E142]
[4000]　　　　　　　　　　Yanquan Road, Chenzhou　[See also Item 47, below]
　　　　　　　　　　　　　Tel: 22379　Zip: 423000

6. 省第六监狱　　　　　　新邵县大理石加工厂　　邵阳市新邵县
LONGXI PRISON　　　　　　Xinshao Marble Factory　Shaoyang Municipality,
(Provincial No.6)　　　　[Marble products]　　　Xinshao County
[>2000]　　　　　　　　　　　　　　　　　　　　[B372/C88]

7. 长沙监狱　　　　　　　a) 新生印刷被服厂　　　长沙市香樟路
CHANGSHA PRISON　　　　　New Life Cotton Quilt　Changsha Municipality,
[3000: women]　　　　　　Printing Factory　　　　Xiangzhang Road
　　　　　　　　　　　　　b) 长沙新民工艺厂　　　[A4/C12/E138]
　　　　　　　　　　　　　Changsha Xinmin Handi-　Tel: 31733
　　　　　　　　　　　　　crafts Factory

8. 桃源监狱　　　　　　　[?]　　　　　　　　常德市桃源县
TAOYUAN PRISON　　　　　　　　　　　　　　Changde Municipality,
　　　　　　　　　　　　　　　　　　　　　　Taoyuan County
　　　　　　　　　　　　　　　　　　　　　　[A423]　Tel: 2964

B. LABOR-REFORM CAMPS

9. 建新劳改农场　　　　　建新农场 Jianxin Farm.　岳阳市毛斯铺
JIANXIN LABOR-REFORM　　(Sales arm is Jianxin　Yueyang Municipality,
FARM　　　　　　　　　　　Trading Co. [建新贸易　Maosi Pu
[>20,000]　　　　　　　　公司], Tel: 24674. Farm　[A568/B151/C21+23]
　　　　　　　　　　　　　office at Mahao [马壕],　Tel: 23708, 23847
　　　　　　　　　　　　　Yueyang, Tel: 22299.)　　Zip: 414000
　　　　　　　　　　　　　[Agricultural products]

229

10. 涔澹劳改农场
CENDAN LABOR-REFORM
FARM
[>20,000]

涔澹农场
Cendan Farm
[Agricultural products]

津市竹田湖
Jin Municipality,
south of Zhutian Lake
[A439/C66]
Tel: 2223, 3254, 2794

11. 临湘劳改农场
LINXIANG LABOR-REFORM
FARM
[<10,000]

临湘农场
Linxiang Farm
[Agricultural products]

岳阳市临湘县
Yueyang Municipality,
Linxiang County

12. 华容劳改农场
HUARONG LABOR-REFORM
FARM
[>5000]

华容农场
Huarong Farm
[Agricultural products]

岳阳市华容县
Yueyang Municipality,
Huarong County

13. 白泥湖劳改农场
BAINIHI LABOR-REFORM
FARM

省白泥湖园艺场
Provincial Bainihu
horticultural Centre

湘阴县白泥湖
Xiangyin County, Bainihu
[A579/C25]
Tel: 938

14. 罗家洲劳改农场
LUOJIAZHOU LABOR-
REFORM FARM
[1000]

罗家洲农场
LuoJiazhou Farm
[Vegetables]

长沙市
Changsha City (suburbs)
[B44]

15. 咪江劳改茶场
MIJIANG LABOR-REFORM
TEA FARM

咪江茶场
MiJiang Tea Farm
[Tea]

茶陵县咪晒坪
Chaling County, Mishaiping
[A282/C34]
Tel: 2655-6, 2667, 2678

16. 省第三劳改支队
PROVINCIAL NO.3 LABOR-
REFORM DETACHMENT
[>5000]

省新生煤矿
Provincial New Life
Coal Mine
[Coal]

耒阳市伍家村
Leiyang Municipality,
WuJia Village
[A337-8/B324/C49]
Tel: 2101, 2363

230

17. 湘潭劳改大队
XIANGTAN LABOR-REFORM
BRIGADE (part of Prov-
incial No.4 or 6 Labor-
Reform Detachment)
[3000]

[?]
[Manganese mining]
(Has transportation
station at Jianshe
Bei Lu. Tel: 21006

湘潭市中路铺
Xiangtan Municipality,
 Zhonglu Pu
[A195]
Tel: 21896 [转]

18. 常德市劳改支队
CHANGDE LABOR-REFORM
DETACHMENT (Provincial
No.4 or 6)
[5000]

湖南柴油机厂
Hunan Diesel Engine
Factory
[Diesel engines]

常德市樟木桥
Changde Municipality,
Zhangmuqiao
[A405/B186/C65]
Tel: 22568   Zip: 415127

19. 常德市劳动管教支队
CHANGDE MUNICIPAL LABOR-
DISCIPLINARY TEAM

[?]

常德市万金障
Changde Municipality,
WanJinzhang

20. 怀化地区第一劳改队
HUAIHUA PREFECTURE
NO.1 LABOR-REFORM TEAM
(part of Provincial
No.8 Labor-Reform
Detachment) [>2000]

怀化毛织厂 [?]
Huaihua Woolen Mill
[Clothing]

怀化地区锦屏
Huaihua Prefecture,
Jinping
[A628]
Tel: 22988

21. 省第九劳改支队
PROVINCIAL NO.9
LABOR-REFORM
DETACHMENT
[>3000]

a) 省长沙火柴厂
Changsha Match Factory
b) 省长沙汽车摩托车修配厂
Changsha Car and Motor-
Cycle Repair Plant

长沙市左家塘赤岗北路
Changsha Municipality,
ZuoJiatang, Chigang N. Rd.
[A123]
Tel: 34151, 34161, 33354

22. 衡山劳改支队
HENGSHAN LABOR-REFORM
DETACHMENT
[>3000]

衡山钨矿
Hengshan Tungsten Mine
[Tungsten wire]

衡阳市衡山县
Hengyang Municipality,
Hengshan County

23. 郴州劳改支队
CHENZHOU LABOR-REFORM
DETACHMENT

郴州市郴县
Chenzhou Municipality,
Chen County

231

24. 零陵劳改支队
LINGLING LABOR-REFORM
DETACHMENT
[>8000]

东安农场
Dong' an Farm
[Agricultural products]

零陵地区东安县
Lingling Prefecture,
Dong' an County

25. 邵阳劳改支队
SHAOYANG LABOR-REFORM
DETACHMENT

湖南省群力煤矿
Hunan Province Qunli
Coal Mine
[Coal]

邵东县砂石乡
Shaoyang Municipality,
Shaodong County, Shashi
[A549/C89]]
Tel: 830, 853

26. 坪塘劳改支队
PINGTANG LABOR-REFORM
DETACHMENT
[3000]

长沙市水泥厂
Changsha Cement Factory
[Cement]

望城县坪塘镇
Wangcheng County,
Pingtang Town
[B56/C13]
Tel: 810326 Zip: 410208

27. 暮云劳改队
MUYUN LABOR-REFORM
TEAM
[>1000]

暮云农场
Muyun Farm
[Agricultural products]

长沙市
Changsha Municipality
[C13]

28. 虹桥劳改队
HONGQIAO LABOR-REFORM
TEAM

[?]

岳阳市平江县虹桥乡
Yueyang Municipality,
PingJiang County,
Hongqiao Township [C28]

29. [?]

醴陵煤矿
Liling Coal Mine
[Coal]

醴陵市
Liling Municipality

30. [?]

矿山新生锑矿
Kuang Shan Antimony
Mine (New Life)
[Antimony]

冷水江市矿山
LengshuiJiang
Municipality, Kuang Shan
[B249/C85] Zip: 417501

C. LABOR RE-EDUCATION CENTERS

31. 长沙妇教所
CHANGSHA WOMEN'S
RE-EDUCATION CENTER
[>1000]

湖南绸厂 Hunan Silk
Factory. (Sales: Zhen
Xiang Trading Services
[振湘贸易服务部] Tel:
44478) [Silk products]

长沙市东风路
Changsha Municipality,
Dongfeng Road
[A118/E138]
Tel: 24011, 26236, 82536

32. 株洲妇教所
ZHUZHOU WOMEN'S
RE-EDUCATION CENTER
[>1000]

[?]

株洲市
Zhuzhou Municipality

33. 长沙新开铺劳教所
CHANGSHA XINKAIPU
LABOR RE-EDUCATION
CENTER
[5000]

湖南开关厂
Hunan Switch Factory
[Electrical switches]

长沙市新开铺路
Changsha Municipality,
Xinkaipu Road
[A105/B24/C12/E138]
Tel: 32411, 32433, 52521

34. 渌口劳教所
LUKOU LABOR RE-
EDUCATION CENTER
[5000]

[?]

[Light industrial
goods]

株洲县渌口镇
Zhouzhou County, Lukou
Town

35. 益阳劳教所
YIYANG DISTRICT LABOR
RE-EDUCATION CENTER
[4000]

[?]

[Machinery]

益阳地区长春乡
Yiyang Municipality,
Changchun Township
[A450/C77]
Tel: 22232

36. 冷水江劳教所
LENGSHUIJIANG LABOR
RE-EDUCATION CENTER
[>5000]

[?]

冷水江市
LengshuiJiang Municipality
(See also Item 30, above)
[C85]

233

37. 衡山劳教所　　　　　[?]　　　　　　　　　衡山县
HENGSHAN LABOR RE-　　　　　　　　　　　Hengshan County
EDUCATION CENTER
[5000]

38. 长桥园艺场劳教所　　长桥园艺场　　　　　长沙市区长桥
CHANGQIAO HORTICULTURAL　Changqiao Horticultural　Changsha City, Changqiao
FARM LABOR RE-EDUCATION　Farm　　　　　　　　[A151/C13]
CENTER　　　　　　　　　[Vegetables and plants]　Tel: 23060
[<1000]

39. 怀化地区第一劳教所　[?]　　　　　　　　怀化地区西冲村
HUAIHUA DISTRICT NO.1　　　　　　　　　　Huaihua Prefecture,
LABOR RE-EDUCATION　　　　　　　　　　　Xichong Village
CENTER　　　　　　　　　　　　　　　　　[A628] Tel: 23158

40. 湘潭市劳教所　　　　[?]　　　　　　　　湘潭市九华乡
XIANGTAN MUNICIPAL　　(Located near Item 27,　Xiangtan Municipality,
LABOR RE-EDUCATION　　above.)　　　　　　Jiuhua Township
CENTER　　　　　　　　　　　　　　　　　[A195/C40] Tel: 22421

41. 娄底劳教所　　　　　[?]　　　　　　　　娄底地区关家脑
LOUDI LABOR RE-EDUCATION　　　　　　　　Loudi Prefecture,
CENTER　　　　　　　　　　　　　　　　　GuanJia'nao
　　　　　　　　　　　　　　　　　　　　[A495] Tel: 2257

42. 邵阳司法局劳教所　　[?]　　　　　　　　邵阳市资江桥下
SHAOYANG JUSTICE BUREAU　　　　　　　　　Shaoyang Municipality,
LABOR RE-EDUCATION　　　　　　　　　　　ZiJiang Qiaoxia
CENTER　　　　　　　　　　　　　　　　　[A524/C86] Tel: 2452

43. 邵阳司法局劳教队　　[?]　　　　　　　　邵阳市白田大队
SHAOYANG JUSTICE BUREAU　　　　　　　　　Shaoyang Municipality,
LABOR RE-EDUCATION TEAM　　　　　　　　　Baitian Brigade
　　　　　　　　　　　　　　　　　　　　[A524] Tel: 2386

44. 零陵地区劳教所　　【?】

LINGLING DISTRICT LABOR
RE-EDUCATION CENTER

零陵地区长茅坪

Lingling Prefecture,
Changmaoping
[A601] Tel: 3224

45. 常德市劳教所　　【?】

CHANGDE MUNICIPAL LABOR
RE-EDUCATION CENTER

常德市南湖坪

Changde Municipality,
Nanhuping
[A398] Tel: 23957, 24221

46. 白马垅劳教所　　【?】

BAIMALONG LABOR
RE-EDUCATION CENTER

【Electric stoves
and furnaces】

【?】

D. JUVENILE DETENTION CENTERS

47. 湖南省少年犯管教所

HUNAN PROVINCE JUVENILE
OFFENDERS DISCIPLINARY
CENTER
[5000]

【Matches and other
handicraft products】

郴州市燕泉路

Chenzhou Municipality,
Yanquan Road
[A348/B373]
Tel: 25717

48. 省第二少年犯管教所

PROVINCIAL NO.2 JUVENILE
OFFENDERS DISCIPLINARY
CENTER
[3000]

【Matches, packaging】

长沙市望城坡

Changsha Municipality,
Wangchengpo
[A4]
Tel: 83313

E. LOCAL JAILS AND DETENTION CENTERS

CHANGSHA

49. 长沙市第一看守所
Changsha Municipal No.1 Jail

长沙市左家塘赤岗北路 [A15]
Changsha City, Chigang North Rd.
Tel: 34327 (Pre-trial investigations)
Tel: 35714 (Reception Center)

50. 长沙市第二看守所
Changsha Municipal No.2 Jail

长沙市螺丝塘 [D48]
Changsha City, Luositang

51. 长沙市长桥收容审查所 [FN?]
Changqiao Shelter and Investigation
Center

长沙县长桥 [A15]
Changsha County, Changqiao
Tel: 48954, 48626, 48941

52. 长沙市郊区拘留所
Changsha Suburban Detention Center

长沙市郊区人民路 [A15]
Changsha (suburbs), People's Rd.
Tel: 35963

53. 浏阳县看守所
Liuyang County Jail

浏阳县百宜坑 [A183]
Liuyang County, Baiyikeng

54. 浏阳县治安拘留所
Liuyang County Public-Order
Detention Center

浏阳县唐家洲 [A183]
Liuyang County, TangJiazhou

XIANGTAN

55. 湘潭市拘留所
Xiangtan Municipal Detention Center

湘潭市 [A195]
Xiangtan City

56. 湘潭市审查站
Xiangtan Municipal Investigation
Station

湘潭市三角坪 [A195]
Xiangtan City, SanJiaoping

236

57. 株洲市收审队
Zhuzhou Shelter and Investigation Team

株洲市 [A228]
Zhuzhou City   Tel: 21741

58. 株洲市看守所
Zhuzhou Municipal Jail

株洲市 [A228]
Zhuzhou City

59. 株洲市拘留所
Zhuzhou Municipal Detention Center

株洲市 [A228]
Zhuzhou City

60. 株洲县看守所
Zhuzhou County Jail

株洲县 [A260]
Zhuzhou County

61. 株洲县拘留所
Zhuzhou County Detention Center

株洲县 [A260]
Zhuzhou County

62. 醴陵市看守所
Liling Municipal Jail

醴陵市五华庙 [A265]
Liling Municipality, Wuhua Temple

63. 攸县看守所
You County Jail

株洲市攸县 [A276]
Zhuzhou Municipality, You County

64. 茶陵县看守所
Chaling County Jail

株洲市茶陵县潘冲 [A280]
Zhuzhou Municipality, Chaling County,
Panchong

65. 茶陵县行政拘留所
Chaling County Administrative
Detention Center

株洲市茶陵县 [A280]
Zhuzhou Municipality, Chaling County

66. 酃县看守所
Ling County Jail

株洲市酃县 [A285]
Zhuzhou Municipality, Ling County

67. 衡阳市看守所
Hengyang Municipal Jail

衡阳市王家湾 [A292]
Hengyang Municipality, WangJiawan

68. 衡阳市白沙洲拘留所
Baishazhou Detention Center

衡阳市白沙洲 [A292]
Hengyang Municipality, Baishazhou

69. 衡阳市收审所
Hengyang Shelter and Investigation
Center

衡阳市白沙洲 [A292]
Hengyang Municipality, Baishazhou
Tel: 22943

70. 衡阳县看守所
Hengyang County Jail

衡阳县东阳乡 [A294]
Hengyang County, Dongyang Township

71. 衡阳县行政拘留所
Hengyang County Administrative
Detention Center

衡阳市衡阳县 [A328]
Hengyang Municipality, Hengyang County

72. 衡山县看守所
Hengshan County Jail

衡阳市衡山县南郊 [A338]
Hengshan County, NanJiao

73. 衡山县拘留所
Hengshan County Detention Center

衡阳市衡山县螺头山水库 [A338]
Hengshan County, Luotoushan Reservoir

74. 南岳区看守所
Nanyue District Jail

衡阳市南岳区长衡路 [A333]
Hengyang Municipality, Nanyue District,
Changheng Road

75. 耒阳市看守所
Leiyang Municipal Jail

耒阳市 [A335]
Leiyang Municipality

76. 耒阳市行政拘留所
Leiyang Administrative Detention
Center

耒阳市 [A335]
Leiyang Municipality

77. 祁东县看守所
Qidong County Jail

衡阳市祁东县石门 [A338]
Hengyang City, Qidong County, Shimen

238

78. 衡东县看守所
Hengdong County Jail

衡阳市衡东县交通东路 [A342]
Hengdong County, Jiaotong East Road

79. 郴州市收审站
Chenzhou Shelter and Investigation
Station

郴州市人民东路 [A348]
Chenzhou Municipality, People's East Rd.
Tel: 23848

80. 郴州市治安拘留所
Chenzhou Public-Order Detention Center

郴州市 [A348]
Chenzhou Municipality

81. 郴州市看守所
Chenzhou Municipal Jail

郴州市 [A348]
Chenzhou Municipality

82. 桂东县看守所
Guidong County Jail

郴州地区桂东县 [A378]
Chenzhou Prefecture, Guidong County

83. 嘉禾县看守所
Jiahe County Jail

郴州地区嘉禾县东头桥 [A372]
Chenzhou Prefecture, Jiahe County,
Dongtouqiao

84. 资兴市看守所
Zixing Municipal Jail

郴州地区资兴市邝家冲 [A375]
Chenzhou Prefecture, Zixing
Municipality, KuangJiaohong

85. 宜章县收容所
Yizhang County Shelter Center

郴州地区宜章县 [A381]
Chenzhou Prefecture, Yizhang County

86. 宜章县看守所
Yizhang County Jail

郴州地区宜章县 [A381]
Chenzhou Prefecture, Yizhang County

87. 常德市收容审查站
Changde Municipal Shelter and

常德市万金障 [A389]
Changde Municipality, WanJinzhang

Investigation Center   Tel: 24369

88. 武陵区拘役所
Wuling District Detention and   常德市武陵区滨湖东路 [A389]
Labor Center   Changde Municipality, Wuling District,
                                              Binhu East Road

89. 武陵区拘留所   常德市武陵区 [A389]
Wuling District Detention Center   Changde Municipality, Wuling District

90. 常德市看守所   常德市东堤 [A390]
Changde Municipal Jail   Changde Municipality, Dongdi

91. 鼎城区看守所   常德市武陵镇 [A390]
Dingcheng District Jail   Changde Municipality, Wuling Town

92. 桃源县看守所   常德市桃源县千梯山 [A423]
Taoyuan County Jail   Changde Municipality, Taoyuan County,
                                              Qianti Shan

93. 桃源县拘留所   常德市桃源县千梯山 [A423]
Taoyuan County Detention Center   Changde Municipality, Taoyuan County,
                                              Qianti Shan

94. 澧县看守所   常德市澧县 [A442]
Li County Jail   Changde Municipality, Li County

95. 澧县拘留所   常德市澧县 [A442]
Li County Detention Center   Changde Municipality, Li County

    YIYANG

96. 益阳县看守所   益阳地区益阳县 [A452]
Yiyang County Jail   Yiyang Prefecture, Yiyang County

97. 桃江县看守所   益阳地区桃江县桃花东路 [A474]
TaoJiang County Jail   Yiyang Prefecture, TaoJiang County,
                                              Taohua East Road

98. 娄底地区收审所
Loudi Shelter and Investigation Center

娄底地区豹兰山 [A495]
Loudi Prefecture, Baolan Shan
Tel: 3629

99. 娄底地区看守所
Loudi Prefectural Jail

娄底地区关家脑 [A495]
Loudi Prefecture, GuanJia'nao

100. 娄底地区拘留所
Loudi Prefectural Detention Center

娄底地区关家脑 [A495]
Loudi Prefecture, GuanJia'nao

101. 涟源市看守所
Lianyuan Municipal Jail

娄底地区涟源市 [A502]
Loudi Prefecture, Lianyuan Municipality

102. 冷水江市治安拘留所
LengshuiJiang Municipal Public-
Order Jail

娄底地区冷水江市 [A507]
Loudi Prefecture, LengshuiJiang Munic.

103. 冷水江市看守所
LengshuiJiang Municipal Jail

娄底地区冷水江市中连乡诚意村 [A507]
LengshuiJiang Municipality, Zhenglian
Township, Chengyi Village

104. 新化县拘留所
Xinhua County Detention Center

冷水江市新化县枫林乡 [A513]
LengshuiJiang Municipality, Xinhua
County, Fenglin Township

105. 新化县看守所
Xinhua County Jail

冷水江市新化县上渡乡 [A513]
LengshuiJiang Municipality, Xinhua
County, Shangdu Township

106. 邵阳市看守所
Shaoyang Municipal Jail

邵阳市戴家坪 [A523]
Shaoyang Municipality, DaiJiaping

107. 邵阳市收审所
Shaoyang Municipal Shelter and
Investigation Center

邵阳市三里桥 [A523]
Shaoyang Municipality, Sanliqiao
Tel: 2797

108. 洞口县拘留所
Dongkou County Detention Center

邵阳市洞口县 [A543]
Shaoyang Municipality, Dongkou County

109. 城步县拘留所
Chengbu County Detention Center

邵阳市城步苗族自治县新田路 [A545]
Shaoyang Municipality, Chengbu Miao
Autonomous County, Xintian Road

YUEYANG

110. 岳阳市收审一所
Yueyang Municipal No.1 Shelter
and Investigation Center

岳阳市花板桥 [A553]
Yueyang Municipality, Huabanqiao
Tel: 24235

111. 岳阳市收审二所
Yueyang Municipal No.2 Shelter
and Investigation Center

岳阳市湖滨 [A553]
Yueyang Municipality, Hubin
Tel: 24530

112. 岳阳市看守所
Yueyang Municipal Jail

岳阳市岳城 [A553]
Yueyang Municipality, Yuecheng

113. 岳阳市治安拘留所
Yueyang Municipal Public-Order
Detention Center

岳阳市 [A553]
Yueyang Municipality

114. 汨罗市行政拘留所
Miluo Municipal Administrative
Detention Center

汨罗市 [A570]
Miluo Municipality

115. 平江县看守所
PingJiang County Jail

岳阳市平江县 [A580]
Yueyang Municipality, PingJiang County

242

116. 岳阳县看守所
Yueyang County Jail

岳阳市岳阳县 [A591]
Yueyahg Municipality, Yueyang County

117. 临湘县治安拘留所
Linxiang County Administrative
Detention Center

岳阳市临湘县南正街 [A593]
Yueyang Municipality, Linxiang County,
Nanzheng Street

LINGLING

118. 永州市拘留所
Yongzhou Municipal Detention Center

零陵地区永州市太平路 [A601]
Lingling Prefecture, Yongzhou
Municipality, Taiping Road

119. 永州市看守所
Yongzhou Municipal Jail

永州市麻元村 [A601]
Yongzhou Municipality, Mayuan Village

120. 祁阳县看守所
Qiyang County Jail

零陵地区祁阳县交山村 [A609]
Lingling Prefecture, Qiyang County,
Jiaoshan Village

121. 祁阳县行政拘留所
Qiyang County Administrative
Detention Center

零陵地区祁阳县 [A609]
Lingling Prefecture, Qiyang County

122. 东安县看守所
Dong'an County Jail

零陵地区东安县 [A611]
Lingling Prefecture, Dong'an County

123. 东安县拘役所
Dong'an County Detention and Labor
Center

零陵地区东安县 [A611]
Lingling Prefecture, Dong'an County

124. 双牌县看守所
Shuangpai County Jail

零陵地区双牌县迎宾路 [A614]
Lingling Prefecture, Shuangpai County,
Yingbin Road

125. 蓝山县看守所
Lanshan County Jail

零陵地区蓝山县环城路 [A619]
Lingling Prefecture, Lanshan County,
Huancheng Road

243

126. 新田县看守所
Xintian County Jail

零陵地区新田县 [A621]
Lingling Prefecture, Xintian County

HUAIHUA

127. 怀化地区收审所
Huaihua Prefecture Shelter and
Investigation Center

怀化市 [A628]
Huaihua Municipality
Tel: 22715

128. 怀化市行政拘留所
Huaihua Municipal Administrative
Detention Center

怀化市 [A628]
Huaihua Municipality

129. 黔阳县看守所
Qianyang County Jail

怀化地区黔阳县白虎脑 [A642]
Huaihua Prefecture, Qianyang County,
Baihunao

130. 大庸市看守所
Dayong Municipal Jail

大庸市凤湾 [A655]
Dayong Municipality, Fengwan

131. 桑植县看守所
Sangzhi County Jail

大庸市桑植县尚家坪 [A668]
Dayong Municipality, Sangzhi County,
ShangJiaping

132. 桑植县拘留所
Sangzhi County Detention Center

大庸市桑植县尚家坪 [A668]
Sangzhi County, ShangJiaping

133. 慈利县看守所
Cili County Jail

大庸市慈利县打鼓台 [A663]
Dayong Municipality, Cili County,
Dagutai

134. 慈利县拘留所
Cili County Detention Center

大庸市慈利县打鼓台 [A663]
Cili County, Dagutai

244

135. 湘西自治州收审所
Xiangxi Autonomous Prefecture
Shelter and Investigation Center

湘西土家族苗族自治州吉首市 [A673]
Xiangxi TuJia and Miao Autonomous
Prefecture, Jishou Municipality
Tel: 3345

136. 湘西自治州看守所
Xiangxi Autonomous Prefecture Jail

吉首市 [A673]
Jishou Municipality

137. 湘西自治州行政拘留所
Xiangxi Autonomous Prefecture
Administrative Detention Center

吉首市光明路 [A673]
Jishou Municipality, Guangming Road

138. 保靖县看守所
BaoJing County Jail

湘西土家族苗族自治州保靖县 [A684]
Xiangxi TuJia and Miao Autonomous
Prefecture, BaoJing County

139. 保靖县拘留所
BaoJing County Detention Center

保靖县 [A684]
BaoJing County

140. 永顺县拘留所
Yongshun County Detention Center

湘西土家族苗族自治州永顺县 [A686]
Xiangxi TuJia and Miao Autonomous
Prefecture, Yongshun County

141. 龙山县看守所
Longshan County Jail

湘西土家族苗族自治州龙山县 [A690]
Xiangxi TuJia and Miao Autonomous
Prefecture, Longshan County

142. 古丈县看守所
Guzhang County Jail

湘西土家族苗族自治州古丈县柑子坪 [A693]
Xiangxi TuJia and Miao Autonomous
Prefecture, Guzhang County, Ganziping

MAPS

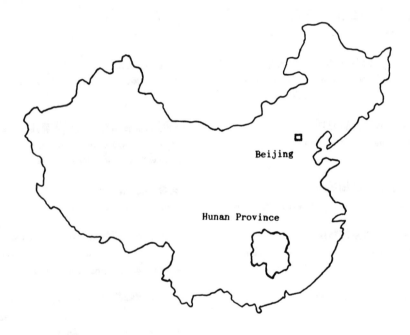

Beijing

Hunan Province

CHINA

CHANGSHA CITY

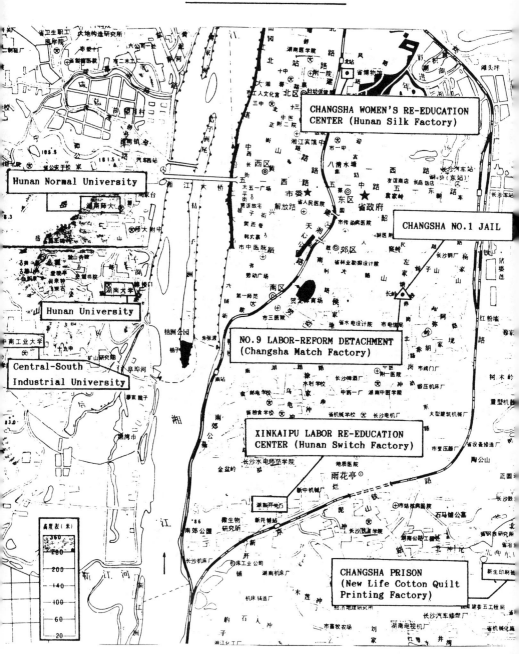

Hunan Normal University

Hunan University

Central-South Industrial University

CHANGSHA WOMEN'S RE-EDUCATION CENTER (Hunan Silk Factory)

CHANGSHA NO.1 JAIL

NO.9 LABOR-REFORM DETACHMENT (Changsha Match Factory)

XINKAIPU LABOR RE-EDUCATION CENTER (Hunan Switch Factory)

CHANGSHA PRISON (New Life Cotton Quilt Printing Factory)

248

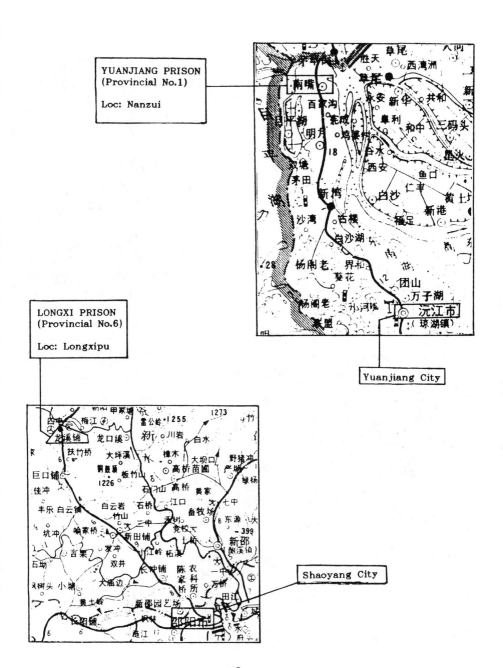

YUANJIANG PRISON
(Provincial No.1)

Loc: Nanzui

LONGXI PRISON
(Provincial No.6)

Loc: Longxipu

Yuanjiang City

Shaoyang City

249

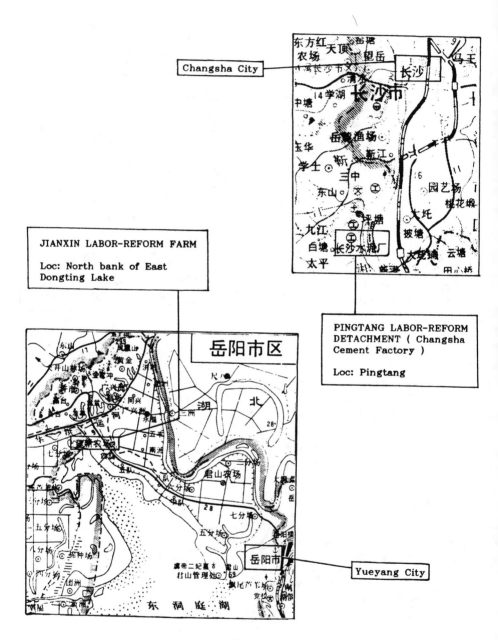

Changsha City

JIANXIN LABOR-REFORM FARM

Loc: North bank of East
Dongting Lake

PINGTANG LABOR-REFORM
DETACHMENT (Changsha
Cement Factory)

Loc: Pingtang

Yueyang City

长沙市

岳阳市区

湖　北

东　洞　庭　湖

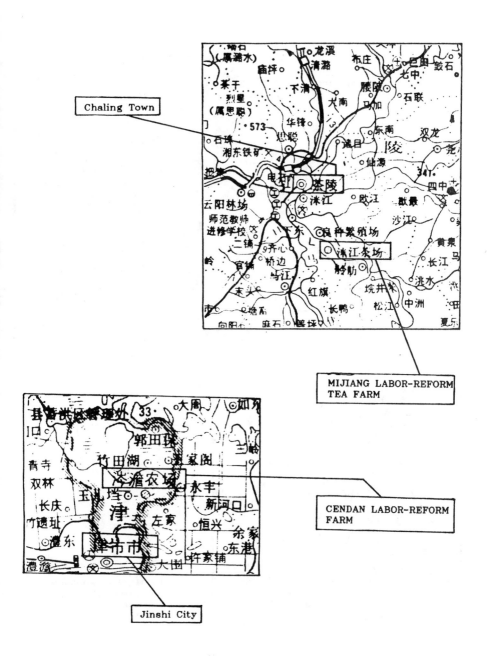

251

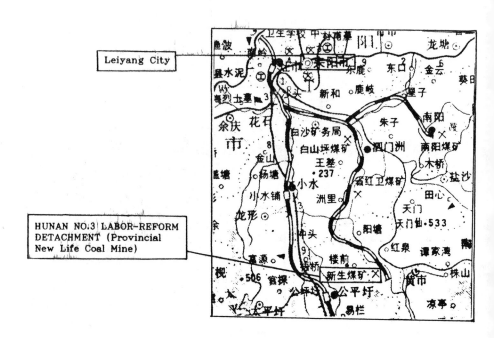

Leiyang City

HUNAN NO.3 LABOR-REFORM
DETACHMENT (Provincial
New Life Coal Mine)

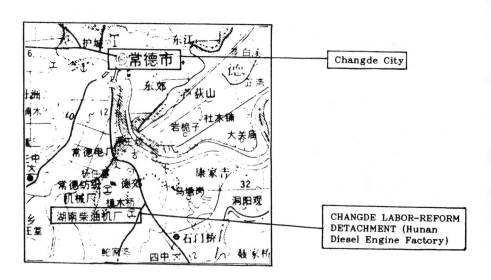

Changde City

CHANGDE LABOR-REFORM
DETACHMENT (Hunan
Diesel Engine Factory)

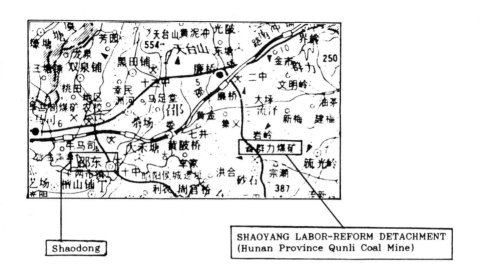

Shaodong

SHAOYANG LABOR-REFORM DETACHMENT
(Hunan Province Qunli Coal Mine)

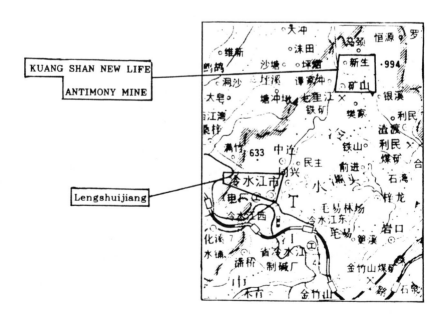

KUANG SHAN NEW LIFE
ANTIMONY MINE

Lengshuijiang

253

Index